STRUCTURAL INEQUALITY

To Tom Mitchell

Regards

Victoria Kaplan

Because you do so much to
hand the keys to young
men and women so that
they can unlock the door!
(pgs 34-35)

Sharon Tomkins Porter

STRUCTURAL INEQUALITY

BLACK ARCHITECTS IN THE UNITED STATES

VICTORIA KAPLAN

Rowman & Littlefield Publishers, Inc.
Lanham • Boulder • New York • Toronto • Oxford

ROWMAN & LITTLEFIELD PUBLISHERS, INC.

Published in the United States of America
by Rowman & Littlefield Publishers, Inc.
A wholly owned subsidiary of The Rowman & Littlefield Publishing Group, Inc.
4501 Forbes Boulevard, Suite 200, Lanham, Maryland 20706
www.rowmanlittlefield.com

PO Box 317
Oxford
OX2 9RU, UK

British Library Cataloguing in Publication Information Available

Library of Congress Cataloging-in-Publication Data

Kaplan, Victoria.
 Structural inequality : black architects in the United States / Victoria Kaplan.
  p. cm.
 Includes bibliographical references and index.
 ISBN-10: 0-7425-4582-2 (cloth : alk. paper)
 ISBN-13: 978-0-7425-4582-3
 ISBN-10: 0-7425-4583-0 (pbk. : alk. paper)
 ISBN-13: 978-0-7425-4583-0
 1. African American architects. I. Title.

 NA738.N5K37 2006
 720.92'396073—dc22   2005037176

Printed in the United States of America

♾™ The paper used in this publication meets the minimum requirements of
American National Standard for Information Sciences—Permanence of Paper
for Printed Library Materials, ANSI/NISO Z39.48-1992.

In memory of Gerald D. Baker

November 4, 1950–August 27, 2004

CONTENTS

FOREWORD

We shape our buildings, thereafter our buildings shape us.

—Sir Winston Churchill

Architects are fond of this quote and others like it that attest to the important role the profession plays in creating communities. How this observation by Sir Winston is applicable in twenty-first century, multicultural societies has been the subject of great debate for a very long time. The profession's self-image builds on this notion: we have a vital role in helping create the physical environment that enables people's lives. While architects generally recognize that we are not alone in this effort, we do feel a huge obligation to serve the public by creating a beautiful environment. That obligation joins with our legal obligation, by virtue of the licenses granted architects, to protect the public's "health, safety, and welfare."

The architecture profession is consistently challenged in its efforts to serve these dual roles in society. Being an architect is far more than "drawing blueprints," something the profession hasn't done for decades. Insufficient understanding among the public of the complexity of decisions architects make, a lack of understanding of the value created when architects are fully engaged in creating communities, the challenge of matching an architect's skills and experiences with the demands of a project assignment, and the low levels of compensation are but a few of the issues we face. Granted, the profession bears a responsibility to inform the public, and the clients who retain an architect's services, of the complexity and criticality of these issues.

This reality is deeply rooted in the profession's history, dating back to the Renaissance and the royal patrons who supported the work of architects. Continuing the primary elements of that patronage system to this day has not required the architectural profession to really explain itself to the public it serves. As American society continues to evolve from the narrow slice of humanity represented by its colonial founders, demonstrating the relevance and value architects bring to solving the challenges facing a multicultural society will require the profession to engage in some serious internal discussions. The implications of these long-standing modes of architectural practice take on different meanings if you are not a white, male architect.

This work by Victoria Kaplan is exceptionally interesting on two levels. At one level, Kaplan has revealed the challenges and issues faced by every architect. At the second level, she then addresses how these challenges are amplified for architects of color. At the first level, difficulties resulting from a lack of access to capital plague every architect. While this may seem a minor issue, lack of capital makes meeting payroll and covering capital expenses such as acquisition of computer hardware, software, and the training to use them a difficult investment for businesses that often have to wait 120 days or more to get paid for their work. The critical role social networks play in securing project assignments, clearly continuing the traditions of patronage from the Renaissance, challenges architects in many ways. Entering new markets, either geographic or project types, often stretches such networks. It's not unusual for highly qualified architects to market their credentials for long periods of time before successfully securing an assignment. For a profession that requires years of schooling followed by a multi-year internship and a nine-part examination to obtain a license, these issues of access to capital, restrictions of social networks, validating credentials, and the like are extremely frustrating.

Given these issues, I admire all those who choose to pursue this profession. As Kaplan explains so well, architects persist in their work because they believe in their ability to make the cities, towns, and buildings where people live, work, and play better places than when the architects began their assignment. In that sense, architects enter the profession because they are "called" to the work, doing it because of their joy in the act of creation and reveling in the joy the results bring to others.

As an exploration of these universal aspects of the architectural profession, Kaplan does every architect and the public a service. She explains these issues of architectural practice from a sociological vantage point, forcing us to examine obstructions to present-day practice from an outsider's perspective. And this is where the second level of the book comes into play, explaining how these same issues effectively cut the profession and society off from an untapped resource: people other than white males who seek to join the architectural profession in creating the communities and buildings we aspire to see built.

American society has seen huge transformations in recent decades. Ethnic cultures have exerted tremendous influence on nearly every aspect of our society. Without a lot of thought, each of us can name a non-European influence on food, fashion, theater, dance, art, movies, music, language, sports, holidays, and other aspects of the United States' social traditions. We would miss those aspects of our lives should they disappear from our cultural landscape. In fact, as Americans we pride ourselves on the multicultural nature of the U.S. society. We trumpet the virtues of the American way, where everyone has an equal chance to succeed in life through hard work and their intelligence. As pointed out in the very personal stories of the real-life experiences of black architects Kaplan collected in her research, the reality of an equal access society is not yet the normal state of affairs.

As Kaplan explores here, architects are challenged each day by many issues that make success difficult to achieve. The everyday challenges all architects face become huge *barriers* to the success of black architects as well as other architects who are not white males. Added to the list of architects' challenges, black architects must deal with more restricted social networks and fewer opportunities to access capital markets than their white, male counterparts. The even more infuriating barrier is the nearly continuous questioning of their qualifications relative to their white counterparts. While the direction of nearly all other aspects of American society has been influenced by other cultures, architecture continues to resist any change that would alter its white male dominance.

It's not unreasonable for readers to ask themselves why this is so. As a white male with more than thirty years of experience in the architectural profession, I cannot offer a definitive answer. What I do know for certain is that if the profession is to thrive in the decades ahead, we cannot continue to ignore entire sectors of our society and fail to welcome them to join the architectural profession. As the data from the U.S. Census so clearly demonstrate, nonwhite segments of the population are becoming the "majority" in our society. If Sir Winston is correct, the built environment we create must reflect those cultures. As the social networks of clients who make building decisions shift to reflect the cultural makeup of society, becoming more diverse, we can anticipate they will choose "people who look like themselves" to prepare the designs. If there are no architects of color from whom to choose, will the profession remain relevant in a future society? Can a profession that celebrates new ideas, new approaches, and innovation fail to draw upon an entire sector of society at times when we need every good idea to solve the problems we face? But in the end, will society tolerate buildings that ignore the cultural values they hold dear?

As Kaplan observes, it is really hard to talk about an emotionally charged issue such as racism in an American society that prides itself on equality. It is very hard to talk of racism within a profession that prides itself on serving society and welcoming new ideas. As the stories in this book illustrate so vividly, we have a long way to go before we realize the benefits of true multiculturalism in the architecture that is this generation's contribution to future generations. Will we be the generation of architects who seriously begin making changes in the educational system, licensing requirements, and firms that support inclusion of young people of color as welcome members of our great profession? We must take on these issues while preserving the standards we have evolved to protect society.

We can only realize Sir Winston's vision of architecture's impact when all of society contributes to its creation. Evolving the profession so it reflects society's composition will take real effort, sustained over many years. We can only make changes if we talk, meaningfully talk, to each other and take seriously those barriers that prevent bringing everyone's talents to focus on making change happen within the profession.

That is the real value of Kaplan's work: to prompt the discussion so that white architects and white clients understand that by joining the nonwhite members of our society we can leave this planet better than when we found it. Isn't that the obligation of each generation of architects? How can we fail to respond to our responsibility to the future?

R. K. Stewart, FAIA
Partner, Gensler
American Institute of Architects 2007 President

ACKNOWLEDGMENTS

There are several people who made this book possible. Without the encouragement of Joe Feagin and Alan McClare, senior editor at Rowman & Littlefield, it would not have happened. Their trust, and belief in the importance of this subject, provided me the courage to go ahead and do it.

I have gratitude, respect, and many thanks for all the architects who took time to talk to me and tell their stories. It was an honor to spend time with each of them, and I hope I have done a good job of relating their tales. I would particularly like to thank Melvin Mitchell, FAIA; Marshall Purnell, FAIA; Harry Robinson, FAIA; and Jack Travis, FAIA; for their willingness to answer questions, keep me on the right path, and get me out of jams. And to Donald King, FAIA, thanks for being a great coach and a good friend. I also want to thank the members of the AIA Seattle Diversity Roundtable for their support and enthusiasm.

To my friends Susan and Peter Grote, Eric Newman, and Linda Wilson, thanks for the endless editing you did with great wit, humor, and sensitivity to both race and architecture. Thanks also to Julie Miller for moral support and welcome retreats.

The Millennium Fund clients taught me more than they will ever realize about the realities of institutional racism; my only regret is they did not recognize the contributions they made to my life.

Finally, thanks to my pals at Pacific Coast Yacht Service for keeping me sane during the months of what otherwise would have been very solitary writing.

1

INTRODUCTION

If we are going to do anything about changing the individual, let us first admit that it is easier to have lived in a leper colony and not acquired leprosy than to have lived in America and not acquired prejudice. You don't start changing until you first admit you have it.

—Whitney Young, address to Urban League, June 1968

I never looked at having my own firm just to be the boss. When I was growing up, there wasn't an architect in my community to be a mentor; I wanted to change that. We need more representation of the possibilities. As long as there aren't any black architects, people can think it's because they're not smart enough, or they have no talent. People make up their own reasons. We need to teach by example, by being visible. The more people there are, outside the mainstream, to take away the myths and stereotypes about black people, the better.

—Donald Nelson

Racism is a difficult subject, one most people in the United States do not want to think about. This is especially true for whites; we are not encouraged to learn about racism, nor to consider its toxicity.[1] As Cornel West says, "We confine discussions about race in America to the 'problems' black people pose for whites, rather than consider what this way of viewing black people reveals about us as a nation."[2] We get stuck, in part, because we are not clear how to make the distinction between guilt and responsibility. Unsure how to assume responsibility for change, we are also uncomfortable feeling guilty.

The people whose lives you will hear about in this book are highly educated professionals with extensive experience. They work hard and have standing in their communities; they are talented people who, despite all their education and polite respect from their colleagues, are being limited in what they can achieve because of the color of their skin. The subject is the architecture profession, but in many ways architecture is a metaphor for the larger society. Architecture is a good site for evaluating structural inequality because it remains a bastion of white males. Black architects make up only 1 percent of the membership of the American Institute of Architects (AIA), and women less than 25 percent.[3]

The existing data on black architects, or for that matter, any architects of color, are extremely limited; data on women in the profession are only slightly more available. In the spring of 2005, the AIA commissioned a member survey with the goal of collecting data by gender and ethnicity. The results will enable the Institute to understand the demographics of the current membership and, as R. K. Stewart suggests in the foreword, to serve existing members and expand the membership in more inclusive ways. In the meantime, I have looked to the existing sources to provide additional perspectives on the profession.

The AIA Minority Resources Committee conducted a focus group in 1990 to determine the gaps between the perception and reality of the capabilities and attitudes about minority architects.[4] The AIA report on the results of this focus group does not contain data on the numbers or ethnicities of the focus group attendees.

Myths about minority architects:

capable of doing only a small percentage of the work
not able to handle large projects
not qualified/tokens/culturally limited
unreliable/lack experience and leadership qualities
only do government work/Minority Business Enterprises (MBE) have advantages due to set-asides
only want MBE work

Truths about minority architects:

feel isolated/highly stressed
as competent as majority architects/equally qualified
determined/can work miracles with limited dollars

risk takers/creative/tenacious and determined to overcome obstacles
Since they are visible, they feel pressured to work harder and longer, to strive
   to be better, and to get the recognition they deserve. They feel isolated,
   anxious and stressed.

Although the data are now fifteen years old, there has been little change. The small universe of contemporary accounts on diversity in architecture confirms there has been minimal progress.[5] The same results could have been achieved in any sector of U.S. society. A major contributing factor to the gap between perception and reality comes about because blacks and whites in this country remain segregated. In our daily lives, we have little of the sort of contact with each other that would enable us to understand each other's views of the world; we do not share our lives with each other. We do not understand the vast differences in our cumulative experiences. Whiteness is so dominant in this culture we are not even aware of the degree of difference.[6]

When I started working in economic development fifteen years ago, I could not have understood the issues I am now addressing. Despite a dedication to social change, I did not really have a core understanding of modern racism. Much as the whites referred to in Joe Feagin's sociology research thought attainment of middle-class status protected people of color from oppression, I was completely sheltered from the reality of race-based oppression.[7] It was not until I worked every day in what amounted to partnerships with business owners of color that I began to understand how whiteness shields us from the truth about racism.

For the past decade, I managed a small community-development venture capital fund on the West Coast. The goal of the Fund was to provide access to capital for businesses that did not have it. As the manager, I was responsible not only for finding businesses to invest in, but also for providing technical assistance once we invested. My staff or I spent an average of one day a week with each of the businesses we invested in. Based on my experience in business counseling and finance, and with the assistance of the investors and an advisory board, we worked with small businesses shut out of mainstream capital markets. Not coincidentally, most of these businesses were black owned.

I could not have known when we started the Fund how much I would learn from my clients. I did not yet understand the pressures entrepreneurs of color face above and beyond what is experienced by all small-business owners. I had no idea the ways I would need to appreciate the difficulty of being bicultural in order to be effective. At that time, I did not realize there *was* more than one culture to be learned. I did not have a comprehensive understanding of the dominant culture, and the oppression that results from being other than "the norm."

This research on inequality in the architecture profession was inspired by those ten years of funding, building, mentoring, and dismantling businesses. If I had not done what amounted to fieldwork for the past ten years, I would not have known the extent of the differences I have encountered. I also would not have appreciated the joys of sharing across cultures, nor the pain of learning racism from the perspective of my clients. While acting as mentor all those years, I was also a student.

Institutional, or systemic, racism is so embedded in our culture it no longer requires individual actions to be effective. As a result, many Americans believe the existence of *middle-class* blacks proves racism is no longer a problem. Further, there is a sense well-educated blacks are actually better off than their white counterparts. As discussed in many works cited in this book, it is difficult for whites to understand what it feels like to be discriminated against on the basis of skin color.[8]

The structure of the dominant culture in the United States—that is, the systems of education, health care, economics, social relationships, politics, and so forth—continues to facilitate discrimination against citizens who are other than white and at least middle class. Using the lens of the profession of architecture, this book lays out one way to look at that culture.

Institutional racism creates barriers I cannot see because they are not in my way. I can be pretty much assured the power structure of any mainstream business organization I might wish to join will look like me. I can expect if I succeed at a business venture, I will not be held up as a credit to my race, but rather as a successful individual. I can drive through any part of my town and know if I were to get pulled over for being different, it would be for my own protection and not that of the neighborhood. My friends and clients of color are not privy to the same expectations.[9]

The power of institutional racism is that the overt, in-your-face black and white racism of the first 150 years of the republic has been replaced by something far more sophisticated and far more insidious, what Bonilla-Silva refers to as "reasonable racism."[10] Michelle Fine, another sociologist who has done extensive work on issues of whiteness and race-based discrimination, presented a useful theoretical basis for how whiteness is developed and plays out in institutions. There are four underlying assumptions to this construct:

1. whiteness is being manufactured through institutional arrangements, "as if" hierarchy, stratification, and scarcity were inevitable;
2. whiteness is coproduced with other colors in a symbiotic relationship, where "white" stands for merit and advantage and "color" represents deficit and lack;

3. whiteness and color are relational and need to be studied as a system, rather than just considering the other and not the whole; and
4. the institutional design of whiteness creates racial identities and produces racial tensions.[11]

Racism is built into the fabric of our institutions. Individual acts of racism no longer need to occur for there to be continuing oppression of people of color. To understand the extent of systemic racism, it is vital to look at the ways a variety of sectors of our society interact to maintain white dominance. This book will examine the profession of architecture from the perspectives of education, professional practice, public policy, business management, and social networks.

WHY ARCHITECTURE?

This investigation into inequality in architecture began with my doctoral dissertation, an ethnographic case study of the lifeworld of one entrepreneur of color.[12] I was concerned with the ways his experiences as a black man—particularly as a black man in architecture—had shaped his life. The work focused on his frame of reference about the triumphs and tribulations he had experienced as the sole owner of an architecture firm.

As I searched for ways to conduct an academic examination of the work of the Fund, I wanted to give voice to a business owner of color to tell his story, a story not heard in academia. While the literature on racism and entrepreneurship is useful and illuminating, there is very little in print about racism as experienced at the firm level.[13] Grace Carroll made this point in an article in the *Journal of Comparative Family Studies*:

> Unfortunately, studies focusing on Black families and Black people in general have been fragmented and are typically pejorative. Cultural deviant models have predominated. . . . Research has not been much concerned with describing and analyzing actual everyday behaviors, attitudes, and coping mechanisms of African Americans with an ecological and functional perspective.[14]

The universe in this work was the intersection of institutional structures, public policy, and social networks. The ethnographic case method is an effective way to consider whole worlds that create the context in which the research informant operates. It provided a way to evaluate the effects not only of the institutions of education and government, but also of a myriad of professional and community networks.

Ethnography asks questions about the lifeworld of research participants. It tries to create a picture of their world, from their perspective, as seen through the eyes of the researcher. Questions that are of concern include: What are the things people care about? What are the ways they have addressed particular issues in their interactions with the dominant culture? How have they overcome barriers that institutional racism has placed in their way? What problems have they been unable to solve? How do they make meaning out of their lives within the business?

In using the ethnographic method, there are also questions for the researcher to answer. How do my values work for or against doing this work? In what ways am I, will I always be, an outsider, and what are the ways I am similar to my informants? How can I remain true to their words and still retain my own identity? This is the heart of ethnography: finding the balance between the informant's story and the researcher's worldview.[15] This approach called for a research subject who would be willing to have me with him or her in the office on a regular basis for an extended period.

As I began to look for a participant, I called on my economic development colleagues for suggestions. The name of one business owner was mentioned by all of them—an architect who had owned his own firm for nearly two decades. Like so many of the people I have spoken to about this research in the past two years, the idea of conducting research about a black architect probably would not have occurred to me.

I contacted him, and he agreed to meet with me. In our first conversation, we talked about the Fund's work with black-owned businesses. We discussed racism as I had observed it with Fund clients and he had lived it within the business. He was enthusiastic about the idea of establishing a place in the literature for voices like his. He told me, "I would be interested in joining your research because I have always thought my story should be told. I have white employees and professional colleagues who don't think it's a struggle for me to run this business. They can't see that being black—especially in this profession—is not the same as being white. If I try to tell them something that happens in the firm is racist, they don't believe me. I've always wanted to find a way to make these stories visible." I did not expect to gain his trust in the first meeting, nor to find such reinforcement for what I wanted to do. Now two years and twenty architects later, I understand the importance and the novelty of having a sympathetic white ear.

I spent three months in the firm. At the time, it was a twenty-person firm including eight women and nine people of color. The observations were carried out in the office and at meetings around town, where I observed the daily life of the firm and the owner.

The architect who participated in my dissertation suggested I read Melvin Mitchell's book, *The Crisis of the African-American Architect: Conflicting Cultures of Architecture and (Black) Power*.[16] He told me, "The thing about the Mitchell book is that there was nothing new, but it was nice to know I'm not alone. There are other people who feel the way I do and who view things the way I do. Mitchell makes it clear how racism is in this field."

There is a daily deluge of slights—not being fully accepted as a competent architect, despite decades of experience; not being included on the bid list for highly visible government projects, despite having the credentials to complete them; having only one or two professional colleagues with backgrounds or skin tone the same as his, despite having worked in the same city for over twenty years; and many more—that add up to a clear sense of being discriminated against on the basis of race. One of the reasons we developed a rapport early is that I did not discount the impact of racism on his practice.

As I followed him through his day at work, it was clear to me he was a well-respected architect, well-known among his colleagues, but being black had limited his growth and access quite apart from his competence. This is a complaint of many black professionals; they complete professional training, get certified in whatever way the profession requires, and then have to spend an inordinate amount of energy defending those credentials because they are black.[17] As Cornel West says,

> It's a version of the predicament faced by the wolf who would have to gnaw off a limb to escape from a trap. Hence, the appeal of that comforting old lie: I'm not a black *x* (poet, president, whatever), I'm an *x* who happens to be black. Alas, circumstance won't have it so. Nobody happens to be black: this is a definitional truth. For a world in which blackness is elective or incidental—worlds where you can "happen to be" black—is a world without blackness, a world, that is, where the concept has been dismantled or transfigured beyond recognition.[18]

ARCHITECTS IN THIS BOOK

The dearth of data on black architects led me to consider broadening my evaluation. This expanded research ultimately included twenty black architects. I began the selection process by putting together a list of the architects who surfaced in my academic research as the most visible in the community of black architects. I also asked advice of my dissertation research participant, who postdissertation had become my colleague and friend, and spoke with Dennis Mann, the codirector of the University of Cincinnati Architecture School's Center for the

Study of Practice. Mann and codirector Bradford Grant were responsible for the development and production of the *Directory of African American Architects*.[19]

The preliminary selection criteria were based on observations I had made in my academic work. I was looking for firm owners, with employees, who had been in that practice at least five years, knowing they would have experienced the rigors of professional competition, financial management, and employee management. Geographic diversity was important because the availability of social networks, and the attitudes about hiring black professionals, vary considerably in different regions of the country; metropolitan areas with large black populations tend to be more lucrative markets than locations with more limited black communities. Generational diversity was vital to get a sense of how different political experiences had affected the participants' perspectives on racism, architecture, and community. The pre–civil rights movement years, the movement decades, the Reagan years—all had distinct impacts on the cultural, social, and political contexts of the country and, specifically, on the ability of black architects to compete. Finally, working with architects who had achieved a high level of professional accomplishment, evidenced by publications, awards, and word of mouth, would provide a reasonable way to isolate the effects of racial oppression from the business problems all architecture firms encounter. Any architect who gains a measure of prominence is likely to be an architect who can sustain a practice; the instances of isolation and marginalization experienced by black architects were unlikely to be attributable to being in practice per se.

Eleven of the first twelve architects responded positively to a letter of inquiry. The remaining nine were recommended as the project proceeded. Four are from the West, three from the Midwest, four from the South, and nine from the East. Fifteen of the twenty architects have at least a master's degree, most in architecture. Twelve have been elected to the AIA College of Fellows. They range in age from thirty to seventy-five, with an average in the midforties. Four of them are female.

Seventeen are firm owners or co-owners; two are full-time academics, and eight teach part-time while practicing; five maintain offices in more than one location. Three have more than fifty employees (a "large" firm by AIA standards); one is a sole practitioner.

My interactions with each architect began with an unstructured interview. I met seventeen of the participants in person; the other three I spoke with on the phone. I did follow-up work with fourteen. The subsequent encounters ran from additional, formal unstructured interviews to social interactions. The interviews focused on educational experience; pre-firm ownership professional experience;

a variety of issues about firm ownership, including finding and retaining clients, financing the firm, doing government projects, and managing employees; and social networks.

The majority of the information the research participants shared with me was conveyed in stories. Many of the stories connected the architects with each other; some were short and personal, others long tales about government red tape and other management nightmares—but all had the common theme of racism in the profession.

The operating assumption in starting to develop this book—that people who did not know me or my history would be willing to take otherwise productive time to sit down with me and tell me about their lives—was reasonable given my dissertation work. The community of black architects is small, and the communication system is effective. As I began the interviews, news of this project spread quickly to others on my list. Still, I was concerned about whether or not I would be able to gain the interviewees' trust enough to get their stories.

Once I began the process, everyone I met with was gracious and took time away from busy schedules; they each began telling me stories within the first five minutes. I was curious about why they were so at ease sharing these stories with me. I was having lunch with one of the deans of black architecture, and I asked him why he thought his colleagues were so forthcoming. "Oh," he said, "we think these stories are really important, and you're all about telling them. As far as we're concerned, you're family." This sentiment was a confirmation that these voices need to be heard.

One last note about the research participants: the real names of the architects have been used when they are quoted in other publications; but in the interest of confidentiality, the names of the interviewees have been changed.

I assured the interviewees I would celebrate black architects. I believe telling their stories, daunting as some of them are, *is* a celebration. The men and women I interviewed for this book are so devoted to the profession they have been willing to put up with conditions that have driven less-determined professionals from the field. They persevered and have succeeded in building firms that have produced both first-rate buildings and a legacy for those black architects coming up. This book is a way to make their stories visible.

Early on in this research, one of the senior East Coast architects said to me, "If you're going to write a 'boo-hoo poor us' book, please don't bother. No black architects will want to read it, and it has the potential to do more harm than good for the white readers." Rather than writing a "terrible plight" book, this book describes the social, political, and economic context within which black architects practice. The big picture of this society is broken down into smaller pieces and evaluated for their impacts on individuals who are determined to push past the barriers. One of the women put it this way:

> I don't want to talk about these issues because I don't want to look too far and I don't want to think too hard about this stuff. I have reservations about talking to you. If you have things in your career and in your life that deal with racism and sexism, there would be a lot of stuff. It would be based on emotions. I may not want to see it the way I say it. I don't say everything because why should I? It becomes the headline. (Sharon Young)

The headline should not be about how hard life is for black architects, but rather how little understanding people have of the deeply ingrained inequality that exists in the United States. At the beginning of the twenty-first century, we have swung back around to convenient ways of blaming those who we have ensured will have to struggle. The media focus on issues such as "reverse discrimination," economic disparity between black and white households, and failing public schools could be useful in dispelling the nineteenth-century bootstrap myth. Instead, rather than focus on the political and social systems that contribute to sustained economic and social disparity, the media have reinforced the idea that oppression results from sloth and indolence rather than being the product of a skewed system. In addition to being important per se, the stories in this book fit into the larger narrative about the reality of daily life for people of color in the United States.

These stories are revealing. If nothing else, black architects—and for that matter all architects who are not white and male—remain invisible to most of us.[20] Their stories are moving, inspiring, and disconcerting. In Feagin's years of interviewing middle-class blacks, he has found over and over again that in contemporary America, race still trumps class.[21] The people I interviewed are well-educated experienced professionals. They are clear about what is important to them, and they have found ways to earn a living doing what they love. I am hard-pressed to think of many people who can say that about their lives.

Without exception, all have told story after story of the ways their professional development has been stymied by racism. They are pragmatic and realistic about what they can achieve—aesthetically, economically, and culturally—given the continuing climate of racism in this country. If they talk about it to white folks, they usually get accused of whining or, worse, are totally ignored.[22]

> Whites don't want to hear about it. If I'm at a dinner meeting seated at a table full of white architects, if they ask me a question that I believe has something to do with

race, I'm going to answer it truthfully. Some of them will stay with me and keep the conversation going, but always some will start another conversation. They don't want to hear it. They say, "Things have gotten so much better." (Nicholas Rose)

ECONOMIC, POLITICAL, AND SOCIAL CONTEXT FOR BLACK ARCHITECTS

Although the dictionary definition of race might lead us to believe otherwise, the concept of race is a social construction.[23] It has shifted across time, as the social, political, and cultural climates have changed. In their discussion of the historical development of the racial state, Omi and Winant point out, "Throughout the nineteenth century, many state and federal legal arrangements recognized only three racial categories: 'white,' 'Negro,' and 'Indian.'"[24] In California, conflicts arose over how to categorize Mexicans and Chinese. In the end, Mexicans were defined as white, and Chinese as Indian.

Although this seems ludicrous to us now, it does serve to remind us that the politicization of race is an American tradition. While the 1990 Census allowed Americans to choose only one of five race categories, the 2000 count let people choose more than one of six categories, increasing the possible number of race classifications to sixty-three.[25] Although in some ways this reflects a cultural acknowledgment that race in America is no longer merely bipolar, it does nothing to address in any substantive way the manner in which the norm in the United States remains white and middle class.

"If we project the relative changes in wealth [for black families] over the last 15 years into the future, it would take 200 years for the median wealth of a black family to be *half* that of a white family."[26] As long as black family wealth is 10 to 12 percent of white family wealth, all the hard work in the world will not create social or economic equality for blacks. Economic disparity remains a barrier to the ability of blacks, of any socioeconomic class, to achieve their full potential.

Oliver and Shapiro did the first extensive writing on the importance of looking at wealth, rather than income, when evaluating the relative economic success of blacks and whites.[27] Their work provided a way to think about racial economic inequality based on private wealth. Their thesis was that wealth brings advantage—in housing, education, health care, and generally in a sense of security. This is a very different picture from that developed by considering only income. The wealth gap creates limits for black architects, and other business owners of color, in part by limiting their access to investment capital, social networks, and other assets that would facilitate the success of their firms. An understanding of the disparity is not complete without the wealth analysis.

Conley followed in the path of Oliver and Shapiro in looking at the effect of wealth on the economic disparity between whites and blacks.[28] He went further, though, attempting to make some distinctions between race and class, and their respective impacts on access to opportunity. "Wealth, not occupation or education, is the realm in which the greatest degree of racial inequality lies in contemporary America."[29]

Public policy decisions contribute to the ongoing economic disparity. The changing political landscape has had a profound impact on black architects. Affirmative action, a systematic attempt ostensibly to minimize the disparity of opportunities between whites and people of color, has been a double-edged sword. Black architects, seldom chosen for corporate commissions, have been dependent on government work to grow their firms and maintain cash flow.[30] The access to public projects has waxed and waned over the past fifty years as the belief in "leveling the playing field" has gone in and out of favor. Additionally, when black-owned firms do get the work, there is a stigma associated with "just doing government work," creating the perception they are not qualified to do anything else.

Since the beginning, the profession of architecture has been dependent on a system of patronage. Building a profitable firm requires establishing personal relationships as a way to broaden contacts—social networks—to increase access to the people making decisions about hiring architects. Not only have blacks been limited in their ability to create those contacts with corporate executives and others in a position to hire architects but, as many interviewees told me, "People hire architects who look like themselves."

Social network analysis provides a framework for recognizing the importance of looking at the big picture if we are to gain an understanding of structural inequality.[31] This book presents a broad enough view that it will be possible to understand how the economic, political, and social landscapes in the United States come together to maintain an institutional system of disparity between whites and people of color.

PLAN OF THE BOOK

Stevens, in his book *The Favored Circle*, points out the problems with other sociological studies of architecture.[32] According to him, sociologists usually focus on the *products* of the occupation. This approach ignores the possibility that architects may have functions other than designing buildings, and it disconnects them from their social milieu and ignores internal stratification. Stevens's book, grounded in sociology, is very little about buildings and a lot about the social and cultural space the profession occupies. I, too, use "architecture" to refer to the economic, social, and cultural aspects of the discipline—the *context* of the profession rather than the buildings or the aesthetics.

Architecture is a profession steeped in patronage. As early as the Italian Renaissance, there was a split between the designers, those who not only came up with the aesthetic themes for the buildings but also managed the projects, and the craftsmen, those who were responsible for the actual production. Chapter 2 describes this legacy and how it has been reproduced in the United States. From the way the educational system is structured to the practice itself, this distinction between the designers, often considered the "stars," and everyone else has molded the culture of architecture. For black architects, who constitute a small minority, the economic and social disparities that exist in the United States are magnified in the profession.

A majority of the interviewees knew when they were young that architecture was the path they would choose. Following a rigorous academic curriculum and an intensive internship and licensing process, they went out in the world to become architects. Chapter 3 begins with architecture as a calling, and then analyzes the reality of practice. The interviewees' stories serve as a vehicle to look at what it takes to get into a practice and how the dominant culture is reinforced in the field. The chapter ends with discussions of service to community and collaborative joint ventures.

Politics can have a sizable impact on the success or failure of a firm. Affirmative action and set-aside programs have both received adverse publicity and increased scrutiny, and have been the basis of lawsuits. Chapter 4 presents a short history of both set-asides and affirmative action and a discussion of the role government work plays in black-owned firms.

Chapter 5 is a look at the business of running a firm. This is challenging for all entrepreneurs, and black architects have the additional demand of educating potential clients "downtown" that they are competent, and potential clients in "the community" about the products and services architects can provide. The role of industry associations, the difficulties of marketing, the joy of managing employees, and the challenges of growth are included to provide a comprehensive view of firm ownership and management.

As a result of architecture's legacy of patronage relationships, the practice is unusually dependent on social contacts. All business owners use social and professional networks to connect to customers, but this process is complicated for black architects. They need to get visible in the professional community, develop contacts in the architecture community, and find ways to stay connected to ethnic communities—all while trying to keep the business going. Chapter 6 presents an analysis of the importance and development of social networks.

The concluding chapter provides a summary of the stories that have been told and points out the ways the various pieces of the profession fit together to create a context entirely reflective of the dominant culture. The book concludes with suggestions for ways the profession, and the culture, can broaden the mainstream and create new, more inclusive ways.

I believe this book will be useful in helping readers think about racism in a different way. I also believe this book will validate the experience of black professionals and let them know they are not alone. I hope these stories will help all of us understand that the most useful response is to think about what we can do to break the institutional barriers faced by blacks, and all people of color, in the United States.

NOTES

For the sake of flow, there are some expressions I use in this book that are problematic. I want to make these clear from the beginning and acknowledge that their use may be culturally inappropriate. I was taught many years ago using the word "minority" to refer to people of color is a way to further the perception they are "less than." However, the expression "Minority-Owned Business Enterprise" (MBE) is often more workable than "businesses owned by people of color."

I will also use the *United States* instead of *America*, believing that America includes all the countries of three continents. There are a couple instances, however, when "American" is less awkward. For the most part, personal pronouns refer to the gender of the speaker. In the case where there is not a specific reference, I have tried to alternate between the feminine and the masculine.

1. Much of what has become part of my daily vocabulary and understanding remains shocking news to many of my white friends. The daily grind of racial and class oppression is outside the view of most European Americans.

2. Cornel West, *Race Matters* (New York: Vintage, 2001), 5.

3. American Institute of Architects, *AIA Firm Survey, 2000/2002* (Washington, DC: AIA, 2000).

4. Jean Barber, "Profile of the Minority Architect" and Roundtable "Today's Minority Architect: A Major Force," Minority Resources Committee of the AIA, July 1990, 3.

5. See Kathryn H. Anthony, *Designing for Diversity: Gender, Race, and Ethnicity in the Architectural Profession* (Urbana: University of Illinois Press, 2001); Melvin Mitchell, *The*

Crisis of the African-American Architect: Conflicting Cultures of Architecture and (Black) Power (Lincoln, NE: Writer's Club, 2001); and Garry Stevens, *The Favored Circle: The Social Foundations of Architectural Distinction* (Cambridge, MA: MIT Press, 1998).

6. See Margaret Andersen and Patricia H. Collins, eds., *Race, Class and Gender: An Anthology* (Belmont, CA: Wadsworth, 1998); Stephen L. Carter, "The Black Table, the Empty Seat, and the Tie," in *Lure and Loathing: Essays on Race, Identity and the Ambivalence of Assimilation*, ed. Gerald Early (New York: Penguin, 1993); Robert T. Carter, "Is White a Race? Expressions of White Identity," in *Off White: Readings on Race, Power, and Society*, ed. Michelle Fine, Lois Weis, Linda C. Powell, and L. Mun Wong (New York: Routledge, 1997); and Thomas M. Shapiro, *The Hidden Cost of Being African American: How Wealth Perpetuates Inequality* (New York: Oxford University Press, 2004), for various views on whiteness and blackness in the United States.

7. For an insightful and candid look into the lives of blacks in the middle class, see Joe Feagin and Melvin Sikes, *Living with Racism: The Black Middle-Class Experience* (Boston: Beacon, 1994); and Joe Feagin, Kevin E. Early, and Karyn D. McKinney, "The Many Costs of Discrimination: The Case of Middle-Class African-Americans," *Indiana Law Review* 34, no. 4 (2001): 1311–60.

8. Among many others, see Stephen L. Carter, "Black Table"; Ellis Cose, *Rage of a Privileged Class* (New York: Harper Perennial, 1995); Feagin et al. "Many Costs of Discrimination"; Henry Louis Gates and Cornel West, *The Future of the Race* (New York: Knopf, 1996); and bell hooks, *Killing Rage: Ending Racism* (New York: Holt, 1995), for incisive discussions on the impacts of racism on people of color.

9. See Cose, *Rage of a Privileged Class*; Peggy McIntosh, "White Privilege and Male Privilege: A Personal Account of Coming to See Correspondences Through Work in Women's Studies," in *Race, Class and Gender: An Anthology*, ed. Margaret Andersen and Patricia H. Collins, 94–105 (Belmont, CA: Wadsworth, 1988); and George Simpson and Milton Yinger, *Racial and Cultural Minorities: An Analysis of Prejudice and Discrimination* (New York: Harper & Row, 1985), for discussions on the differences in expectations between blacks and whites in the United States.

10. Eduardo Bonilla-Silva, *Racism without Racists: Color-Blind Racism and the Persistence of Racial Inequality in the United States* (Lanham, MD: Rowman & Littlefield, 2003).

11. Michelle Fine, "Witnessing Whiteness," in *Off White*, ed. Fine, Weis, Powell, and Wong, 57–65.

12. Victoria Kaplan, *Against All Odds: An Ethnographic Case Study of One African American Architect*, Ph.D. dissertation (Santa Barbara, CA: Fielding Graduate Institute, 2004).

13. The work on entrepreneurship and racism falls between the business, sociology, and economic development literature. For a broad view of the topic, see Timothy Bates, *Race, Self-Employment and Upward Mobility: An Illusive American Dream* (Washington, DC: Woodrow Wilson Center Press, 1997); William D. Bradford, "The Wealth Dynamics of Entrepreneurship for Black and White Families in the U.S." (author's manuscript: Seattle, 2001); Nancy A. Denton, "The Role of Residential Segregation in Promoting and Managing Inequality in Wealth and Property," *Indiana Law Review* 34, no.4 (2001): 1199–1211;

Fred Galves, "The Discriminatory Impact of Traditional Lending Criteria: An Economic and Moral Critique," *Seton Hall Law Review* 29, no. 4 (1999): 1467–87; Daniel P. Immergluck, "Progress Confined: Increases in Black Home Buying and the Persistence of Residential Segregation," *Journal of Urban Affairs* 20, no. 4 (1998): 443–57; Manning Marable, *How Capitalism Underdeveloped Black America* (Boston: South End, 1983); Melvin L. Oliver and Thomas M. Shapiro, *Black Wealth/White Wealth: A New Perspective on Racial Inequality* (New York: Routledge, 1997); and Thomas M. Shapiro, *Hidden Cost of Being African American.*

14. Grace Carroll, "Mundane Extreme Environmental Stress and African American Families: A Case for Recognizing Different Realities," *Journal of Comparative Family Studies* 29, no. 2 (1998): 278.

15. Michael H. Agar, *The Professional Stranger: An Informal Introduction to Ethnography* (New York: Academic, 1980); Sherryl Kleinman and Martha Kopp, *Emotions and Fieldwork* (Newbury Park, CA: Sage, 1993); and John Lofland and Lynn Lofland, *Analyzing Social Settings: A Guide to Qualitative Observation and Analysis* (Belmont, CA: Wadsworth, 1995).

16. Mitchell, *Crisis of the African-American Architect.*

17. See Carter "Black Table"; Cose, *Rage of a Privileged Class*; Patricia Dawson, *Forged by the Knife: The Experience of Surgical Residency from the Perspective of a Woman of Color* (Seattle: Open Hand, 1999); Magali Sarfatti Larson, *The Rise of Professionalism* (Berkeley: University of California Press, 1977); and Norma Merrick Sklarek, "Norma Merrick Sklarek," *California Architecture* (January–February 1985): 22–23.

18. Henry Louis Gates and Cornel West, *Future of the Race*, xviii.

19. Bradford C. Grant and Dennis A. Mann, eds., *Directory of African American Architects* (Cincinnati: Center for the Study of Practice, 1995).

20. As R. K. Stewart has pointed out in the foreword, *most* architects are invisible to the general public. Architects of color and women architects are only more so.

21. Feagin and Sikes, *Living with Racism*; and Feagin et al., "Many Costs of Discrimination."

22. Paul Kivel addressed the issue of whites ignoring the complaints of people of color: "When people of color are angry about racism it is legitimate anger. It is not their oversensitivity, but our lack of sensitivity, that causes this communication gap. They are vulnerable to the abuse of racism everyday. They are experts on it. White society, and most of us individually, rarely notice racism." Paul Kivel, *Uprooting Racism: How White People Can Work for Racial Justice* (Philadelphia: New Society, 1996), 93.

23. Manning Marable. "Beyond Racial Identity Politics: Towards a Liberation Theory for Multicultural Democracy," in *Race, Class and Gender: An Anthology*, ed. Margaret Andersen and Patricia Collins (Belmont, CA: Wadsworth, 1995), 362.

24. Michael Omi and Howard Winant, *Racial Formation in the U.S.* (New York: Routledge & Kegan Paul, 1986), 76.

25. Deborah Kong, "The 2000 Census: Looking Beyond Color Lines," *Seattle Post-Intelligencer*, June 29, 2001, A1.

26. William Bradford, "Black Family Wealth in the United States," in *The State of Black America 2000* (Washington, DC: National Urban League, 2000), 105.

27. Oliver and Shapiro, *Black Wealth/White Wealth*.

28. Dalton Conley, *Being Black, Living in the Red: Race, Wealth, and Social Policy in America* (Berkeley: University of California Press, 1999).

29. Conley, *Being Black, Living in the Red*, 52.

30. There is no hard numerical data on the awarding of corporate architecture commissions. However, there is strong anecdotal evidence, not only in the stories in this book, but also in Max Bond, "The Black Architect's Experience," *Architectural Record* (June 1992): 60–61; Thomas D. Boston, *Affirmative Action and Black Entrepreneurship* (New York: Routledge, 1999); Benjamin Forgey, "First Black Designed Building in Downtown DC," *Washington Post*, March 30, 2002, Style C1, C5; Jane Holtz Kay, "Invisible Architects: Minority Firms Struggle to Achieve Recognition in a White-Dominated Profession," *Architecture* (April 1991): 106–113; Karen E. Hudson, *Paul R. Williams, Architect: A Legacy of Style* (New York: Rizzoli, 1993); and Jack Travis, ed., *African American Architects in Current Practice* (New York: Princeton Architectural Press, 1991).

31. Albert-Laszlo Barabasi, *Linked: How Everything Is Connected to Everything Else and What It Means for Business, Science and Everyday Life* (New York: Penguin, 2003).

32. Stevens, *The Favored Circle*, 33.

ARCHITECTURE: A WHITE GENTLEMEN'S PROFESSION?

I maintain that the highest forms of leadership also engage a wide fol-lowing. But architects are particularly disadvantaged in attracting such an audience because concerns about the designed environment are al-most entirely absent from popular discourse.

For example, although about half of all U.S. senators are attorneys, not one is an architect. The public recognizes that laws make our collec-tive life possible but is apparently unaware of the role of the designed en-vironment in our quality of life, and even our survival, as a nation.

—Sharon E. Sutton, *Architecture* (1996)

The architecture profession's legacy is one of patronage, privilege, and power. What started as a trade evolved into a tool of the aristocracy—a true profes-sion. In the Renaissance, as in the twenty-first century, capital was required to complete buildings; political power ensured the construction of edifices that might otherwise not be constructed. The patronage of the wealthy both created the profession and enabled practitioners to see their designs constructed.

Architecture remains a profession set apart from our daily lives in the United States.[1] In part, this is because architecture has maintained a kind of pristine is-land, disconnected from the social contexts and mundane realities of daily life. Although we spend most of our time connecting with the built environment, most of us have very little understanding of how it comes to be and how it affects and reflects our lives.[2]

In the United States, professions are occupations that hold a high status position and are perceived to have special power and privilege. There are certain clearly defined characteristics that set professions apart. They include such things as cognitive standardization on the basis of the training; a common language or jargon best understood by those in the know; and therefore the claim to specialized knowledge. This claim is evidenced both by completion of lengthy educational curricula and professional licensing. Despite encroachment from other disciplines such as engineering and planning, the ability to define both the content of the education and the conditions of access to architecture remain identifying characteristics.[3]

HISTORY

The profession we in the English-speaking West know as architecture began in the Italian Renaissance. The patrons created both the market and the method for the profession. They were no longer satisfied to use craftsmen to construct their buildings; they wanted artists who could understand design and had skills adequate for managing the complex process of building large projects.[4] This required special knowledge and enabled the designers to separate themselves from the physical labor. Architects became the first professionals to get closer in class to their aristocratic employers.[5] As in contemporary America, most people had some exposure to medicine, and some had business with the law, but from the beginning architecture remained segregated from the daily lives of the populous.[6]

From the beginning, the capital commitment required to construct this art form limited involvement to those who were either wealthy patrons or the representatives of wealthy patrons, such as mayors or priests. In other art forms, painting, music, or literature, for example, the value of the "product" is quite apart from the cost of materials, giving the artist a degree of autonomy architects seldom enjoy. Then, as now, the value of a building was determined at least as much by size and cost as by aesthetics.[7]

As Sharon Sutton observed during a presentation at AIA Seattle, "The servitude to power and lack of control over the design process began in the sixteenth century. There was an historical emphasis on monument-making. We are stuck in an ancient legacy."[8] The mystique, and isolation, of architecture remain. Other areas of mainstream European American culture have appropriated styles from African American culture—music, painting, literature, and fashion— but European influences remain the central model of good architectural design.

Often referred to as the "White Gentlemen's Profession," in the United States the field continues to be thoroughly Eurocentric.[9]

THE MOVEMENT OF BLACKS INTO ARCHITECTURE

The modern-day profession of architecture is a direct descendant of that early patronage system. In some cases, Thomas Jefferson being the most notable example, the wealthy dabbled in design. They did not, however, construct the buildings themselves. During slavery, blacks were master craftsmen and were depended on for a variety of building projects. For the most part, these black craftsmen were not identified by name. As Feagin points out, "Positive achievements of whites may be put in the active tense [e.g., 'Jefferson designed these doors'], while those of blacks may be put in the passive tense [e.g., 'the doors were installed in 1809']."[10]

After Emancipation, a small but vigorous class of black landowners developed. They utilized the talents of the black builders for construction on their properties. By the end of the nineteenth century, industrialization, the growth of trade unions, and a volatile economy had decimated the free black planter class. The black master craftsmen had come to depend on them for building projects; the planters' financial demise led to a similar fate for the builders.[11] This was another step in the process that separated African Americans from the work of design. Architecture was becoming more of a profession just as the economic choices for blacks were diminishing. From the beginning, black business owners faced barriers to entrepreneurship that gave unfair advantages to white-owned commercial entities. According to Marable, there were several factors limiting black economic opportunity after Emancipation.

> According to the 1870 Census, less than one-third of southern urban blacks could read; although many had skills in the crafts, they had no experience as entrepreneurs. They had no experience with selling products, or pricing, or managing employees; many states passed new "Black Codes." Any black man who didn't have an employer (and, thus, presumably was self-employed) was considered a vagrant and could be imprisoned. In some states it was possible to be self-employed, but it required a license, which cost black men $100 and was free to whites.[12]

Beginning after the Civil War, the historically black colleges and universities (HBCUs) were established in the South to provide a means for blacks to receive higher education. The establishment of these institutions provided some opportunities for black architects to design new buildings. The Tuskegee Institute, in

Tuskegee, Alabama, was founded in 1881 by Booker T. Washington. He established the first architectural program to which blacks had relatively easy access. Many believe Tuskegee was the beginning for black professional architecture.[13] Washington stood up to the demands of the white philanthropists who were funding the institute that he hire their white architects; Washington insisted the Tuskegee buildings be designed by faculty and built by students. Fortunately and unfortunately, "the Tuskegee campus, 123 years later is still the largest private real estate assemblage and new development deal ever put together inside Black America."[14]

Robert Taylor, an 1892 graduate of the architecture program at the Massachusetts Institute of Technology and likely the first black architecture graduate from a non-HBCU institution, was a valedictorian of his class. When he was unable to find a job practicing in Boston, Washington convinced him to join the faculty at Tuskegee. John A. Lankford, one of Taylor's earliest students, established the first known black professional architectural office, in Jacksonville, Florida, in 1899.[15] Lankford is also credited by some as starting the architecture program at Howard University.

The faculty at Tuskegee stuck to the model of architect as master builder, even when the architecture programs at non-HBCUs were becoming more and more professional, and increasingly separate from planning and construction. Mitchell explains the Tuskegee decision this way:

> The bifurcation of the old master builder and the gentleman architect made sense for the white world. There was a parallel universe of builders, developers, financiers, suppliers, manufacturers and craftsmen. They also had an abundance of wealthy capitalist and industrialist patrons and clients.[16]

While Tuskegee was still focused on the past, Howard University was looking to the future. In an article in the [AIA] National Associates Committee newsletter, Jack Travis writes: "In and around 1919, Howard University opened its doors to a new kind of black architect. The image of the black architect as 'Gentleman,' thus aspiring to the same ideology as white male architects but finding a very different set of circumstances when entering the profession, emerged."[17]

The Legacy of Black Architects

Many of the architects I have spoken with talked about the first black American practitioners. Nelson Norton gave me his view on the pride black architects have in the early pioneers of black architecture.

All architects are aware of their heritage, but I find for black architects the history takes on an added meaning. It's about the "history of the race," about the accomplishments their ancestors were able to make during a time when blacks in many parts of this country were not allowed to own businesses, and following close on a time when they were not allowed to learn to read.

The reverence and respect with which Norton and others speak of their professional heritage is an indication of the magnitude of the accomplishments of the early black architects. They faced seemingly insurmountable barriers and managed to succeed and leave a significant legacy at a time when Jim Crow laws would have it be otherwise.[18]

The attention to legacy is also about making sure black architecture students and practitioners know they *have* a heritage. The profession and the training curriculum are so focused on European architecture as The Model of good design it is vital for architects with a different cultural heritage to understand they have a legitimate claim to the profession. Architects who are other than "the norm," that is, white and male, have to learn on their own to reflect an aesthetic and a philosophy connected to their ethnic heritage. Black architects are stuck in a bind: they are expected to behave like white architects, taught to design like white architects, and then kept out of mainstream markets by selection processes that favor whites.

In 1996, the last year detailed data were available, New York State had 152 black architects, the most of any state. Of that total, only 34 lived outside the New York City metropolitan area. A lot of the early work in New York City was done by architects trained in the architecture school at Tuskegee; the legacy of the Tuskegee architects reached into the heart of the city. Sharon Young, one of the members of the New York Coalition of Black Architects (NYCOBA), convened a session on the history of black architects in New York City during the 1994 meeting of the National Organization of Minority Architects (NOMA). She reinforced Nelson Norton's comment about the importance of understanding the legacy of the early black architects when she introduced the session by saying, "It's important to understand the value of architects who came before us. We need to understand how different firms in different places are connected." Stevens, in the *Favored Circle*, talked about the ways highly successful white architects bequeathed their stardom to associates; the early black architects also left a trail that connected many of the most important black architects of the last century.[19]

In the 1900s, the most prominent black architect was Vertner Woodson Tandy. He attended the Tuskegee Institute and graduated from the program at Cornell. Tandy was the first black architect licensed in the state of New York. White real estate developers had overbuilt Harlem. They needed to sell these properties, so they sold to black families. Tandy had his office on Broadway and 38th. They designed St. Philips church on 138th, the biggest church at the time. This encouraged black folks to move to Harlem.

John Louis Wilson graduated in 1928. He was the first black graduate from Columbia. Wilson worked primarily in Harlem; he designed the 547 units of the Harlem River Houses, one of the first projects on the east coast accomplished through community agitation. Wilson also did the State Office Building, at 125th and 7th Avenue. Built in 1967, it was the tallest black-designed building in New York City until the Max Bond–designed Towers on the Park. Tandy and Wilson were just two of the important pioneers of black architecture in New York.[20]

Sharon Young closed the session saying, "If you don't write the history of black architects, people won't know about it. The stories disappear if they don't get written. We need to be responsible for documenting our passing through here." Her efforts, and those of her fellow NYCOBA members, are attempts to make visible a presence that has been invisible to most architectural historians. One of the ways to increase the number of black architects is to be able to show black youth this long and venerable heritage. As we shall see in the section on education, the legacy of black architecture is invisible to students.

Besides providing reinforcement for black students, there is an additional reason this heritage is so important. In the education system, the references to architectural history are all based in the European, that is, white male, tradition. The legacy of the Italian and German architects especially is studied and emulated in the curriculum. Learning the inheritance left by the early black architects gives contemporary black architects a grounding and a validity based on their own culture. It provides positive reinforcement for practitioners whose education is focused on modeling a western European aesthetic. For European American architects, their heritage is an integral part of the curriculum and the practice. African American architects have to make a deliberate effort to discover their lineage; they have to look to models within their own culture.

As Nicholas Rose said, "I always ask myself, 'What would [Thelonius] Monk do?' I'm trying to draw my heritage."

On the West Coast, the most visible black architect was Paul Revere Williams. Williams became known for his ability to follow through on promises and to create preliminary design schemes literally overnight. He created pragmatic solutions to race problems so he could do his work, despite the fact that he designed spaces, such as the restaurant at the Beverly Hills Hotel, he was not allowed to enter. Williams became the first black member of the American Institute of Architects (AIA) in 1926 and the first black Fellow in 1956. In 1970, he became the first black AIA vice president.[21]

From 1914 to 1921, he worked for various firms. In June 1921, Williams was licensed; he started his own office in 1924. Williams designed the central restaurant and theme structure at Los Angeles International Airport. Williams is also known for designing the homes of many Hollywood stars, including Betty Grable, Cary Grant, and Frank Sinatra. Williams told of the discomfort of potential clients when they discovered he was black. "In the moment that they met me and discovered they were dealing with a Negro, I could see many of them 'freeze.' Their interest in discussing plans waned instantly and their one remaining concern was to discover a convenient exit without hurting my feelings."[22]

Like all the architects I interviewed, Williams just wanted to practice architecture, so he devised ways to make the clients more comfortable. Reese tells the story of how he learned to draw upside down, figuring no white client would ever want to sit on the same side of the table with him.[23] White male architects who had read this story told me *all* architects learn to draw upside down so they can sit across from clients. I read and heard this story a number of times, from a variety of sources. Like so many issues of systemic racism, if Williams believed it was necessary because of race, it probably was. The perception of discriminatory behavior is in the eye of the recipient.

According to statistics from the University of Cincinnati Architecture School's Center for the Study of Practice, in 1991 there were 44 black female licensed architects. By 2004, there were 145. "The informal sorority of black, female architects may be the nation's smallest profession. But hope is building. In about the last 10 years, black women have more than tripled their numbers as licensed architects."[24] These numbers bring a new perspective to the magnitude of the accomplishments of the early black women architects. I was speaking with one of the East Coast architects about the legacy of the early black architects. She told me about her excitement when she discovered the early women in black architecture:

> You need to read Dreck's book.[25] That's where I read about the first two black women licensed architects. I knew how they must have felt. Because there are so few of us, I understood it. I became kind of obsessed with the second one; she was licensed in 1948. I knew she was still alive. She was quoted saying she felt she'd never be able to get what she needed in the United States. She moved to Brazil and did houses for the wealthy and was a project architect for a white-owned firm. (Sharon Young)

Black women in architecture have had to deal not only with the racism in the profession, but also with the sexism. Even now, at the beginning of the twenty-first century, women constitute only 20 percent of all licensed architects.[26] Young told me she understood why black women architects would feel they must move out of the country in order to achieve their goals as architects. The culture of Brazil was welcoming to a black, female professional in 1948; the architect Young spoke of was able to achieve professional freedom in Brazil she never would have experienced in the United States.

Norma Sklarek is one of the most acclaimed women in the field.[27] In 1954, she became licensed as an architect in the State of New York. In 1966, she became the first black woman to be licensed as an architect in California. For her outstanding contribution to architecture, Sklarek became the first black woman to be honored by her peers with Fellowship in AIA.[28] At the time of the award in 1980, only 43 female architects had been named Fellow by the AIA. According to the AIA, in mid-2005, 174 of the 2,199 Fellows were female.

EDUCATION

The basic structure of the professions encourages inequality. The educational and licensing requirements, hallmarks of professional power, perpetuate race and class issues. A student seeking professional training must be able to display a solid educational background and either obtain scholarships or other funding or have sufficient family resources to cover the training.[29] The underrepresentation of students of color in architecture is not unique among professional training programs. It is difficult to make an exact comparison of enrollment or graduation rates by ethnicity across programs because there are limited data for architecture broken down by ethnicity. However, it is possible to get a useful estimate. Unless otherwise noted, the data that appear in this book on blacks in architecture have come from the *Directory of African American Architects*.[30]

According to the 2000 U.S. Census, 75.1 percent of the population (who claimed one race) are white.[31] Data on total law school enrollment for 2004–2005, available on the website of the American Bar Association, show total law school minority enrollment of 29,489, or 20 percent of the total. Forty-eight percent of the total graduates were women. In 2004, 40,018 juris doctor (JD) degrees were awarded. Twenty-one percent went to students of color; 49.5 percent went to women. Of the total degrees awarded to people of color, 32 percent, or 6.7 percent of the total JDs awarded, went to blacks.[32]

The picture is similar in medicine.[33] In the 2004–2005 school year, total medical school minority enrollment was 19,754, or 31.6 percent of the total. In 2004, 15,821 degrees were awarded. Of those, 35 percent were students of color. Of that total, 20 percent went to blacks, or 6.7 percent of the total. While these numbers are low relative to representation in the total population, blacks are better represented in medicine and law than in architecture schools.[34]

Law, medicine, information systems, and engineering, to name a few, all have serious deficiencies in the diversity of the student body. However, one difference, especially between architecture on the one hand and law and medicine on the other, is where the power lies; in the legal and medical professions, the practitioner has some power over the "customer." Although contemporary clients and patients are more likely to argue, or seek a second opinion, than those of even ten years ago, the doctor and the lawyer still have opinions based on extensive precedent-setting literature. In architecture, the practitioner has some control over the health and safety issues, but the client has the ultimate decision-making authority about everything else.

One final distinction in the practice arena lies in the choices lawyers and doctors have to work in institutions located in ethnic communities. As in architecture, professional positions working in ethnic communities are not the best-paying, or highest prestige jobs, but in other fields, those job do exist.[35] With the demise of community design centers, architects who wish to work in community must make their own way.

The educational requirements of professions are mandated by the practice. The goal is to retain the specialized knowledge, contain the standardization, and meet the criteria for professional licensing. By defining the education, the profession can maintain its long-established image.[36]

At the risk of exaggerating a widely held perception of the discipline, I contend that education in architecture, with its focus on the design studio, reinforces the system where designers are perceived as the stars and everyone else disappears out of the view of the public. This system, created and reinforced by practitioners, exacerbates the cultural divide. Sharon Sutton, a vocal critic of both the profession and design education, made a clear statement about the narrow nature of architectural education.

> While architectural practitioners have been accused of a "cultural imperialism," . . . we can see similar myopic practices in architecture schools' visioning of the architectural act, where the "spotlight" is fixed on the design studio. This framing allows a sharp focus on the aesthetic and geometric dimensions, and blurred vision

on the surrounding components. . . . Once the spotlight focuses on "the drawing board design," the other characters, props, and actions on the stage become simply "supporting cast."

An exclusionary definition of architecture—the real Architecture—as design or practice not only leaves us without a knowledge base, it makes it less likely for persons of color and women to get into and be successful in the field by eliminating a whole array of opportunities that would appeal to the talents and interests of a more diverse group.[37]

Sutton's criticism points out how the narrow focus on design precludes attention to other facets of the profession. The "supporting cast" to which she refers includes those who perform a wide range of activities. Site planning, project management, consulting to other disciplines, teaching, academic research, and real estate development are but a few of the alternatives for architecture graduates. The focus on design discourages students from pursuing these other activities. Given the limited number of opportunities for blacks to obtain design jobs, Sutton points out one way institutional racism continues to operate in the training process. Aesthetic concerns are only one part of the whole picture of what the discipline represents, but the focus on design supports the Eurocentric view of what Architecture is about.

The embedded structure of education in architecture is a reflection of the dominant culture. When asked whether his work had been informed by a foreign influence, Jack Travis, a leading proponent of an Afrocentric architecture, responded, in print: "My education—Eurocentric and designed by white males—has given me a narrow view of who I am, where I come from. So, in a sense, my education is the foreign influence in my work."[38]

Travis's words reflect the reality of a professional education process that is broadly Eurocentric. In many programs, students are divided from the beginning into design studios. This system requires students to work closely together as a group. Outside of the HBCU programs,[39] students of color are a distinct minority. Particularly in the master's programs, the studio system assumes a level of cooperation and trust among students that these students often cannot find.

Appendix A, a demographic study of African American architectural education, provides graduation data for 1,400 licensed black architects. Completed in the spring of 2005, the study reveals "37% of African American architects hold at least one degree from an HBCU; . . . there are only seven accredited architecture programs at HBCUs and over 110 other accredited programs."[40] While HBCU programs obviously make a significant contribution to the pool of licensed black architects, over 60 percent graduated from "majority" schools. Almost forty years after Columbia University designed a program aimed at increasing the number of black students, it still tops the list of universities with ten or more licensed African American graduates.

Design Is All

There are several reasons for the Western focus of architecture programs and for the importance placed on design. The patronage model, established in western Europe, was adopted in the United States at the birth of the profession here. The system established a collaborative model between the patrons, the sources of capital, and the architects, those with the ability to provide the design. The architects were the intermediary between the people and institutions wanting to create the buildings and the craftspeople who were able to implement the designs. Design was the medium of status accumulation. As in the Renaissance, the architects achieved status both by their closeness to the client and their distance from the craft. Design, and particularly European-influenced design, became a source of professional and social capital for architects.

With these early efforts to create a clear distinction between the designers and the builders, African Americans, with their tradition of master builder, were left behind. Given that the Western practice is dependent on a patronage system, and there have been few patrons in communities of color, black architects have not been visible. As a result, black elementary and high school students are not exposed to architects.[41] They do not have role models in the profession; they often do not know if they have talent, because they have no exposure to the field.

> Blacks in high schools and colleges have tended to choose careers other than architecture perhaps continuing to perceive architecture as a "white male" profession. Statistically there are relatively few black architect mentors or role models. . . . [W]ithin black families white community architecture still seems to be an especially remote and esoteric profession, one rarely considered by students who nevertheless might have the requisite talents and motivation.[42]

Once they get into architecture school, they are only exposed to the history of European architecture, are not exposed to the history of blacks as builders, and are given no sense of the cultural relevance of the field.[43]

Cultural Clash

The concerns about inequality in architectural education go beyond structural concerns. There are additional cultural issues that are not addressed in the curriculum development, but may be reflected in the statistics on the participation of black students.[44] Yvonne Bell, in her 1994 article "A Culturally Sensitive Analysis of Black Learning Style," provides a new way of thinking about the differences. Although written about learning styles, Bell's work is readily applicable to architecture and to businesses.[45]

Bell says the European worldview is dominant in American education. The African American worldview, and hence learning style, is distinct from the Eurocentric view, which leaves African Americans at a disadvantage in learning in the United States. She points out, "Western behavioral science operates in an oppressive fashion for African Americans."[46] Architectural training provides a vivid illustration of Bell's theory. The design studio model, with its focus on production, is coupled with the presentation of historical work that is almost entirely European.[47] Additionally, there are few black faculty, so black students find few role models.[48]

According to Bell, the European worldview is competitive—"survival of the fittest"—and controlling. Critical thinking and cognitive capabilities are valued. The abilities to use abstract symbols and to conceptualize solutions to problems are prized and rewarded.

The African worldview, by contrast, is relational and spiritual. The survival of the group is placed ahead of the drive of the individual. "Harmony with nature" is valued over the control of nature. A holistic approach using symbols, intuition, complementarity, and spiritual practices comprises the African approach to "knowing." This is in diametric opposition to the logical, rational, cognitive approach rewarded in the dominant culture.

The model is useful as a way to better understand the assumptions inherent in a Eurocentric education system. School is one more place where blacks are required to be bicultural in order to succeed. This is not an issue for white students, especially white middle-class students, who are raised and cultivated in the dominant culture.[49] The culture clash is visually apparent in the architecture curriculum, where European styles alone are represented.

Max Bond is one of the most influential black architects in the United States. In a lengthy article about him in the Washington Post, it is possible to pick out the genesis of his understanding about the importance of learning about other architectural traditions, specifically the validation he got from being exposed to the North African architecture of Tunisia. All the architects I spoke with who had gone to Columbia when Max was on the faculty in the Architecture School still understand the impact of learning about architecture that is not Eurocentric, architecture that is more reflective of their heritage. After Bond graduated from Harvard, he was a Fulbright scholar in Paris. On his way, he stopped in Tunisia to visit his parents. In looking at the architecture in Tunisia, he discovered some basic truths about architecture. As Lynn Duke explains in her *Washington Post* article:

> It was, Bond says, the "architecture of conquest," of one culture asserting itself over another. And suddenly Bond was struck by something: Beyond pure aesthetics, architecture is about power, the power to transmit a culture's symbols, its politics.
>
> That is why, he realized, "when one culture dominates another it brings its literature, its language, its religion and its architecture."
>
> He didn't learn this in school. There had been no philosophical talk about power and conquest and architecture's role. In fact, Tunisia made him realize the limits of his formal studies. But what two Harvard degrees had not given him he would pick up on his own during that summer he calls "a great moment in my architectural development."
>
> He'd been taught that buildings such as those were only "vernacular" architecture. It was a term he often felt was used to marginalize the architecture of the Third World, which often was more functional than artistic, compared with the architecture of Europe and the United States.
>
> He'd been taught that real architecture had its roots in the structures of the European classical era and that ancient ruins like those at Dougga were the source from which this architectural-cultural dogma grew.
>
> "The European architecture was the only architecture that was 'high art,' and that was just accepted," Bond says of his formal training.
>
> "So in Tunisia, one really begins to see, well, wait a minute: This really is not true."[50]

Architecture is so unknown to people outside the industry there is little discourse in the larger community on the relationships between people and space, or physical space and culture. On a walk around midtown Manhattan, one of the East Coast architects was talking about colonial architecture and the ways it reflects the power of the colonizers. He mentioned that, in Nigeria, the village residential architecture is constructed so that generations of families can use the structures effectively, but when they are finished, they can leave the structures to return to the earth. The colonial architecture, on the other hand, is built to last. His practice, in the middle of a major metropolitan area, is both at odds with his cultural training and consistent with his academic training:

> There was a couple from Ghana, clients of mine, who were getting ready to build a million dollar home. In the end, they built a postmodern home. They needed the house to be in context. They were protecting the value of the property, which is different from the design and economic needs of a South Bronx housing project. It's important to remember, though, at the base level, *they're still all just buildings.*

The product is the same between black and white architects. The only difference is the process and the experience of the process. The practice of architecture is more and more about the people and about 1 percent about the plans. (Wendell Marshall)

Marshall was pragmatic about the real estate market and the need to protect a sizable investment. He also expressed a sense of sadness about having to design structures that may or may not have anything to do with the cultural beliefs of the owners. In the case of these particular clients, they all agreed postmodern would be the "best" choice, but it was clear he wished it had been otherwise.

Mentoring

While racism and sexism continue to plague the profession, young black architects are making an effort to get active in promoting a different image. They feel they have a responsibility to teach young people in communities of color; they do what they can to ensure kids know about architecture. It is one way these architects can work to increase the numbers of blacks in the field. One young woman told me,

I've been working with seventh and eighth grade girls in Long Beach. I tell them how we got interested in architecture, and about the process so they know that people of color do this [architecture]. My father was always doodling. He passed away when I was six, but I still have lots of memories of his doodles. My first knowledge of architecture came from the Brady Bunch.

At seven or eight, I started drawing houses. My mother didn't know how to get me involved. My senior year in high school I took my first drafting class, a class, by the way, which is no longer offered in that school due to budget cuts. The first day of class there were two women. The other woman dropped the class the second day. There were a few other people of color in the class. The guys tutored me. The high school drafting teacher asked if I had ever thought about architecture. We agreed I would need to apply to a state school because I couldn't afford a private school. I got into one of them. When I went to school, it was my first time away from home.

At my college, there were not many African Americans, and when I arrived there was one black male in architecture, one my fourth year, and I was the only one my senior year. The next year there were two black men and two black women, then there were three to five each year after that. All that time, almost half the students were women. There were no African American instructors until my fourth year, when Brad Grant came to teach.[51] We didn't care if we'd already taken the class he was teaching, we wanted to take Brad's class. After Brad left, there was one African American instructor.

I got a great education. We had one instructor from India. He brought in cultural issues and encouraged us to study their vocabulary. Then we would try to emulate some of the items we had gleaned. Pretty much everything else was Eurocentric. The dean was open-minded and let us do whatever we needed to do. I have always been functional in my design—concerned with the person in the space and their comfort. The aesthetics came later. There are so many different pieces to the architecture pie. It feeds to my creative side and doesn't bore me. There are always different things to do, think about. I'm still doodling. (Danelle Graham)

The early influences have a lifelong impact. Objectively, this is about people's early exposure to a broad range of possibilities. The exposure to and assimilation of those stimuli are components in the accumulation of cultural capital. In the right market of exchange, cultural capital can be exchanged for social capital, a useful commodity when you are trying to obtain architectural commissions. Subjectively, a wider range of experiences leads to higher expectations of one's own achievement. A reason many black architects work with school kids is to enable the students to have broader expectations about their own potential. These stories emphasize the importance of black architects serving as mentors and working with young people to introduce them to the profession.

Many of the architects I have spoken with know they were able to become architects because, in their youth, they had an adult who believed they could do it. Whether they grew up in families of college-educated professionals or blue-collar, single-parent families, all could point to a person who provided them enough encouragement to focus on architecture.

The black architecture students who graduated and have remained in the profession are devoted to doing what they can to increase the numbers of blacks in practice. They feel an acute responsibility to be mentors for young architects; they understand how vital it is to give young people positive role models in the profession.

To become an architect, you have to be born into it. Architecture is what I enjoy. African Americans don't go into architecture. We try to encourage architecture students. It's not easy for them. There's serious racism in school. In my studio in City College, there were three or four blacks out of fifteen students. At Columbia, there were none. At Yale, there were one or two out of ten. When I was an undergrad, there were four of us; also four in my graduate class. Black architecture students are dedicated; they learn resiliency. I did a great group project. The other partner in the project got an A; I got a B. It's a process of learning to discern who's good and who's bad, and then working with the best. (Wendell Marshall)

Like so many of the architects I have met, Marshall understood the importance, and the difficulty, of focusing on the end goal. He was clear about the existence of racism in the educational system, but also realized early in the process he would do better in the program by concentrating on what he needed to get out of it rather than dwelling on the oppressive nature of the system.

> Part of the problem is the politics of what it takes to do private work. It's difficult to get young people interested in, and remaining in, architecture, because Generation Y wants to design. They're not interested in paying any dues. Besides which, why would young people want to take a vow of poverty? 1.3 percent of the architects in the AIA are African American, and 99 percent of them are doing drafting. (Thaddeus Collins)

One of the great ironies of architectural education is that for all the focus on design, few architects of any ethnicity will actually get to spend their careers designing. Reminiscent of the quote above from Sharon Sutton, the professional reputation of the designers overshadows that of the people who are responsible for the rest of the work. The invisibility of the drafters, project managers, and others makes it difficult to recruit students into architecture programs.

> Eleven people out of this office have started their own practice. We're really proud of that. We don't want people to come to us and be employees for life; that's not why we're here. We're trying to do what we can to increase the number of blacks in practice, and especially the number of blacks successfully in practice. (Nicholas Rose)

The firm Rose co-owns is devoted to mentoring young architects of color. They know that growing the number of flourishing black-owned firms will increase their visibility over time. By supporting these young practitioners, the firm is increasing the market for services for all architects of color.

Sharon Sutton, a professor of architecture in a state university, shared the following letter she received from a woman she had mentored in the late 1970s. It is a tribute to the change a mentor can facilitate in the lives of young people of color.

> Dear Ms. Sutton: I am hoping that you are the same Architect that volunteered at PS 152 in Brooklyn beginning in 1978. If you are please know I am one of the kids who graduated from that school in 1980. . . . [W]e worked on the kiosk that was built on the front school yard grounds. I am writing to you because it is important

I thank you. You see, Ms. Sutton, because you took the time to volunteer at that school and crossed my life path, you left an everlasting impression in my life.

In fifth grade, I made you a heart shaped box out of construction paper and taped candy inside of it. The following year you stamped my yearbook with your Architect's stamp. After many years of being in my wallet, it is now framed in my office and whenever someone asks I tell them the story of this bad-ass woman, an Architect, who changed my life.

I don't know if you remember the economic make-up of that school but I was on the bottom of that scale. I am the youngest of four. My mom was divorced and working at a cardboard factory earning minimum wage. Medicaid and Food stamps made the ends meet. I saw and felt her painful struggle. I became afraid that my destiny would not be very different from hers. What would become of me? The only black and Hispanic women I saw were all single struggling moms like mine. But the hard times made me strong and resilient, a survivor, something that sticks with me to this day. You forced me to raise the bar on what I expected out of life. Being born poor did not mean "No hope, no options."

I believe it was you who made me realize that someday I too could make something of my life and not be a statistic whose life was just a 5-mile radius. In a very real way, you saved my life. I wanted to be like you. . . . I graduated from Pratt Institute in 1990 with a bachelor's degree in interior design and an award for best design student—go figure, the ghetto girl from East Flatbush Brooklyn. I went on to work for, and was trained by, another strong influential woman who recently passed away. The 4 years I spent with her set the tone for the rest of my career to date. I now work for myself.

I am going on 36 and have three children. I always pray that God sends my kids someone like you, someone that opens their eyes, touches their hearts and is a positive influence and role model to achieving their inner dream. My mom taught me the work ethic and how you must take care of your responsibilities even on the bad days—and growing up we had lots of those. You taught me that I had something inside of me and I could work at what I love.

But before college, before all high profile work, there was Sharon Sutton, who without even trying, and did not even know, opened a path in my mind and a door in my creative soul to show me the world and give me the keys to my life with just a piece of paper and a pencil.[52]

The opportunity to make such a huge difference in the lives of young people is one of the things that keeps busy professionals committed to work in the schools. The contact with a successful, black role model can be enough to show disaffected students possibilities they would never otherwise consider. Especially given the reception blacks have received in architecture programs, these models are a ray of hope.

Harsh Realities

There are many stories in print about young architecture students confronted by the harsh realities of race and racism in the profession. From Paul Williams in the 1920s to Max Bond in the 1950s, Jack Travis in the 1970s, and Jennifer Newsom in 2004, the stories are important for understanding reality for blacks in architecture. For white, middle-class students, the idea of a professor saying "People who look like you cannot do what you want to do" is simply unthinkable. Yet for many blacks in architecture, the message has been clear.

> Years later he [Paul Williams] would recall his instructor's response when he declared his intention to pursue a career in architecture. "He stared at me with as much astonishment as he would have had I proposed a rocket flight to Mars." His instructor demanded, "Who ever heard of a Negro being an architect?" He pointed out that people of Williams' race built neither fine homes nor expensive business buildings and that he would therefore be obliged to depend entirely on white clients for his livelihood.[53]

Williams was determined to continue in his path. In fact, he spent most of his career designing fine homes for wealthy white clients.

Max Bond presented another story about the response of potential mentors to the idea of black architects:

> At Harvard, those many years ago (not long after a cross-burning incident outside Bond's dorm), a friendly white professor took him aside to offer some advice: Forget it.
>
> "There have never been any famous, prominent black architects," Bond recalls the professor saying. "You'd be wise to choose another profession." Even in retelling it for the umpteenth time, Bond looks stunned at the patronizing gall. "He thought he was being helpful," he says.
>
> It did not matter to the professor, or perhaps he did not know, that a classical architect named Julian Abele, who was black, had designed the main Harvard library. And Bond knew Hilyard Robinson, the low-key modernist whose Langston Terrace Dwellings, built in 1937 on Benning Road in Northeast Washington, would ultimately be put on the National Register of Historic Places.
>
> And had the professor been paying attention to the doings out west, he might have heard of Paul Williams, the flashy Los Angeles architect whose clients included Lucille Ball and Frank Sinatra. (Bond spent a summer working for Williams, even handled the tiling project inside Sinatra's house.)
>
> So Bond knew it was possible to practice architecture. He persevered. He earned both his bachelor's and master's degrees in the field, becoming one of the scant few such men (or women) of color in his profession.[54]

Max Bond was not to be dissuaded by the idea that being a black man and an architect was impossible. Like so many of the architects in this book, he had a different perspective about both his potential and his heritage.

One of the architects on the West Coast told me about the troubles he had even getting into the pre-architecture program in high school. It is hard to think about how "lucky" the students were who had a champion. One of the legacies of institutional racism is the perception that students of color are not capable of fulfilling their dreams.

> I had mentors on the East Coast. In 1968, Max Bond was the first African American architect I'd ever seen. In high school we were encouraged to be engineers so we could always get a civil service job. I got no encouragement to be in the program at the technical high school. In fact, my mother got me into the program. She told the counselor off so I could qualify to take the test to get into the program even though the public school system I was in was predominantly minority. (James Patterson)

Through these stories, it is easy to understand the importance of role models in the lives of black architects. Even for students who came into the educational system with support at home, and the confidence to believe in their skills, the fact they knew of black architects who had come before them gave them the strength to continue on their path.

Jack Travis's story of his first encounter with racism in architecture is told in Mitchell's book. As demoralizing as the previous accounts are, it may be possible for the reader to discount them as historical tales. Travis was in architecture school in the '70s, and the story was still the same.

> The first black American architect I met was a professor at the undergraduate university I attended. I was in my third year. Mr. Fellows was his name. He was a simple man with a small practice and a real sense of social responsibility. I hated him. Not for who he was, but for what he represented. I was devastated at the picture of a "black architect" that he painted for me. My future as I had envisioned it and the future he'd shown me were so very different. It never really occurred to me that my color might make my dream to practice architecture improbable.[55]

For talented black students who find their way to architecture without black role models, the first encounter with the truth about racism in architecture can be devastating. Sadly, and tellingly, the final story about the shock of the first recognition of racism in architecture school is from 2004. While we may wish things have changed dramatically, or believe these are just isolated incidents of racism in the profession, the oppression of black students continues:

> I decided to organize *Black Boxes: Enigmas of Space and Race* after a professor claimed that African-American architecture was an oxymoron. In defense of his course content, which included Brunelleschi, Mies van der Rohe, and Le Corbusier, he told us students, "Why aren't we studying black [architecture]? Because it doesn't exist!" He said this in front of a class of 40 Yale School of Architecture graduate students: that architecture made by someone of color, like me, was unimaginable.
>
> His comment, unyielding and unapologetic, slapped me back into my seat. Right then, I realized the irony of my existence. I was in love with this thing, "architecture," yet the foundations of this discipline were blind to the possibility of my contribution, and of the contributions of my forefathers and foremothers. I was both inside and outside the Western canon at the same time. Architecture couldn't see me, even though I was sitting in the room.[56]

Systemic racism is a major contributor to the invisibility of black architects.[57] As difficult as this impact of oppression is for all blacks, for people who stake their professional future on their visual acumen, being invisible is a cruel irony.

As I met black architects and conducted interviews across the country, I was struck by the similarity of the stories I was hearing about the experience of architecture school. Having heard these accounts from almost everyone I spoke with, the surprising thing to me is how many black architecture students graduate and become licensed architects. The statistics, from the AIA website of the National Associates Committee, are dismal. Nineteen percent of the Associate AIA members are people of color, but they comprise only 6 percent of licensed AIA members. A mere 11 percent of all registered architects are people of color. The most telling thing is how difficult it is to find statistics on architecture school attendance, graduation, and licensing rates by ethnicity.[58] If it is difficult for white readers to understand the impact of being one of two or three black students, or sometimes the only black student, in the class, it would be useful to think about how it would feel to be one of the only white students in a classroom. Even for black students who had attended predominantly white schools before college, and had become adept at switching from their ethnic culture to the dominant white culture, it could be a profoundly uncomfortable situation.

> There were only two other African Americans in my classes. I finished my bachelor's degree, but I was ready to leave the profession, convinced I could never go anywhere as a black architect. I had missed the deadline to get into law school that year,

and it would be eighteen months before I could start, so I stayed in architecture and got my master's. That was thirty-one years ago.

The reason young architects leave the profession? They get out of school, go to work for SOM [Skidmore Owings & Merrill, one of the world's largest architecture firms], and realize they aren't going anywhere. (Nicholas Rose)

Until I began this research with architects, most of my work with business owners of color had been with individuals who had not grown up middle class, had not attended college, and had not completed a long internship to gain a professional license. The stories from people whose credentials were analogous to mine made the reality of institutional racism clear to me in ways my clients' did not. Although Thaddeus Collins insisted that classism is more insidious than racism in the struggle for black architects, I was seeing the racism without the filter of class. Although there are differences in the class origin among these twenty people, two-thirds of them have at least a master's degree. Through all that education, and all that accumulation of cultural and social capital, the stories of these architects help illuminate the insidiousness of institutional racism in the United States. The myth of picking yourself up by your bootstraps is exploded by the understanding of the barriers highly educated, competent, motivated professionals face in their attempts to work in their chosen profession.

COLUMBIA

Max Bond appears in many sections of this book. His firm, Davis Brody Bond, was chosen to manage the construction of the memorial at the World Trade Center site. It will be their responsibility to take the design and implement it. Although he was in the middle of negotiations on that project and was unable to take time to meet with me, he graciously referred me to two of his younger East Coast colleagues. As a result of those referrals, his membership in the small community of AIA Fellows,[59] and his many years of teaching in architecture schools, Bond is connected to almost all the architects interviewed for this book. He received his bachelor's in architecture from Harvard College in 1955 and his M.Arch. from Harvard University in 1958. He was chairman of Columbia University's Graduate School of Architecture and Planning from 1980 to 1984 and dean at the School of Architecture and Environmental Studies at City College of New York from 1985 to 1991. But in 1968, as a faculty member at Columbia, he was solving a crisis that made him a hero to a generation of black architects.

It is useful to know what was happening in the United States in 1968 to understand the situation at Columbia University. A timeline on the New York University (NYU) Library website helps to lay out the context.[60] The Vietnam War was in full swing, and the antiwar movement was growing. In March of that year, Eugene McCarthy, avowed peace candidate, got 40 percent of the vote in the New Hampshire Democratic presidential primary, Robert Kennedy announced his candidacy for president, and President Johnson announced he would not run again.

In April, Martin Luther King Jr. was assassinated in Memphis. As word of King's death spread across the country, demonstrations and violence broke out. Campuses all over the United States were affected by antiwar/civil rights demonstrations. Students made demands for administrations to take a stand against the war; in many colleges and universities, there was a movement to increase the number of people of color both on faculties and in the student body.

There are different versions of why the strike at Columbia was called, but on April 23, 1968, a student strike shut down Columbia University.[61] Some accounts allege the strikes were called to put an end to administration plans to build a university gymnasium in the adjoining black neighborhood of Harlem, a move many opposed as an unreasonable encroachment into the community. Some say it was an attempt to protest the university's ties to the U.S. defense establishment, and some say it was an act to force the colleges (particularly the professional schools) to address long-term racial inequality in both the student body and the administration.

The architects I met who benefited from the strike demands told stories about the special case of the class of 1968 at the Columbia University Graduate School of Architecture. Even thirty-five years later, the stories were still told with love and the conviction that successfully increasing the number of students of color requires a deliberate, thoughtful process.

> We were the beneficiaries of the 1968 strikes in the professional schools at Columbia. Max was the one who really designed the program for increasing the number of minority students. He was also the one who insisted on having faculty devoted to mentoring us. It never would have happened that way if it hadn't been for Max. It worked because we had faculty we knew we could talk to and rely on, and because we formed study groups early on so that none of us could be singled out. A lot of us are still around, and most of us have done quite well in our careers. (Elwood Jackson)

The problem of trying to increase black enrollment is a reflection of how systemic racism influences organizational culture. Until the professional schools at Columbia were shut down by strikes, there was not a serious effort to diversify either the student body or the faculty. Although the administration at Columbia was responding to a crisis situation, they crafted a very successful response. Max Bond and others knew if they really wanted to increase black enrollment *and* graduation, they would have to create an environment that was welcoming. One way they did that was by making sure students were encouraged and supported in the exploration of other-than-European architecture and archetypes. The real key to making it work, though, was the architects they hired to be on staff specifically to mentor the students of color.

> I started school at Drexel. It was an eight-year night school program. I only went through the fifth year, then I transferred to Columbia. It was September 1968. Prior to that time, there were only two or three minorities in the Architecture School. That year, there were thirty-two minority students in a school of three hundred, where the year before there had been three. We were mostly African Americans or Afro Caribbeans. Max Bond interviewed us. Carl Anthony, who's now an architect in San Francisco, was working at Columbia on the janitorial staff. (In the '50s, all the Pullman porters had master's degrees!) He ended up studying in the school of architecture. He and Max Bond went to the dean and suggested they team up with the AIA to recruit minority students.
>
> They went on a recruiting trip. They started with HBCUs. The thirty of us were a little older than the average. We formed study groups so we couldn't be isolated and driven out. That way, everybody had to work for each other to make it. I wouldn't have graduated if it hadn't been for the other students. (Thaddeus Collins)

The importance of having mentors of color, and having study groups with other students who were part of the diversity program, was emphasized by all who spoke about that experience. It created not only a bond between the thirty of them, but also a sense of responsibility to continue the tradition of mentoring. The members of the generation of black architects who grew up in the civil rights movement continue to be actively involved in serving as role models for younger black architects, many as faculty members. The understanding of the struggle for civil rights has remained with them.

There is also a recognition of the role Max Bond played in creating opportunities for black architecture students to be exposed to architecture that more nearly reflected their own cultural experiences. He made sure they had the chance to see there was more than Eurocentric design.

> I was working on a project in Washington, DC, and applied to the master's program at Columbia. They were trying to increase the number of people of color in the program, and there were scholarships available. One of my friends in the program and

I went to Africa together on the trip Max Bond put together. It was exciting to see buildings that were so different from what we spent so much time on in school. It was the first time I understood how I could really connect who I am to what I design. (Sharon Young)

TEACHING

Half of the architects discussed in this book are either teaching in architecture programs concurrently with practicing or have taught in the past. Teaching often began as a way to bring money into the firm, but was also a way to give back to the community by ensuring students of color would have a role model who looked like them. The architects' participation in the curriculum is also one way to bring change to the profession. Out of 1,200 architecture professors in the United States, there are about 110 who are black. Of those, eight or ten are women.[62] Although their numbers are small, they are uniquely situated to act as change agents in the discipline.

> I've done lecturing at HBCUs about my history and about the firm and the kind of work we're doing. I work with seniors about their expectations going out into the world. Until the late '80s, I taught at Morgan State. There are seven accredited HBCU programs. Fifty percent of licensed black architects come from Howard, Hampton, Florida A. &M., and Tuskegee. It's important for these students to have black faculty. It made a huge difference for me when I was in school. (Thaddeus Collins)

Given the small numbers of black architecture students, it is vital they have exposure and access to black architects who are in practice. They need to see it is possible for them to succeed in their chosen profession. As discussed above, these students continue to receive messages to the contrary. They remain isolated.

> I teach interior design to the undergraduates at the Fashion Institute. I also teach interior design to graduate students at Pratt, and I run an independent studio class at Pratt that's mostly Asian students. In the summer, I teach at Parsons. I've also been involved in twelve mentorship programs. The latest is a Steelcase[63] program for fourth graders. They live in the Polo Grounds Housing Project, which is the worst project. In the 1960s, you had to qualify to get in. Those kids come to school already in trouble. There's too much pressure on these kids, but there's talent. They can't see that their sense of worth is challenged. (Leroy Vaughan)

I was in Vaughan's office when he got a call from a young black man who was interested in going into architecture. Vaughan stopped everything else he was doing to focus on the conversation. He listened respectfully to the questions and then kindly and patiently made a number of suggestions for networking and for what courses to take to increase the likelihood of being accepted into a program, and he urged him to draw anything and everything all the time to get his "eye" used to looking at and seeing shapes and spatial relationships. It was so clear from the look on Vaughan's face that, even though he had said these same words many times to many young students, he relished the opportunity to make this connection.

> When I was in school, Max [Bond] was the department chair at Columbia. He was my mentor. After I graduated and had started my own office, I taught at City College to supplement this practice. I taught at Columbia briefly and then taught four years at Yale. I know what it meant for me to have Max available. I have tried to make a difference for the students coming up. (Wendell Marshall)

The recognition of the importance of mentoring and sharing the joy of architecture is spread throughout the ranks of black architects. The most effective way to increase the numbers of black architects is to make sure young people are exposed to the profession and to role models within the profession. Danelle Graham said of her work with young girls,

> I feel a responsibility to the youngsters coming up behind me. Architecture is a way to express your creativity to the world. I see it as a way to give back to my community. My parents were always giving back. I have time, energy, and enthusiasm about architecture. It makes me feel good. (Danelle Graham)

The reason these architects keep going back to the classroom, and keep working with children and students, is the knowledge they have of how much difference a role model can make. Most of them were isolated in architecture programs; they all had at least one mentor who encouraged them to finish. The full-time faculty members, outside of the HBCUs, also find themselves isolated. They may look to activities outside the university for that community connection.

> I teach design studio, ethics, and community leadership practices. I've got a grant from the Ford Foundation, which is working on an interdisciplinary community development project with black youth. As an academic, I'm an outsider within the infrastructure of power. I look on it as the Power of the Other. There are nine hundred practicing black architects and one hundred academics. Racism is more covert

in academia. They have to believe your ideas are good to get tenure, but once you've got it, they have a hard time getting rid of you! I was the first black woman to be a full professor in architecture in America, and the second African American woman to be a Fellow. My struggle to earn what others are given continues.

A lot of people think of architecture only as "conceiving buildings." As a result, academic architects aren't thought of as real architects. Architects have no power because they're always relying on clients for money. I haven't practiced since 1984, but just the fact that I did once still gives me credibility as an architect. Academia has its own perverse racism.

It's not easy to stand your ground and keep a focus on the struggle for equality. There are times when I am so conscious of the energy it takes to keep pushing on the administration, on my colleagues. It really leaves me exhausted, but I have to do it. Things will never improve if we don't just keep on. (Tina Taylor)

Particularly in "majority" schools, just the act of making the struggle visible is an act of courage. Taylor articulated a theme that was repeated by others: systemic racism does not disappear by itself. Addressing structural inequality is a full-time job for those black academics who are willing to take it on.

Black architecture students have their own invisible struggles. Eugene Newman has followed the progress of generations of black students. Their ability to connect their ethnicity to their studies has been compromised by changes in the profession.

The hard thing for black architecture students is that they've always been involved in the community through their church or other activities, and suddenly the curriculum is completely divorced from community issues. White architects are not connected to their legacy in the same way because the training is so Eurocentric.

The use of computers has led to a loss of context for architecture students. They used to be able to go out and wander around the site and see what was next door and really get a feeling for where they were placing a design. Now they sit in the office, with a site plan and a computer-aided design program, and design/plan in the absence of a clear understanding about the site. (Eugene Newman)

Being able to connect to communities is an important part of who these students are. Having faculty of color who are sensitive to a wider range of needs is an important part of the effort to increase minority enrollment.

If architecture is to survive in a technologically sophisticated, multicultural society, it must come out of the cocoon of a medieval guild culture where each person learns at the side of another person, thus perpetuating all the intellectual limitations and cultural biases of the mentor. Simply having more people of color or women as mentors on a sinking ship is not the answer. What is needed is a new vision of the field in which there are greatly expanded career opportunities diverging from two equally valued paths. A narrow path leads to practice while another much broader one leads to the research that creates a vital context for the few who practice.[64]

While this quote appears to be in conflict with earlier acknowledgments of the importance of mentoring, it is about the necessity for change in the profession. Systemic change requires more than just making sure black architecture students have support. If there were more students of color, and an emphasis on the way a variety of cultures impact aesthetics, individual attention and respect would be accorded all students.

Despite the difficulty of bringing the profession into the twenty-first century, there is a recognition that architecture requires a tolerance for flexibility, and the understanding that this is an iterative process. Given the staid culture of the profession, it is ironic the practice requires the agility, and the maturity, to make change seemingly endlessly.

One of the flaws in architectural education is about the assumptions you'll be an apprentice. It calls for transparency and invention, minute by minute trying to find your place in society. You can take some of someone else's success and build your own on top of it. You have to be willing to try. In architecture, mistakes are endemic. You have to look at several alternatives to come up with one idea. "Failure" is built into the process. The winning scheme is related to the failures. You've got to be flexible and look at the alternatives. (Wendell Marshall)

NOTES

1. Garry Stevens pointed out that the way we think of architecture as a profession reflects an Anglocentric view of the field. It removes architecture from any consideration of the social context in which it operates. He said, "In Italy, architecture functions more as a mechanism for entering a cultural elite than as anything else. Where the United States and the United Kingdom have 120 to 150 architecture students per million population, Italy is educating a staggering 1,700 per million. The 97 percent or so of architecture graduates who never enter practice no more think of themselves as belonging to a profession of architecture than a Bachelor of Arts graduate in the English-speaking world thinks of himself or herself as belonging to a profession of 'arts.'" Garry Stevens, *The Favored Circle: The Social Foundations of Architectural Distinction* (Cambridge, MA: MIT Press, 1998), 29.

2. See Amos Rapoport, "Cross-Cultural Aspects of Environmental Design," in *Human Behavior and Environment: Advances in Theory and Research*, ed. Irwin Altman, Amos

Rapoport, and Joachim F. Wohlwill (New York: Plenum, 1980), for an extensive analysis of the connections between place and culture.

3. See Magali Sarfatti Larson, *The Rise of Professionalism* (Berkeley: University of California Press, 1977), and Stevens, *Favored Circle*, for more extensive investigations into the attributes of the architecture profession.

4. Magali Sarfatti Larson, *Behind the Postmodern Facade: Architectural Change in Late Twentieth-Century America* (Berkeley: University of California Press, 1993); Magali Sarfatti Larson, "Patronage and Power," in *Reflections on Architectural Practices in the Nineties*, ed. William S. Saunders, 130–43 (Princeton, NJ: Princeton Architectural Press, 1996); and Stevens, *Favored Circle*, present illuminating perspectives on the beginnings of architecture.

5. The irony of this is not lost on professionals who, by all reports, earn less than their comparably educated peers in other fields.

6. See Lily M. Hoffman, *The Politics of Knowledge: Activist Movements in Medicine and Planning* (Albany: SUNY Press, 1989); and Magali Sarfatti Larson, *Rise of Professionalism*, for more on the relationship of professionals to citizens in the community.

7. Larson, "Patronage and Power."

8. Sharon Sutton, presentation to the AIA Seattle as part of a series of luncheons celebrating chapter members who are Fellows of the AIA, June 2004.

9. The epithet "white gentlemen's profession" was coined by Dixon in the title of a reflective article in *Progressive Architecture*, a magazine no longer in print. I am certain, however, the name was first used informally a long time before John Morris Dixon. "A White Gentlemen's Profession?" *Progressive Architecture* 75, no. 11 (November 1994): 55–61.

The Eurocentric nature of the profession has been extensively discussed in the literature. See Kathryn H. Anthony, *Designing for Diversity: Gender, Race, and Ethnicity in the Architectural Profession* (Urbana: University of Illinois Press, 2001); Richard K. Dozier, "The Black Architectural Experience in America," in *African American Architects in Current Practice*, ed. Jack Travis (New York: Princeton Architectural Press, 1991); Jane Holtz Kay, "Invisible Architects: Minority Firms Struggle to Achieve Recognition in a White-Dominated Profession," *Architecture* (April 1991): 106–113; Melvin Mitchell, *The Crisis of the African-American Architect: Conflicting Cultures of Architecture and (Black) Power* (Lincoln, NE: Writer's Club, 2001); Stevens, *Favored Circle*; and Sharon E. Sutton, "Finding Our Voice in a Dominant Key," in *African Americans in Current Practice*, ed. Jack Travis, 13–15 (New York: Princeton Architectural Press, 1991).

10. Joe Feagin, *Racist America: Roots, Current Realities, and Future Reparations* (New York: Routledge, 2001): 120–21.

11. Richard K. Dozier, "The Black Architectural Experience in America" (1991).

12. Manning Marable, *How Capitalism Underdeveloped Black America* (Boston: South End, 1983), 142.

13. Richard K. Dozier, "The Black Architectural Experience in America," *AIA Journal* 65, no. 7 (1976): 162–68; Robin D. G. Kelley, "Into the Fire: 1970 to the Present," in *To*

Make Our World Anew: A History of African Americans, ed. Robin D. G. Kelley and Earl Lewis, 543–613 (Oxford: Oxford University Press, 2000); Mitchell, *Crisis of the African-American Architect*; and Dreck Spurlock Wilson, ed. *African American Architects: A Biographical Dictionary, 1865–1945* (New York: Routledge, 2004), all include interesting discussions of the early years at Tuskegee. It is important to note there are black architects in the Midwest and the West who do not feel the special tie to the early program at Tuskegee. Architects in the East and the Southeast are more likely than those west of the Mississippi to identify their professional lineage with Tuskegee.

14. Mitchell, *Crisis of the African-American Architect*, 34.

15. Dozier, "Black Architectural Experience in America" (1976).

16. Mitchell, *Crisis of the African-American Architect*, 40.

17. Jack Travis, "Hidden in Plain View," *National Associates Committee Quarterly* (Spring 2003): 2.

18. From *Webster's Collegiate Dictionary:* "Jim Crow: a practice or policy of segregating or discriminating against blacks; so called from the name of a song sung by Thomas Rice (1808–1860) in a minstrel show." Blacks were excluded from public transportation, made to sit in special Jim Crow sections of theaters and white churches, educated in segregated schools, punished in segregated prisons, nursed in segregated hospitals, and buried in segregated cemeteries. Marable, *How Capitalism Underdeveloped Black America*.

19. See Wilson, *African American Architects*, for extensive biographies on the early black architects.

20. From the author's session notes, November 2004.

21. See Anthony, *Designing for Diversity*; Karen E. Hudson, *Paul R. Williams, Architect: A Legacy of Style* (New York: Rizzoli, 1993); Mitchell, *Crisis of the African-American Architect*; Jennifer Reese, "Paul Williams, An Architect," *Via* (September–October 1999), 52–55; and Travis, *African American Architects in Current Practice*, for a broader perspective on Williams's life and work.

22. Jennifer Reese, "Paul Williams, An Architect," 52.

23. Jennifer Reese, "Paul Williams, An Architect," 52.

24. Mary Reilly, "African Americans, Especially Women, Build up Their Numbers in Architecture," University of Cincinnati, January 2, 2004, at www.uc.edu/news/NR.asp?id=1222 (accessed September 5, 2005).

25. Wilson, *African American Architects*.

26. *Diversity in the Architecture Profession*, AIA National Associates Committee, May 6, 2004, at www.aia.org/SiteObjects/files/NACDiversity/WhitePaper.pdf (accessed September 15, 2005).

27. See a profile of Sklarek at www.ni.essortment.com. See also, Norma Merrick Sklarek, "Norma Merrick Sklarek," *California Architecture* (January–February 1985): 22–23.

28. In an interview, Sklarek said it was one of the only times in her life she didn't mind being referred to as a fellow.

29. In the high school I attended, in an upper-middle class, white city neighborhood in the West, if one of my classmates expressed an interest in going to professional school,

every effort was made to help her plan a course to attain her goal. One of our Fund clients went to inner-city schools in the Midwest. He told his high school counselor he wanted to be a doctor. She laughed and told him that would never happen and to forget about it. The social and cultural capital we start with has a lasting impact on how, and how well, we progress as adults. See Karen Aschaffenburg and Ineke Maas, "Cultural and Educational Careers: The Dynamics of Social Reproduction," *American Sociological Review* 62 (August 1997): 573–87; Dalton Conley, *Being Black, Living in the Red: Race, Wealth, and Social Policy in America* (Berkeley: University of California Press, 1999); George Farkas, Robert P. Grobe, Daniel Sheehan, and Yuan Shuan, "Cultural Resources and School Success: Gender, Ethnicity and Poverty Groups within an Urban School District," *American Sociological Review* 55 (February 1990): 127–42; and Matthijs Kalmijn and Gerbert Kraaykamp, "Race, Cultural Capital and Schooling: An Analysis of Trends in the United States," *Sociology of Education* 69 (January 1996): 22–34.

30. Bradford Grant and Dennis A. Mann, ed. *Directory of African American Architects* (Cincinnati: Center for the Study of Practice, 1995).

31. U.S. Census Bureau, Census 2000.

32. Statistics on law school enrollment and graduation can be found at www.abanet .org/legaled/statistics.

33. Given how little data are available about architecture students, the mass of data on doctors and lawyers is remarkable. It seems to suggest the relative attitudes about both diversity and disclosure in each profession. Although it is likely law schools and medical schools receive higher levels of government funding than architecture schools and, therefore, are required to keep more detailed data, the difference is nonetheless striking.

34. Data on medical school enrollment and graduation were published by the Association of American Medical Colleges. See "Minorities in Medical Education: Facts & Figures 2005" at services.aamc.org/Publications.

35. I have done no research on funding of community legal and medical clinics, but I am certain economic support has diminished in the past decade. Our societal abandonment of services in communities of color is a hallmark of institutional racism; lack of access to critical services is a way to guarantee the disenfranchised will remain so.

36. Nowhere is the power of the institution more insidious, and more vigorous, than in education. This notion is supported in the writing of Louis Althusser, "Ideology and Ideological State Apparatuses: Notes Towards an Investigation," in *Lenin and Philosophy and Other Essays* (New York: Monthly Review Press, 1971), 127–86; Phyllis Cunningham, "The Adult Educator and Social Responsibility," in *Ethical Issues in Adult Education*, ed. Ralph G. Brockett (New York: Teachers College Press, 1988), 134–41; Larson, *Rise of Professionalism*; and Peter Jarvis, "Meaningful and Meaningless Experience: Toward an Analysis of Learning from Life," *Adult Education Quarterly* 73, no. 3 (1987): 164–72.

Althusser describes the vehicles for teaching the "rules"—that is, the essence of the dominant culture. Since the educational institutions are the purveyors of the dominant culture, it stands to reason there are cultural barriers built into the fabric of these institutions. Althusser says everyone is socialized to maintain the dominant social order through the way they are educated.

The system is set up to take care of people who already have some idea how to take care of themselves. Curricula are designed to foster and perpetuate the dominant culture. As Cunningham says, "Those with more education get more education." Magali Sarfatti Larson adds that "monopolizing training is important, but monopolizing it at the university level brings a built-in legitimation of monopoly in terms of cognitive superiority." Larson, *Rise of Professionalism*, 48.

Those who have already been socialized into a culture that is sympathetic to the dominant culture, or into the dominant culture itself, are more likely to acquire the fruits of education than those who have not. Jarvis, "Meaningful and Meaningless Experience."

37. Sharon E. Sutton, "Practice: Architects and Power," *Progressive Architecture* 73, no. 5 (1992): 66, 67.

38. Susan S. Szenasy, "Designers and Multiculturalism," *Metropolis* 14, no. 3 (October 1994): 114.

39. See Dennis Alan Mann, "Making Connections: The African-American Architect," *Journal of the Interfaith Forum on Religion, Art & Architecture* (Fall 1993): 22–23, 31, and Mitchell, *Crisis of the African-American Architect*. See also appendix A, a working paper written by Bradford Grant and Dennis Mann, for the distribution of black students by institution.

40. See appendix A.

41. As will be discussed in chapter 3, the community design centers were ostensibly a way for architects to work and be visible in the community. There are still groups across the country, the AIA Seattle Diversity Committee among them, addressing the issues of both the social responsibility of architects and the need to make the profession more visible in communities of color. They are particularly sensitive to the criticism that "professionals" have a tendency to go into communities and talk instead of listen. See Hoffman, *Politics of Knowledge*, for a helpful discussion of this issue.

42. Mitchell, *Crisis of the African-American Architect*, 269.

43. See Anthony, *Designing for Diversity*; Max Bond, "The Black Architect's Experience," *Architectural Record* (June 1992): 60–61; Holtz Kay, "Invisible Architects"; Harry L. Overstreet, "The Bastion of Hope," in *African American Architects in Current Practice*, ed. Jack Travis (New York: Princeton Architectural Press, 1991): 12; Sutton, "Finding Our Voice in a Dominant Key."

44. "The race record of architecture education is a continuing disgrace, and if anything, things seem to be worsening." Lee D. Mitgang, "Saving the Soul of an Architectural Education: Four Critical Challenges Face Today's Architecture Schools," *Architectural Record* (May 1997): 124. In 1992, there were 2,172 African American architectural students, 5.9 percent of the national total. By 1996, the number had dropped to 2,018, or 5.4 percent. Just 3.2 percent of all architecture faculty—123—were African American. Of those, forty in the entire nation were tenured. "Put bluntly, it's hard to imagine that this

profession can ever lay claim to leadership in shaping the built environment when it remains so unreflective of late twentieth-century America."

In the 1997–98 academic year, 36 percent of the 33,673 undergraduate and graduate students enrolled in architecture programs were women, but only 5.8 percent of the nation's architecture students were African American; little changed during the 1990s. There were 873 (21 percent) women faculty in 1997–1998—but only 166 were tenured. In the entire nation, there were 117 African American architecture faculty and just 37 were tenured—a drop from five years earlier, when there were 126 African American faculty total and 44 were tenured. Lee D. Mitgang, "Back to School: Architects Sound Off on 10 Critical Issues Facing Architectural Education," *Architectural Record* 187 (September 1999): 112.

45. Obviously, there are exceptions to this characterization. As with any model, this work does serve to remind about the dangers of making assumptions about management and leadership styles, but it still provides a useful perspective.

46. Yvonne R. Bell, "A Culturally Sensitive Analysis of Black Learning Style," *Journal of Black Psychology* 20, no. 1 (1994): 48.

47. See Anthony, *Designing for Diversity*; Mitchell, *Crisis of the African-American Architect*; Sutton, "Finding Our Voice in a Dominant Key"; and Susan S. Szenasy, "Designers and Multiculturalism."

48. Interesting discussions on the lack of role models can be found in Anthony, *Designing for Diversity*; Mitchell, *Crisis of the African-American Architect*; Mitgang, "Saving the Soul of an Architectural Education"; and Mitgang, "Back to School."

49. This will be discussed in greater depth in chapter 6. Also see Donna Langston, "Tired of Playing Monopoly?" in *Race, Class and Gender: An Anthology*, ed. Margaret Andersen and Patricia Collins, 126–35 (Belmont, CA: Wadsworth, 1997), and Henry Louis Gates and Cornel West, *The Future of the Race* (New York: Knopf, 1996), for additional perspectives.

50. Lynne Duke, "Blueprint of a Life," *Washington Post*, July 1, 2004, C4.

51. Brad Grant is currently the dean of the architecture program at Hampton University.

52. April 15, 2005. Thanks to Sharon Sutton for sharing this letter.

53. Hudson, *Paul R. Williams, Architect*, 11.

54. Duke, "Blueprint of a Life," C4.

55. Jack Travis, quoted in Mitchell, *Crisis of the African-American Architect*, 261.

56. Jennifer Newsom, "Does African-American Architecture Exist?" Metropolismag.com, January 7, 2004, at www.metropolismag.com/cda/story.php?artid=63 (accessed September 12, 2004).

57. See Holtz Kay, "Invisible Architects"; Peggy McIntosh, "White Privilege and Male Privilege: A Personal Account of Coming to See Correspondences Through Work in Women's Studies," in *Race, Class and Gender: An Anthology*, ed. Margaret Andersen and Patricia H. Collins, 94–105 (Belmont, CA: Wadsworth, 1988); Overstreet, "Bastion of Hope"; and Sklarek, "Norma Merrick Sklarek," for additional discussions on being invisible.

58. In an article entitled "Why Diversity Matters in Architecture," found on the AIA website, Fall 2003, the American Society of Association Executives says, "Trends show that our pool of *future members*, customers, staff, and *our members' customers* will primarily be from groups that are currently underrepresented." Although everyone agrees "diversity" is important, there has not yet been an effective initiative to increase diversity in the profession.

59. The AIA College of Fellows recognizes architects who have made significant contributions to the profession. According to the AIA Office of Member Services, as of July 2005, there were 2,199 Fellows, of whom 55 were black. Short of the annual Gold Medal, membership in the College of Fellows is the highest honor the organization bestows on its members. More than half of the architects in this book are Fellows.

60. www.nyu.edu/library/bobst/collections/exhibits/arch/1968/Index.html (accessed September 2005).

61. A Google search on the strike produced many personal accounts, newspaper articles, and academic studies.

62. These numbers were derived from combining data in Mitgang, "Back to School," and Grant and Mann's *Directory of African American Architects* listing of African American faculty.

63. The Steelcase Corporation is a designer and manufacturer of workplace furniture and fixtures. Part of its corporate giving program provides support for a variety of educational programs in the design fields.

64. Sutton, "Practice: Architects and Power," 67.

3

OUT IN THE WORLD: THE REALITY OF PRACTICE

We went to the same schools and got the same awards as the white architects, and I have to prove myself at what I'm doing over and over again. It's sad because the world wastes so much energy on racism. It's such a waste to go through this foolishness so many times. As a profession, we have not attacked the problem of shelter, which means a lot of people suffer. Our meager efforts are few and far between. There's no excuse for this.

They know who the enemy is and how to protect against it. The life we've had to lead along with the profession is sad. I'm tired of hearing I'm a great role model. I hope and pray there will be a time when African Americans are able to just practice architecture like everyone else. (David Norman)[1]

ARCHITECTURE AS A CALLING

All I ever wanted to do was design. (Isaiah Stewart)

Doing this research with architects has made me think about the differences between the architects I have met and the business owners I have worked with the past ten years. Almost all the architects knew when they were little they wanted to be an architect. In some cases, they had to fight to get into programs in high school; for others, the desire to be an architect was nurtured and encouraged by family (usually a mother or a grandfather) or a special teacher; but for all of them, architecture is a calling.

Most of the other black business owners I have known did not have a clear set of business objectives or a professional goal in mind when they started a business. They also did not have the advantage of professional training in a Euro-centric system, such as architecture school, to teach them about the necessities of being bicultural.[2] As a result, many of them have been less able to develop an understanding of what it takes to thrive in the predominantly white business culture.

With architects, black and white, the idea of practice seems to have been a dream for a lifetime. Obviously, there are exceptions to this singlemindedness, but a lot of the stories about being introduced to architecture are variations on a theme. Many professionals are "called" to their field; in the case of black professionals, they are rarely able to act on that urge without a mentor or some other outside influence that either leads to, or facilitates, the calling. In an article on designers and multiculturalism, Susan Szenasy quotes Donald King:

> My father's father was a brick mason. He also worked in steel erection. In the 1920s, '30s, and '40s, many construction trades were closed to African Americans. Sometimes he passed as a Native American to get work. My grandfather, father, and uncle tried unsuccessfully for years to work as construction contractors. My mother's interest was in the "softer" arts and she encouraged me in drawing and painting. She often worked as a domestic and would bring home rare gifts of the discarded toys of her employer's children. The toys included model building blocks and, in one case, a model city of movable wood block buildings on a canvas mat of streets and sidewalks. This was my favorite. With these influences, I unknowingly became interested in architecture when I was five or six years old.[3]

Despite firsthand knowledge of the struggles blacks encountered trying to work in their chosen fields, the lure of architecture—and the support of his mother—moved King to pursue his studies in the profession.

I had a friend in elementary school who started drawing buildings in the second or third grade. He continued drawing all the way through school. Because of the neighborhood we grew up in, and the schools we attended, it was always expected he would go to college and have the opportunity to study architecture. The past twenty-plus years he has had his own firm. He was the only student I went all the way through school with who knew, early on, what he wanted to do for a living.

For the most part, black students do not grow up with the same expectations.[4] The presence of institutional racism has ensured public education in this country is set up so that black children are expected not to succeed.

Race remains an influential and easily identifiable status in this society, and race-based micropolitical processes occurring in the school and classroom may be, as the findings [of their study] suggest, important in the evaluation and rewarding of background attributes.[5]

Even in "integrated" schools, the teacher serves as a gatekeeper, making unconscious determinations of who belongs in what level and who is deserving of what rewards. As with so many issues about institutional racism, teachers and administrators who are decent, well-meaning public servants unwittingly help maintain the systems that foster disparity. Given how difficult it is for students of color to get what they want and what they need in public school classrooms, the black architects' tenacity and dedication to find what they needed is all the more inspiring.

Most architects knew they wanted to be an architect at a very young age. I knew at age nine or ten. I think 60–70 percent of architects knew when they were young. If your goal is to be rich, don't do architecture. But if your goal is to do something you love, and want to get up and go to work, go into architecture. Architects are smart enough and bright enough to be successful at anything. Sometimes when I come home excited about a new contract, my wife will say to me, "Isn't that the same group that didn't pay you last time? What are you so excited about?" You want to make enough to break even so you can continue to satisfy your desire to be an architect.

I'm married to my profession; my wife is my mistress. (Thaddeus Collins)

This commitment to the profession does not seem to dim over time. Thaddeus Collins has been practicing almost thirty-five years and still has a wide-eyed enthusiasm when he talks about being an architect. He readily acknowledges the pay is lousy, the hours long, the clients often challenging, but he never thought about pursuing any other kind of work.

Unlike law school, you never find anyone who was pressured to go to architecture school! We're all here because we want to be architects. My father's a judge, my brother's an attorney, and my wife is an attorney. When I was trying to decide on a major in college, my father gave me the best advice: do what you enjoy. I had an academic interest in architecture, but my extracurricular activities were in journalism. You have to love architecture to continue in this business. (Roland Davis)

With so many attorneys in the family, Davis might have been tempted to go into law, but he knew in college he would be happier practicing architecture. Ninety percent of the architects I interviewed said they remain devoted to the field. Despite the struggles with systemic racism, the intense competition for projects, and the limited remuneration, they all look forward to their work.

If there was a single point in my life that I could recall saying I wanted to be an architect, it was after seeing the *Life* magazine spread on Brasilia in the early 1960s. The sprawling modernist new town planned by Lucia Costa and populated with the gleaming architecture of Oscar Neimeyer truly captured my spirit. The thought of designing an entire city with new buildings flooded my imagination. I immediately went to work on *my* city.

I located a site on the West Coast of the United States at the mouth of a navigable river; of course at twelve the fact that the land was already occupied by a city named Salinas had no relevance. Later, in high school, I became a fan of John Steinbeck and his stories set around the area. By the age of fifteen, I had refined my city and, with the support of my tenth grade art teacher, built a model and designed several of the city's buildings.

In eleventh grade, I wanted to redesign the central business district of my hometown in Michigan, with a plan from an urban planning and design firm. The same art teacher encouraged me to build a model and produce renderings of the building designs. The plan led to my first paid work in architecture, at seventeen, and my first job as an apprentice draftsman with a local firm. (Edward Lamont)

Once Lamont was hooked on architecture, there was no going back. He was fortunate to have the support of a high school teacher who encouraged him to think bigger and to keep going. That early reinforcement served him well as he went out into the real world of architecture. He still remembers fondly the firm that took him in when he was in high school; they nurtured his love of the profession and gave him the experience and the courage to take the next step.

In Lynne Duke's *Washington Post* article on Max Bond, she tells of his introduction to architecture as a child in Alabama. Early exposure helped form his understanding of the importance of context for young architects.

He [Max Bond] had found his own passion years earlier, when his parents lived in Tuskegee, Alabama, where the elder Bond taught at Tuskegee Institute. . . . He became especially enamored of the huge airplane hangars at a military complex next to the Institute. That was the training base for the storied black pilots, the Tuskegee airmen. Something about campus buildings fascinated the young Bond, who lived in Tuskegee between the ages of 5 and 9. He watched a dormitory being built and wondered how it happened. The architectural bug had caught him.[6]

Even one of the architects who was less rhapsodic about his journey into architecture has grown to have an intense connection to the profession. Especially for firm owners, it is not just about getting up and going to a job everyday.

My father was a surveyor in Nigeria when Nigeria became independent. He also did some architecture and construction. When he decided to work for a big firm, he wanted me to take over his business, but I went into advertising. I had no experience hands-on in production. My sophomore year, I switched to architecture. I did it in part because I already knew about architecture.

You look at work in all sorts of ways. Architects need to be an advocate for the clients. We need to find ways of elevating the spirit of the tenants. One example of advocacy is putting security cameras in the housing project we worked on. Sometimes minimalist design, the kind of thing that might be considered high-end, "good" design, doesn't give people a sense of being settled. Small interventions can make a big difference; it elevates their sense of place and involves everyone. It's important to include everyone as a development team. That way HUD [the U.S. Department of Housing and Urban Development] no longer owned this project, the tenants did.

I feel we have to give our work a meaning beyond bread and butter. We are socially based. Our raison d'etre is to bring value and design to people who normally wouldn't get it. There's a spiritual value and connection to make; it's a way to empower clients. (Wendell Marshall)

Marshall finds joy in the service he is able to render his clients. His sense of community is satisfied by being able to use the firm to serve communities of color. For him, the calling is about using the talents and skills in his firm to contribute to the lives of the end users of the buildings they design.

Fifteen of the twenty architects I met are either sole owners or co-owners of the firms in which they practice. They all have their own take on the profession. As Thad Collins said to me, "I think you'll find that all our careers have been different. All the architects have approached architecture from different perspectives in order to make it do what they want it to do." Even across the differences, the love of architecture and the devotion to the next generation of black architects was unequivocal with everyone I interviewed. Like all architects in practice, in the end the sum of the practitioner's experience comes together with the needs and wants of the client to produce architecture. All architects want the opportunity to create their best work for every client.

THE PROFESSION OF ARCHITECTURE

Architecture, as a discipline, has not seriously considered social and political issues, while social history has developed without much consideration of space or design.

—Dolores Hayden, *Power of Place*

There is ongoing discussion in a wide variety of quarters about the disconnect between architecture—predominantly white and male—and the increasingly multicultural reality of twenty-first century America. The face of both clients and consumers is changing, and the profession is not doing a good job of reflecting those changes.[7]

In order to maintain respect for the accepted canon, difference must be disdained. There certainly are changes in fashion, but those take place within acceptable design limits.[8] This notion is one of the results of the homogeneity of the architecture profession, and the homogeneity of the canon is a manifestation of power. To paraphrase Stevens, the value of professional capital is only relevant in that profession. Those who are privileged in that profession make the wisest decisions about how and whether to invest their capital. As the profession changes, the value of existing capital is liable to change; the power in the field rests with the ability to define and manage change and, thus, maintain the existing balance of privilege.[9]

Until other voices are allowed to be heard, it will likely continue to be a struggle for architects of color to be fully accepted by corporate clients. Holtz Kay's article, "Invisible Architects," begins with an anecdote about I. M. Pei and Cesar Pelli, two of the twentieth century's most successful and recognizable architects. Pei, who is Chinese, and Pelli, an Argentine, are so successful they are "no longer considered a minority."[10] According to Holtz Kay and others, the naming of an architect as a "minority" creates the perception of less than—less talent than their white colleagues, less experience, and so on.[11]

Allowing other, different voices has the potential to challenge the status quo in the field. The way a profession develops unique character is by very deliberately defining a standard for performance; to succeed, practitioners must consciously adhere to and excel at that standard.[12] As Jack Travis observes in an online article about his practice:

> We do not have a focus in design that radically departs from a European tradition that brings any other cultural influences forward. . . . The lack of significant recognition

of women and minorities has resulted in division within the profession between those who maintain a reverence for the notion of architecture as art and an aesthetic expression for uplifting the spirit incapable [of serving] as a catalyst towards solving social problems, and those of us who seek inclusion for a more comprehensive and unified effort towards problem solving in our ever-changing society.[13]

The legacy of professional architects versus the builders lives on in the way the educational experience is structured, and in the low numbers of people of color in the practice. Many of the architects I met have no delusions about their chosen profession. They understood from the time they began their studies that including ethnic diversity in a practice would require a conscious choice. They spoke often about the profession and pointed out how the need for economic capital means the clients are either financially privileged or are institutions. Further, clients tend to hire people who look like themselves, which in architecture usually means white men.

The attempt to bring diversity into the profession has not been particularly successful to date. Unlike music, art, dance, textiles, and literature, there is no "Black Architecture." Within the "family" of black architects, there remains ongoing and considerable discussion about the existence of Black Architecture. The spectrum is broad, from the opinion that there is no such thing, to the belief if you are black and an architect, your work is automatically influenced by your cultural heritage, to the few practitioners who make a clear statement their work consistently mirrors their culture.[14]

Some of the older generation of black architects believe the dominant culture of the architectural establishment keeps the African American influence out of design.

> Class warfare impacts architecture. It's like jazz combined with African music. There are people who would look at the combination of African and American architecture as an abomination. Look at Frank Gehry. An African American could never have gotten away with this kind of design. What if we used the same technology with African themes? The private sector with money fear that more than anything else.
>
> I grew up in the era when there were black entertainers and white entertainers, and then came Chubby Checker crossing the "color line." White folks can't afford to have that happen to *all* our cultural icons. (Thaddeus Collins)

The design culture of architecture remains somehow sacrosanct, not to be diluted by outside influence. In *The Crisis of the African-American Architect*, Melvin Mitchell says, "The need for a complete integration of all black art forms with architecture must take place . . . through new realizations that presumptively 'white' Modern Architecture can be no whiter than today's American music and other cultural art forms."[15] The melding of black cultural influences (what some might characterize as cultural appropriation) with other white arts and culture has not happened in architecture.

The last word on this subject belongs to Nelson Norton. His emphatic statement substantiates the belief that the dominant white culture is vulnerable to and terrified of change from "outside" influences.

> Fifty years ago, the reason professional athletes were all white was because it was believed blacks couldn't perform at that level. Once it is made clear the playing field is level, black people will rise. White people look at professional sports and get scared the same results will happen in other areas. It has to be communicated to black people that the field is level and that they can achieve results. Those areas where it's made clear are areas where blacks will overcompensate, because they're good at things like culture, intuition, interpersonal dynamics, etc.
>
> White folks believe civilization as we know it would go down the tubes if white people lost control. (Nelson Norton)

This is a rigorous profession for all practitioners. The wages are low, the hours are grueling, the expectations of clients are impossible to meet, and design considerations are always tempered by budget constraints and considerations for public safety. And yet it is difficult to make changes.

GETTING A JOB

Many architects told me stories about going to look for a job. When they got to the office for the interview, they were told "Oh, that job is already filled." Some continued to look for employment, and others started their own firms.

> We were involved and engulfed in the personal history of this country, but we couldn't go to school and study. When I was at the University of Nebraska, I was one of the first black people on the basketball team. There were no blacks in the Big 7. I was the only black architecture student in the school of architecture. You were just so involved in so many things. I got sent up north to Nebraska to get out of Kansas because at the Kansas schools you couldn't eat in the restaurants. I was the first African American to play basketball in the Southern Conference. When the team went to play in Tennessee, Arkansas, and Texas, I wasn't allowed to play so they would leave me at home.

I went to Florida A. & M. and the University of Nebraska. My architecture professor was hard on me and told me "You have to be twice as good as the white guys."
I told him, "All I need you to do is teach me architecture—I don't need you to tell
me about my social problems." When I finished, I had a job offer in New York and
three in Los Angeles. I came home to Kansas to see my parents and decide what I
wanted to do. A black guy who was a World War II vet came by to visit. He was
home seeing the family, and trying to get a job. No one would hire him in our hometown. I didn't like anyone to tell me what I couldn't do, so Monday morning I went
out looking for a job.

I had one white architect tell me I could come back on Wednesday to talk to his
partner. Wednesday I went back, and the partner said to me, "I've always wondered
what we would do if we had a colored fellow apply for a job." I couldn't believe he
would actually say that.

When I came home from the interview, I still wasn't sure what I wanted to do.
My father and I had a long talk, and he helped me realize what I really wanted to
do was practice on my own. He and I built all my furniture, and I started my own
office. I was determined to prove it could be done. (David Norman)

The desire and intention to practice architecture provided the motivation to
open an office against all odds. While the climate *is* improved for young black architects, systemic racism remains. For those who found employment in firms, the
struggle to level the playing field in the profession continued. Reflecting the evolution of racism in the United States, the discrimination in hiring is less overt
than it was in the pre–civil rights movement years. This does not mean racism is
over; it means it is more difficult to define and divine. What was once overt and
one-on-one is now less visible, more sophisticated, and systemic.[16] The statistics
on firm membership by ethnicity are sparse. According to the 2000/2002 AIA
Firm Survey, 8 percent of licensed architects were people of color, despite the
fact they were 30 percent of the total U.S. population. They made up 6 percent
of principals and partners at firms.

There was a big class divide in graduate school. I was trying to get my portfolio together so I could get a job, and no one else in my class seemed particularly concerned. Over spring break (when everyone else was at the beach), I interviewed
with SOM and got the job in New York City. My friends all said, "We hate you because *you* got a job." I needed that job.

I was at SOM three years, in the design department. During that time, the department went from 500 to 175. There was one other African American designer,
and he got laid off. As soon as I got there, I wondered, "Where are all the women?"
When I had my exit interview, I asked, "What policies do you have in place to make

sure African Americans and women are hired and promoted so when I leave there will still be some on the staff?"

They said, "We're on a par with our peers [as far as hiring women and people of color are concerned]." I responded, "Does that satisfy you? Why is it that when it comes to designing, CAD, etc., you seek to be number one, but when it comes to hiring you're content to be on a par with everyone else?" (Roland Davis)

He left without getting an answer, but the answer is apparent in the numbers. It would be easy to forgive firms for not advancing more people of color by pointing out how few graduates, and experienced practitioners, there are. But it is a vicious circle: Why would talented young blacks want to go into a profession that is so clearly unwelcoming? Why are there not more people of color advancing within firms?

As his time in Paris wound down, [Max] Bond sent letters to five architecture firms in the United States, seeking interviews. With his credentials and early experience, he received enthusiastic responses from all five. He made appointments.

At each firm, his arrival, the black face behind the impressive qualifications, stirred "this moment of confusion." Then somebody would come out and say, "There must be some mistake. We don't have work." Eventually, he did get work. But he was wiser, even hardened by the rejections, "another one of those rude awakenings."[17]

In a 1993 article, Dennis Mann, a faculty member in the architecture school at the University of Cincinnati and the coauthor of the *Directory of African American Architects*, related a different version of the same discriminatory practices.

Another young graduate from . . . the early 1950s and now a successful architect on the West Coast related his own experience to me. . . . After graduation he telephoned a local architect in Cincinnati to arrange a job interview. He described his interview in the following way:

"When I stepped out of the elevator, Mr. X., who was standing at the far end of his office, looked up from his papers at me and turned a beet red. I guess he hadn't expected to see a black architecture graduate since I probably didn't sound 'black' on the telephone. My interview consisted of Mr. X spending the entire time trying to convince me that architecture was not the profession for me. He said I would be much happier as a doorman or a porter. I knew immediately that Cincinnati was not the place for me. I left for California as soon as I could."[18]

These stories from the 1950s remain relevant today. Although modern racism is considerably less overt, these collective memories are a part of the legacy of black architects. Across all ethnicities, the memories are part of what defines "culture." If we are able to have an objective look at our own collective memories, we can begin to understand they are an active part of both our general outlook on the world—our "lifeworld"—as well as affecting the details of our everyday life.[19]

> I graduated in 1950. I had a rough time finding a job. Even after graduation from school, with a professional architectural degree, it was tough to get a job. I applied and went to about twenty different offices. I don't know if the rejections were because I was a black person, because I was a young woman, or because of the economic recession at that time. I've tried not to pay too much attention to that. I knew I was smart, and I knew what I wanted to do. I needed a job, so I just kept going.
>
> I finally went to work for the City.[20] You needed three years of experience before you could take the licensing exam. It was a four-day exam, twelve hours day one, nine the other days, on architecture and engineering. I passed the entire exam. I was licensed in New York City in 1954. Everyone was mad I passed the test. My boss at the City wasn't even licensed. (Olivia Tucker)

As Tucker told me this story, I sensed she had felt the people around her were saying, "How dare she pass that exam the first try?" If there were expectations for blacks and women, they certainly would not have been about superior intelligence, scholastic ability, or professional excellence. Like so many other black professionals, Tucker knew what she wanted to do, and she worked very hard to be able to do it. The barriers made it more difficult, but they also stiffened her resolve.

Another architect who finished school in the middle of the civil rights movement had a different story with the same theme. Attention to disparity issues waxes and wanes.

> In the late '60s and early '70s, I had no problem finding work. Individuals and the profession in general were encouraging people of color to participate in architecture. I was awarded one of the first AIA minority scholarships. Racial attitudes were different then, and the profession's attitudes were different, too. It's as if the architectural profession's social conscience was a "fad," sometimes in fashion and sometimes out. I established my own firm primarily for the opportunity to practice as an architect. I knew I would never have the opportunity to design and manage projects unless I was the principal. (Edward Lamont)

One of the great ironies of the racism in architecture is the simultaneous invisibility and hypervisibility that happen for architects of color. For those of us European Americans who do not have to consider whether or not we will be seen and singled out, these stories can be difficult to digest. Lamont learned shortly after he got out of school not to pin his hopes on the vagaries of political attitudes. By establishing his own firm, he had to face a different set of problems, but at a minimum he created a situation where he would not have to worry about whether or not a firm owner would hire a black architect.

DEALING WITH RACISM

> *The work of black architects seldom appears in the pages of professional magazines. In academia, they hold few professorships and rarely appear on awards juries and panels of architectural events. There are no prominent black architectural writers or editors. And—perhaps the ultimate insult of invisibility—there are few exact statistics to certify these figures.*
>
> —Jane Holtz Kay, "Invisible Architects"

The social and political realities black architects face in establishing and maintaining a practice are modulated by attitudes and perceptions embedded in social, political, and economic systems. For the most part, contemporary racism is no longer about one-on-one name calling, and increasingly about the difficulty of effecting social change, the difficulty of making deeply ingrained racism visible.[21] Systemic racism is exactly that: built into the system.

Institutional, or systemic, racism "creates a built-in system of privilege, shapes everyday social relations, and forms change over time. Specific racial group histories differ, but different race groups share a common experience of racial oppression."[22] Institutional racism is a little like high blood pressure. It exists, and its effects can be measured, but it is often invisible to the victim. I do not mean to imply institutional racism is not destructive and oppressive. Often people of color who have always been oppressed no longer recognize it as oppression, and whites who have grown up in this system also do not recognize it.

In architecture, cultural racism is also at work. Robert T. Carter defined it as "the conscious or subconscious conviction that white Euro-American cultural patterns and practices, as reflected in values, language, belief systems, interpersonal interaction, styles, behavioral patterns, political, social roles, economics, music . . . etc. are superior to those of other visible racial/ethnic groups."[23] The focus on Eurocentric architecture, both in the educational curriculum and in practice, leaves other views invisible at best, and ostracized at worst.

Despite the myth white America has created, being educated and middle class, or upper-middle class (or even upper class, but that is not an issue for the architects in this book), does not protect blacks from systemic racism.[24] This myth is particularly visible in architecture, but for those who are looking, it is observable across the American landscape.

Feagin et al. reported on extensive interviews with middle-class African Americans about what workplace life is like for them in corporate America. They were told that from a black, middle-class perspective, "it is often the less-qualified whites who get special privileges over better-qualified people of color."[25] In seeking to understand this viewpoint, they reported, "In the U.S. economy, many racial barriers are linked, directly or indirectly, to white 'good-ole-boy' networks which are commonly at the core of workplaces."[26] The more profitable and interesting work generally goes to those firms who are already known and are a part of the industry power structure.[27] This is an issue for all but the most successful, the "star" firms; all firms struggle with business development problems. Because they do not have access to private developers with wealth, nor to corporate decision makers, this problem is more pronounced for black firms.

The fact of not getting commissions for design work, as opposed to having jobs that are strictly functional buildings with tightly restricted budgets, is a source of frustration and resentment for black architects. Because design holds such an exalted place in American architecture, the dearth of design projects increases the invisibility of black architects.

> How do you get the exposure if you can't get the exposure? You can't get the repeat commissions; people can't ever see our work, so they don't think we have the vision. We can't afford the photographers and we can't afford the writers. We don't have a publicist in our office and we don't have the relative at the magazine.
>
> Clients categorize architecture in terms of new buildings. That's how they decide whether an architect can see or can't see. Our society believes black architects can't see. Remodels and renovations are okay for us, anything but design. (James Patterson)

One of the most insidious things about the racism in the architecture profession is that it not only renders the practitioners invisible, but it leaves their work invisible as well. Repeatedly, I was told that black firms have relatively little trouble finding work; they just cannot find the kind of work that will allow them to put their design prowess to the test.

Straddling Two Communities

I also did not understand the cognitive dissonance between professional success and needing to justify that success to the black community. I have heard anecdotally over the past fifteen years about the struggles black business owners have between functioning effectively in the predominantly white business community and being an active member of the black community.[28] Edward Lamont said,

> Then there's the ongoing oppression on top of everything else. It's always a question of economic power. As an African American, I have to try twice as hard. If I have legitimate complaints about racism, they're often tossed off as whining. Whiteness is always better; there's very little value in being other than white. As an architect who's black, my qualifications don't count.
>
> On the other hand, if you *are* successful, people in the community complain you're "white," and then you still have to do all the management stuff. . . . How do you take this business vocabulary back into the 'hood? How do you deal with the organizations in the 'hood, and how do you explain to your white staff the differences between the reality of our business and the reality of many in the community?
>
> Black architects just weren't there. Outside of the community design era, they weren't visible. There wasn't a critical mass, so there was a lack of support for African American architects. (Edward Lamont)[29]

Here is the catch: They are trained as part of the white architecture culture, with a focus on design. If they attempt to compete on that basis, they are generally kept out of the most visible, profitable work. If they work to market their services in communities of color, they may get interesting projects, but their work is discounted by the profession as "only" being work in communities of color, not interesting or important enough to be credible.

Even the black architects we think of as wildly successful struggled with racism. Given the professional acclaim and financial rewards Paul Williams garnered, it would be easy to forget the degree to which racism remained part of his life. He left a substantial written record of his life and his practice. Karen Hudson, Williams's granddaughter, employed many quotes from that material in her book *Paul R. Williams, Architect: A Legacy of Style*. She writes,

> The opportunities he coveted would be forever out of his grasp if he allowed himself to be discouraged at this juncture. . . . No longer was architecture an assumed profession born of a love of drawing; it became a well thought-out commitment. . . . "If I allow the fact I am a Negro to checkmate my will to do, now, I will inevitably form the habit of being defeated."
>
> "Virtually everything pertaining to my professional life, during those early years, was influenced by my need to offset race prejudice, by my effort to force white people to consider me as an individual rather than as a member of a race. Occasionally, I encountered irreconcilables who simply refused to give me a hearing, but, on the whole, I have been treated with an amazing fairness."[30]

It is easy, and less painful, to believe things have improved dramatically since the days Paul Williams was in practice. When people who have heard about this research have said to me, "Yes, but it's so much better than it used to be," I generally reply, "That is true. Architects no longer have to design buildings with separate sets of bathrooms and drinking fountains!" The racism has only become less overt and more insidious.[31]

> My wife and I went to an AIA convention on the other side of the state. We were the only people of color at the meeting. We took one of my white employees with us to the meeting. We would introduce ourselves to other people at the meeting—all white—and they automatically assumed he was the firm owner. It was like they assumed *I* couldn't possibly be the firm principal. (Edward Lamont)

As white people, it is comforting to believe the changes are sufficient. Rather than taking the time to try to understand how our culture is designed to maintain continuing oppression of nonmajority citizens, most of us shout that we are *not* racists, and move on.

An architect on the East Coast talked about the ways racism has an impact on his practice:

> Let me tell you how the racism and rage impact my work. When I have a *cold*, I can't be creative. How much time do I have to focus on something that can't be productive? I find a positive way to vent the anger, to give back. I try to find a way to get more of a critical mass to make change. You have to take it, deal with it, move on, and use the energy to produce. Our words have power and become reality. The Thought is the commodity we produce. The clients can benefit from that.
>
> That gray zone exists everywhere. It's up to us to find a way to work both sides against the middle. The thinking time defines particular trends. You have to make it overt for people to start thinking about oppression without them having to take much time. Black people *are* affecting culture, which leads to affecting the way we think, which leads to why things feel and look the way they do. Changes will just happen whether we think about them or not, so we have to think about them. We need to be deliberate rather than just letting things happen. (Wendell Marshall)

Marshall implied how easy it would be to let racism disrupt the creative process. If it is difficult to perform with a cold, it would be paralyzing to deal with the racism if he let it get to him. He is well aware it exists, and has a desire to address it and to make change, but he is pragmatic. He knows one of the assets of understanding two cultures is the ability to pick and choose methods from each culture in order to accomplish his goals. He fashions a process, keeping in mind how it will affect the outcome. He wants his efforts toward social change to be beneficial for his clients.

In order to educate people about racism, and about the contributions blacks are making, he wants to find overt ways to get the message across. Marshall was in advertising as an undergraduate; he understands marketing well enough to know that quick hits get people's attention. He pointed out that the evolution of this culture will happen whether or not we pay attention; we need to think about how we want it to change, and assume some power over the changes.

Client Relations

There are still places where hiring a black architect causes problems for white clients. The expectation of solidarity in the business community can be difficult, but not impossible, for an architect of color to overcome. It seems incredible that white clients would still have to justify hiring a black architect. However, outside of major metropolitan areas, a scarcity of black professionals, coupled with a tightly knit good ol' (white) boys network, can mean the act of hiring a black architect is an act of courage.

> The hard part about running a practice is access to dollars and access to clients. If we have white clients, they have to explain to the community why they hired me. Bank of America pledged $15 million to the minority community in this town; none of it has been spent. We couldn't get a line of credit in our hometown. (David Norman)

Racism can create barriers to growth for black-owned firms. Although twenty-first-century institutional racism is less overt, more sophisticated, and more insidious than the in-your-face racism of the previous 250 years,[32] the scars of those years are still readily visible in the stories of the older architects. In some parts of the country, the racism remains clearly identifiable. Despite the changes, these stories continue to inform modern practice both for the older architects and for their colleagues. David continued,

> Folks were always in your face. "How are you going to hire people?" I said, "What do you mean?" They said, "Who will you find that will work for you?" I said, "I'm paying salaries, providing jobs and opportunities the same as any other firm." If somebody confuses the architecture profession with the mythical people, well we live those patterns and we're not mythical. One of my white clients told me, "Your work has to be good because I've gotten a lot of criticism for hiring you." As though my work wouldn't be good!

We're working on our third contract for the local newspaper. I got a call from the editor, my friend and client, who said, "Can you come have lunch with me at my club that you can't belong to?" By the time I got there, he had already had a big Scotch. "Five businessmen in town had a meeting with me last night. They said, 'What do you mean hiring a nigger to do your work?' I told them it's my money, and that guy you're calling a nigger is the best architect in town."

I've submitted bids and had people come back to me and say things like, "You don't have the experience. You're the only principal in the firm. What if something happened to you?" This society remains so racist. I've been in business forty-two years. I'm proud of the things we've done. I've done more than anyone thought I would do, but my greatest legacy is my daughters. I worked hard to create a reputation for quality work even when I was getting the crap beat out of me.

I'm not going away. If there's something you think I lied about, you tell me. (David Norman)

This story is a good example of the dedication these professionals bring to their work and the lingering shadow of racism in the profession. On one hand, David Norman's continuing determination is a cause for celebration. His is a community that continues to place barriers in his way. On the other hand, it is unconscionable that a firm with a track record of first-rate work still has to put up with the continuing struggle of proving themselves to the business leaders in his hometown.

The architects I spoke to whose firms are focused on communities of color have a steady flow of work and agree there is more than enough work to keep them busy. It gives them the opportunity to explore the ways culture can be reflected in the built environment and enables them to explore their ethnic heritage, and that of their clients, through design. Edward Lamont, whose firm works in a number of communities of color, pointed out that working in ethnic communities can bring up difficult issues:

One of our long-time clients is a social service agency in the Asian community. I was on their board for a while and gave them free space planning. Twenty years with the same client agency; I'm on my third executive director. Because of all the cultural issues, they are a challenging client. The agency, and the facilities planning committee, which reflects the whole staff, are a mix of people from a variety of backgrounds—Chinese, Japanese, Vietnamese, and Cambodian.

Over the years, we've done a lot of work in the Asian community. I hate to say it, but I think in some of these immigrant communities, it is culturally appropriate to be racist. I worry about how to get change to the next generation. It's so difficult to get away from a cultural pressure. It's like they recognize African Americans are discriminated against, and if they want to be accepted as Americans they have to adopt the model they want to be part of, so they discriminate against African Americans. In some parts of that community, there are big class differences. I'm committed to positive change, but it can be depressing to think about the mean-spirited things people do. Before September 11, a backlash was already boiling. I've since realized when you dehumanize people, it's easier to bomb them. (Edward Lamont)

Maintaining a diverse firm and serving a diverse customer base can be very satisfying. Especially for an architect such as Lamont, who grew up in community design centers, multiculturalism is an essential part of who he is. However, it requires a conscious decision and a long-term view in order to avoid getting stuck in the daily skirmishes that come with diversity. Working with the social service agency described above requires Lamont to hone and maintain his diplomacy skills; it also enables him to remain aware of and sensitive to cultural difference. This is vital in a practice that attempts to reflect those differences in the designs they deliver to the client.

Paul Williams articulated the relationship that forms between the architect and the client. In these times of complex and changing building codes, collaboration with other professionals, and increasing land and materials costs, it seems somehow quaint, but it is a statement that gets to the heart of how this work gets done:

Each day, in my office, I consult with men and women who are leaders in the financial, intellectual and cultural worlds. An exchange of ideas occurs. From the moment when the first sketch is conceived, until the day when the building stands completed, there is, of necessity, a close bond between client and architect.[33]

For a society that does very little interracial socializing, it is not a surprise black architects have trouble getting private and corporate commissions. The majority of the people with the money to hire architects likely do not know any people of color personally, much less architects of color. This is one reason so many of the architects I interviewed stressed the need for a critical mass. If there were more black architects, it would be a little easier to be more visible. As discussed in the last chapter, at least other professionals, particularly doctors and lawyers, are visible in communities of color.

There is also the ongoing issue of developing clients over time. As in any industry, it is cheaper to get more jobs out of a previous client than it is to find new ones. Because of the perception that a black-owned firm cannot handle the work, and because of the lack of capital in the black community, few black firms get to work on buildings from scratch. After twenty years, Edward Lamont's firm still has very few opportunities to design new construction. Lamont said, "That's only happened every three years. It's like the difference between golfing with a foursome and going to the driving range. When you only get a shot every three years to show off your design skills, it's hard to maintain a design flow." Lamont continued, using the example of the job that really got the firm going:

> Take our first client. We got to do a major skilled nursing facility because they liked me. It was our first big job, $10 million. Two of us did it by ourselves, with no other employees, just some subs. It's tough to get a new client to have that kind of faith in you.[34]

I asked others about the energy it takes to find clients, given the perception that black architects do not know how to design.

> I appreciate challenges. You live day to day, but you believe the work will come—living day to day. I started this office in 1993; I had worked for Max Bond. I graduated from Columbia in 1984. I started a firm with a Chinese American classmate. It was the mid-'80s. His Chinese family bought property, and we designed upscale houses.
> I did that for five years. He moved into construction, and I went to work for Max. Eventually, I left and started this firm, but by then I had decided I wanted to focus on projects in the community. We have done a lot of education to teach potential clients what we can do for them, and show them by example we are competent. (Wendell Marshall)

> When I start to think about the racism in this system, I can't afford to be bitter. Eleven people out of this office have started their own offices. We have twenty-five people now. We know what our capabilities are, and we have to keep moving forward. Why did they hire the East Asian woman for a design project when they wouldn't hire her when she worked for me? Any minority who's not black is perceived as more qualified—East Asians, Asians, women. They'll hire anyone but a black architect. The excuses they make are things like, "They can be confrontational, they have deep voices, they intimidate us." When you're not in the room, you can't make them hire you. (Nicholas Rose)

The cumulative impact of daily acts of racism takes a toll on blacks in the United States.[35] For black architects, the anger lives just under the surface. The pragmatic response, the one taken by Marshall, Rose, and others, is to acknowledge it and move on. Their great strength is the recognition that anger and bitterness only harm them; they would rather spend their energy fighting for good architecture than spinning their wheels in the mire of systemic racism.

Lynn Duke, in her article in the *Washington Post*, provides a picture of how Max Bond has chosen to address the effect of racism in his life.

> His [Max Bond's] father wasn't the worst example, he says, but many of the African American men he knew in his father's generation were gripped by bitterness because of the limitations that racism had placed on their lives. He saw men being squeezed by their bitterness, almost debilitated by it.
>
> Obviously, racism had impacted his life. And the battle against it was part of the Bond family's daily life. (One of Bond's cousins, by the way, is Julian Bond, chairman of the NAACP.) But the younger Bond did not want to fall into a private hell of "If I were white" and fill in the blanks: The jobs would have opened up; his work would have been published more, causing more work to come. All that may be true, he says, but it gets nowhere to wallow in the hypothetical.
>
> "I would argue that, yes, maybe if I'd been white I'd have done this and that," he says. "But on the other hand, I never wanted to be white. I always felt I was fortunate to be black" and thus have a broader frame of reference on the world.[36]

Just to succeed in their chosen field, these men, and their black colleagues, have had to make a conscious decision to focus on their practice and not on the institutional oppression they face. Their continuing success is a testimony to the wisdom of that decision. Each of the architects I met has made a commitment to make a contribution by serving as a successful role model for young black architects. They are devoted to making change, quietly and deliberately, by taking their rightful places in the profession.

When these black firms go out in the market and try to broaden their client base, they are often rebuffed on the basis of being black. Marketing and firm development are difficult endeavors for all architecture firms, but the white-owned firms, particularly the white, *male*-owned firms, do not have the additional onus of race working against them.

> We've bid on jobs—that we are totally capable of doing—only to have the owner say, "For that kind of fee, I could hire a white architect." Earning respect in this profession is the worst. I shouldn't have to go through that. You either get no respect, or you think things are going well, and then you find out what they're up to.
>
> My partner and I have practiced together for twenty-six years; the firm has been here for thirty-one. Our big project downtown is the only building we, or any black architect, has gotten to design downtown, the only one. Our firm has only done one new building downtown—after thirty-one years. We have a tremendous amount of talent. We've been successful in this firm, but if we were white we'd be the size of SOM. (Nicholas Rose)

At the same time Rose focuses his energy on supporting the firm, he is always conscious of the ways life would be different absent racism. It is frustrating, knowing they are a talented firm capable of doing a broad range of work, and seeing how they have been kept from doing it.

Even the largest black firms are not shielded from the daily slights. The owner of a large firm in the Midwest said,

> The largest percentage of our work is university work. In the education studio, we're divided into sports and recreation, student centers, classrooms, and everything else. We also have a health care studio and an interior design studio. In all of those, we've won awards and made contributions that allow us to compete with any firm in the marketplace. Most hiring committees are used to hearing minority firms say they've *participated*. We say we *did* the project. There's a lot of skepticism. That's as opposed to white firms who say they did a project and it's just accepted.
>
> I actually had a project selection committee member ask me, "Did you really do these projects?" And I said, "Yes, I specifically put together the slides that are projects we've *done*." At least he said it out loud. Most people just think it. Then we don't get the job but we can't be exactly sure why. (Donald Nelson)

These stories are more evidence of the insidious racism in the profession. Despite my years of experience, and my stated objective of writing about institutional racism, I was still shocked by the way black architects have been treated. A potential client would never think to question the integrity of a white-owned firm.

When opportunities to get involved in corporate work do open up, black firms are routinely shuffled to the bottom of the list. Worse, they are assumed to be unable to complete projects on their own.

> A couple years ago, we made contact with one of the big corporations that was planning a long-term construction project, and the diversity officer told us to bring our financials and apply for work as a subcontractor. [The "prime contractor manages a project. Other firms, the "subcontractors," have contracts with the prime.] They had made the assumption firms of color would be small firms and would not be willing to walk away. We walked from the process. We wanted to be a prime not a sub, and we weren't going to provide our financials so the competition could see them.
>
> One problem with getting corporate clients is the need to overcome the perception of our firm as a firm that only works in communities of color. Some large clients think they will wait to hire us until they have the "right" project in the central area. When do we start to build a new portfolio? We could try to hire someone from outside who comes in with clients. Everyone who hires an architect hires because they

know the person. The corporate folks say, "We think we know you, we hear good things about you, we don't know what you've done." Clients do projects with architects they know. (Edward Lamont)

The corporations that establish requirements for "minority participation," that is, a mandate that a certain amount of any construction project will include nonmajority contractors, believe they are doing the right thing by making an effort to employ contractors of color. There are a couple of fundamental flaws in these programs. There is an assumption the applicants will be small businesses, desperate for work, and unable to compete for any but the smallest jobs. For a seasoned architecture firm, those assumptions are insulting at least, and racist at most. However, the minority-owned businesses that really *are* small are subject to what amounts to harassment in the process. They are forced to give the client proprietary business information that can be used against them and can be lifted by competitors.

Black-owned firms have a challenge overcoming the perception they work only in ethnic communities. The corporations who do consider them for projects will generally look to them for projects that are in those communities; they are unwilling to consider black firms for "mainstream" projects. One of the most insidious aspects of institutional racism is the ways access is effectively blocked by the perception that blacks of any occupation are not as competent, skilled, and so forth as whites in comparable positions.

All the architects I have interviewed have been generous with their time and their stories. They have all said how important it is to tell these stories, but I am always conscious of the fact many of these stories are painful and humiliating to relive. I tried to be sensitive to the fact that discussing oppression of any kind can be disturbing and enervating. I am certain, though, that the more we are able to talk about it, and tell the stories more broadly, the more difficult it will be for the "isms" to retain their power. As long as the stories are invisible, it is easy to believe we have solved our race problem.

A profession referred to as the white gentlemen's profession is as difficult for women as it is for nonwhites. The statistics on women in the profession are slightly less dismal than the statistics (when you can find them) on people of color, but things are still pretty grim. According to the AIA National Associates Committee, 40–50 percent of architecture graduates are female; 33 percent of Associate AIA members are female. Women constitute 20 percent of all registered architects and 11 percent of AIA licensed members.[37] Women of color have a particularly difficult time gaining credibility and status. One of the women interviewed for an article in a regional design publication writes,

What is the experience of cultural discrimination in architecture? It's when any of these alternative cultural values are practiced, they are seen by the majority culture as incidental or unimportant (not recognized or respected) to the extent that they diverge from the norm. If the primary design determinants are not valued, the design is not valued, and the designer is not valued. This "blind spot" in the eye of the cultural majority results in fewer opportunities for those with diverse viewpoints.

If women adopt the cultural male traits of aggression and competition, they are seen as unfemale and ostracized; if they keep the traditional female quality of cooperation they are seen as not authoritative enough. This double bind can cause women to leave to start their own offices or leave traditional practice for tangential fields which aren't so [white] male-dominated.[38]

One of the women I interviewed has had her own firm thirty years. The firm has made a name for itself, and has been successful in a number of niche segments. However, her experiences as a black woman in a racist, sexist profession remain a source of pain. As with her male colleagues discussed above, she looks for ways to keep moving and not focus on the daily slights.

Where could I start? If you're black or female, and you go into certain professions known to be dominated by white men, you can't think about it at all. Okay, I'll tell you one story. When I started my office and got my first health-care facility, I got two tiny ones and a medium one. Then I decided to try to get a clinic that was part of a State hospital. I had to be interviewed. I knew someone on the State selection committee, so I got an interview. The first meeting was with the doctors involved in the project. There were thirteen or fourteen of them.

The person from the State, an East Indian, knew the people at the hospital. He went with me to the interview. We walked into the meeting room; there was a long table full of white men in white jackets. You can't think about this stuff. If you thought about it, you'd be crazy.

I was sitting down next to the guy with the funding.

One of the doctors said to him, "You mean, she works for the architect?"

The Indian said, "No, she *is* the architect."

They kept talking about me like I wasn't there.

"You know this project requires someone with a degree and some experience."

"She has a degree in hospital design."

They were so unbelieving. It wasn't as though they destroyed me or anything. By the time the project was over, those guys were my friends. At the end they had no problem seeing me as the architect.

To be black and female in a profession that's not welcoming requires you to focus and do what you can do best. It's their problem, and you can't think about it. I can't get this work because. . . . It's always in the back of your mind. (Sharon Young)

This quandary is one of the reasons I wanted to pursue this research. It is difficult to imagine the feeling of the continual affront of not getting the work, and the inability of the clients and colleagues to understand the toxicity of the ways they wield their power. When it comes to race and gender, the Golden Rule truly becomes "Those with the Gold, Rule."[39]

HIGHLY VISIBLE AND COMPLETELY INVISIBLE

We are so spent by trying to get into the system that there is little time remaining to critique the historical conditions that make our climb so difficult. Rather than develop a self-defined praxis of architecture that would make a real difference in the lives of our people, we mimic the values and goals that have created our oppression. How can we resist the tendency to mirror the dominant culture? How can we improve our access to the rewards to which we are entitled as citizens of the United States and still unmask the structural inequities that make those rewards possible? How can we develop political clarity when we are so isolated from one another and so driven by the need to prove our worth and make ourselves visible?

—Sharon E. Sutton,
"Finding Our Voice in a Dominant Key"

As R. K. Stewart points out in his foreword, the profession has not done an effective job of making itself known and understood. To some degree, most architects are invisible. Asked to name five architects, most people are hard-pressed to get three. The problem is worse for black architects.

One of the great ironies for black architects is that they are simultaneously invisible (their work is passed over, they are not invited to compete, etc.) and highly visible (they are expected to be at work precisely on time, have to carefully manage every detail of a project, etc.), unlike their majority counterparts, many of whom can easily heighten their visibility to get work and do not have to be concerned about whether they have done everything perfectly.

For those of us European Americans who do not have to consider whether or not we will be seen, and singled out, these stories can be hard to believe. I did not come to my work in community development finance equipped to understand this visibility problem. Only through hearing about it repeatedly from my clients and witnessing it when we were out together did I begin to recognize my own freedom of movement. Architecture is no different. The fact of having an advanced education and having served an extensive internship just like their white counterparts does not protect black architects from being singled out and treated differently than their white colleagues.

> I started teaching at NYC Community College in Brooklyn, and worked at SOM. I was highly visible. If two of the guys were talking, no one noticed. If guys were talking to me, it was assumed it was small talk. My employers seemed to think I wasn't productive despite the fact I accomplished more than most of the employees. (Olivia Tucker)

This anecdote of Tucker's reflects the male privilege her colleagues possessed. Peggy McIntosh wrote in the 1980s her observations of white privilege and male privilege in an academic setting.[40] She came up with a list of the ways white privilege manifests in everyday life. Visibility/invisibility is mentioned a number of times. Unfortunately, the article is as relevant today as it was when it was written. The more I have come to recognize racist behavior and actions in the world around me, the more I feel as white people we wear a special cloak that identifies us as white and alters our vision so we do not have to see the slights happening around us; we usually do not know when we have created them. We struggle not to understand truths that are clear to blacks: whether we *mean* to be "racists" or not, the system is so well-designed that we can participate in maintaining systemic racism without even knowing. By actively *not* noticing, we can participate in our own success without realizing or recognizing how our actions cause others to become invisible.[41]

In a 1985 article in *California Architect* magazine, Norma Sklarek talked about the frustration of being visible as a black woman employee.

> In 1960, I moved to California. When I first moved to California, a coworker who lived in the same neighborhood was driving me to work. He was late every day for the previous two years. It took only one week before the boss came and spoke to me about being late. Yet he had not noticed that the young man had been late for two years. My solution was to buy a car since I, the highly visible employee, had to be punctual.[42]

Sklarek was a role model for other black women who were determined to practice architecture; she was clear that being an architect was more important to her than spending her life responding to either racist or sexist behavior in the workplace.

Just as blacks' complaints about racism are often dismissed as whining, their frustration, anger, and fear of oppression are often discounted or ignored. I was discussing the reality of racism with one of the architects when he told me this story:

> There was an incident, I can't remember whether it was at Brown or Columbia. Some students in the dorm hung a Confederate flag out their window. A black woman student went to the administration and complained. They told her there was nothing wrong with them hanging the flag out their window. She went back to her room, and hung a big swastika out her window. Both flags were down before the end of the day. Sometimes we can only get seen in contrast to others. (Nicholas Rose)

Paul Kivel and others have pointed out that "black" is seen *in relation to.* That is, the political state of blackness is only defined by considering whiteness. In his book *Uprooting Racism,* Kivel points out:

> Genetic differences among humans can be explained by the distribution of genetic variables, but don't correspond with any useful category of race defined genetically, by skin color, or any other physical characteristic. Because there's nothing biological about whiteness, it ends up being defined by contrasts to other groups, becoming confused with ideas of nationality, religion and ethnicity.[43]

The work of black architects is often discussed relative to black contributions to other art forms. Black cultural contributions to music, dance, literature, and art make a stark contrast to architecture.

> If we're obscure in the present, our past is completely invisible. The economic core of architecture can't approach other professions. None of us earns what doctors and lawyers make. Some of the issues are difficult for all architects. We [black people] have been exceptionally able to do uplifting things that are culturally based. How we measure success has infiltrated mainstream culture. We have molded American culture. When something more refined, like architecture, comes out of black culture, it's assumed to be more Eurocentric. As black architects, we get no credit.
>
> Rather than assimilating, we could have a distinctive identity, talent, expression, etc. As we make individual decisions we either get involved or not, we're either Jack Travis or not, we either have a style that evokes an African American aesthetic or not. It's discussed in a spiritual or an intellectual way, but we need to start getting clear about it and getting our work to be more visible. (Tom Miller)

Miller is among those who are lobbying their fellow black architects to come up with effective ways to work together to get their work in front of more potential clients. It will require a monumental task in a profession that has successfully resisted attempts to introduce a more diverse approach to design.

SERVICE TO THE COMMUNITY

June 24, 1968, Whitney M. Young, the executive director of the Urban League, addressed a national meeting of the AIA. In an articulate and civilized manner, he excoriated the architects and the institution for their total disregard of the problems facing low-income communities and communities of color.[44] In the middle of a long and moving address about racism in America, he singled out the architects:

> You are not a profession that has distinguished itself by your social and civic contributions to the cause of civil rights, and I am sure this does not come to you as any shock. You are most distinguished by your thunderous silence and your complete irrelevance.
>
> You are employers, you are key people in the planning of our cities today. You share the responsibility for the mess we are in in terms of the white noose around the central city. It didn't just happen. We didn't just suddenly get this situation. It was carefully planned.[45]

For black architects, community service can be complex. In terms of deciding the most strategic way to allocate their volunteer time, they have to balance the need to be visible in two or three very different places.

> Working in "the community" is complicated because I have so many communities where I need to be visible. I want to work in my "own" community, and I try to work in the white business community, and then I do volunteering in the architectural community by serving on AIA committees.[46] It's a lot of volunteer work. Sometimes I wonder when I have time for my firm. (Edward Lamont)

Forty years ago, architects who wanted to work in communities had the option of working (either as employees or, often, as volunteers) in community design centers (CDCs). Begun in Harlem in 1964, the community design movement was an effort to provide design services to low- and moderate-income communities, and also to ensure the quality of those services.[47] Whitney Young's speech provided the impetus for the idea to spread. In 1968, when Young addressed the AIA, the cities of America were burning. There were demonstrations outside the Democratic presidential convention in Chicago, and there had been riots in many major cities across the country.[48] Community design was one way the profession could get involved in rebuilding central cities.

Work in the CDCs was a good way to connect social justice activism with professional skills, but the endeavor was not without political problems. There was considerable conflict between the community residents and the activists who were trained as architects and planners.[49] It is challenging to create community organizations that can bridge the divide between the professionals who have a theoretical concept about what will be best for a community and the people who live there and know what they want.[50] Even so, the movement did serve a useful purpose for both the residents and the staff.

Of all the architects I interviewed, Edward Lamont was the person whose life was most affected by working in community design. Edward Lamont's first experience in a CDC was in 1968 in Detroit, the site of some of the worst race riots in the country. Working with one of the senior associates from the firm where he was employed, he volunteered at the Urban Design and Development Group, a CDC working in the inner city. "We worked at night, in a nearly abandoned midrise office tower, on neighborhood development plans to rebuild a broken city," he said.

When Lamont moved west, in late 1968, he continued his work in community design. For him, and many others, it served as a way to understand the politics of both urban problems and architecture; it also fostered his understanding of, and interest in, culturally relevant design. As Amos Rapoport said, "Since culture is variable, designed environments respond to variable definitions of needs and priorities as expressed in varying schemata: environments are culture specific."[51] In the CDC movement, architects were encouraged to include design elements that reflected the communities they served.

Lamont learned early in his career that there are ways to design apart from the dominant culture's approach. He believed all art forms play a role in cultural identity, but most people do not think about how architecture can also be a reflection of ethnicity.[52]

Throughout the years of his formal education, Lamont maintained and expanded his sense of cultural identity through his work in the community design movement. He talked about his experience:

> After a stint as a drafter in a West Los Angeles firm, I found my way to Watts and the Urban Workshop community design center. In Watts, I continued the community building work I had begun in Detroit. We produced comprehensive neighborhood improvement plans and provided free and low-cost services for new and renovated housing and community facilities. A burned-out Safeway store was salvaged and converted to a much needed community theater. Housing designated to be demolished in the area of an expanded LAX airport was saved and moved to Watts for freeway replacement housing.
>
> The late '60s, and my work in Watts, was a coming of age in my professional growth, and organizations like the Student National Coordinating Committee (SNCC)[53] and

the Black Panther Party galvanized my political awareness. It was pretty radical to leave professional work and go to Watts to work in a converted lumber warehouse. (Edward Lamont)

The contribution of CDC training allowed architects to bring together the two pieces of their lives, as architects and as people of color concerned about community. For black architects, this disparity between who they are as people and what they want to do professionally often is at the center of a lifelong struggle. The CDCs provided a way to make a community contribution *and* practice architecture.

When Lamont moved back to Detroit to complete his undergraduate work, he worked in his third community design center. By then, he had realized the value to him and to the community of continuing this work: "Four years following the battle of 12th Street, Detroit was still undergoing repair and redevelopment. I went to work on many neighborhood improvement projects, in-fill housing, and the first project of my own design and project management, St. Paul AME Church, the church my grandfather attended in Port Huron." This special connection to his grandfather tied together all the important aspects of his life in one project.

The shift in public policy from providing services and aiding community development, aimed at empowering low-income communities and communities of color, to a "blame the victim" mentality in the Reagan and Bush years brought about the demise of most CDCs.[54] The experiences in that system created a lasting impression about the need to work in community, and also about the importance of creating design sensitive to cultural difference. According to the ACD, the CDCs that were able to stay in business over the past twenty-five years tended to be those where diversity was valued and maintained, both in the staff and in the community work.[55]

COOPERATIVE JOINT VENTURES

Architecture has given me a chance to express my individuality, but I've never been allowed to practice 100 percent. If you look at joint ventures, most of what you'll see is who's getting the crap kicked out of them. (David Norman)

Joint ventures are a good example of the ways inequality plays out in the profession. The ongoing battle for recognition on the part of black practitioners is highlighted in the bidding process on large projects. Although these firms know they have the capability to provide competent management, they are often perceived by potential clients as being more appropriate as subcontractors than as prime contractors. Benjamin Forgey described the situation in an article in the *Washington Post*:

> In particular, the market for major commercial buildings, where prestige and big money reside, remained sealed to African-American practitioners. Washington was being rebuilt but African-American architecture firms were excluded until, during the 1980s, they began getting jobs as minority associates of white-owned firms.
>
> In such arrangements, however, the lion's share of the creative design work—and the credit—inevitably goes to the architecture firm that leads the team. The secondary stuff keeps an office busy, but, no matter its quality, it generally gets ignored. The jobs can, of course, be helpful in establishing reputations, yet for African-American architects, the invisible barriers remain.[56]

Joint ventures can be a productive relationship. At their best, they are a pairing of firms with complementary strengths. Often a firm with strong design skills will partner with a firm with good project management. For all firms, joint ventures are hard to manage; they require clear agreement up front about who is going to be responsible for what, what the fee will be, and how the fee will be divided.[57] As with so many other aspects of architectural practice, I was unsure of the ways these relationships are problematic for firms of color.

Few relationships between firms are true joint ventures. In practice, even when the firms are close to equal, the prime is the sole signer of the contract with the owner. Richard Franklin, a presenter at the 2004 NOMA meeting, talked about the potential for joint ventures:

> Associating with other architects is a new trend for black architects. We used to go out for jobs alone. We are competing with larger and larger entities, firms that provide both architecture and engineering. The ability of communities to impact projects has diminished, which means we have to be even more active in political activities to moderate the impact on our community. We have a social responsibility in a time when the architect's role is being diminished due to process; we lose communication with the client through the project manager. We are now competing with architects from around the world. Most of us are too small to compete on big projects without putting together teams.

As Holtz Kay and others have noted, all black-owned firms have run into the same problem. It is difficult for them to move into the role of prime, both on public-sector and private work.[58] Joint ventures present a useful illustration of how discrimination works against black architects.

> [With invited competitions] they suggest invited signature architects bring along a black or female architect as the "associated architect." *This is usually a truly ugly and demeaning state of affairs for most black architects.* The stated rationale that such exposure will lead to similar opportunities for black architects as primes is rarely the reality.[59]

They are *perceived* to be less competent than their white, male colleagues, so they are not trusted to run a large project. It is almost as though the organizations putting together the competitions unconsciously decide black-owned firms cannot do the work, so why consider hiring them to be the prime? This attitude on the part of developers is facilitated by white-owned firms. It is one of the many ways the culture of architecture remains Eurocentric and male-dominated.[60]

When joint ventures work the way they are supposed to, both firms receive equal credit for their efforts. Commissions for large municipal projects bring with them visibility and marketing opportunities for architecture firms. This is particularly important for black firms; they are always having to fight the perception they are not competent to be primes on big jobs. The effort that goes into breaking down the stereotypes about black firms requires a lot of energy, political savvy, and tact. When they *do* get these important projects, they expect to receive equal billing.

> We did a large, visible job a couple years ago that was a joint venture. We spent a long time hammering out the agreement over what the relationship would be, who would do what, how we would make it work, and what kind of public relations we would do. Then there was a piece in one of the architectural magazines that cited our partners as the designers of the building. I've written a letter to the editor, because it's important to us they know it was a joint venture and we were *not* subs on that job.
>
> We had another joint venture relationship with a white firm. We thought things were going pretty well, and next thing we knew they came for a meeting and brought along a new design firm. After we had been working together for quite a while, they had the nerve to bring someone else to a meeting in my office to talk about design. We had a short meeting. I told them, "I am the final decision maker on this project," and I told them to leave my office. (Nicholas Rose)

Even after agreements have been written, contracts signed, and project work begun, black firms still have to suffer the insults Rose described. Like much government work, joint ventures can be an asset and a liability. They offer the possibility to work on projects that might not otherwise be accessible, and they often preclude getting the credit for work that is done.

> We're good at teaming with other firms. We can do a variety of projects. We're an excellent joint-venture company; we no longer have to be the subs. There's no firm our size that has its hands in as many projects successfully in the city, and now we're getting to be the prime—and we've never been sued. We're proving it again on this job for the City. We are the prime on this job, and the designers' firm works for us. This relationship is *not* a partnership; the design firm is a sub to us. One of the newspapers already got it wrong and called it a partnership. We're working on a letter to them that will be polite, but will let them know this is an important misstatement. (Edward Lamont)

Without understanding the larger context of racism in the profession, it would seem this emphasis on correcting publicized materials is overblown. But with a sense of the big picture, it is easy to understand these architects' insistence on an accurate representation of the relationships. Winning these big commissions requires a great deal of time and energy; being the lead firm is fraught with both symbolism and marketing value. Black architects get column inches so seldom, especially in national magazines, that seeing their accomplishments erased in print is a slap in the face.

NOTES

1. Garry Stevens, a sociologist and an architect, discusses this question at length in *The Favored Circle: The Social Foundations of Architectural Distinction* (Cambridge, MA: MIT Press, 1998). This quote about protecting against the enemy is not just conspiracy theory on the part of one black architect. As Stevens says, "Against the idea that individuals succeed or fail on their natural talents, one must weight the fact that there is extraordinary continuity in the dominant classes from generation to generation." Stevens, *Favored Circle*, 68.

He continues further on in the book to discuss the ways those who are "favored" remain at the top. By serving as masters/mentors, these star architects transfer to the next generation both their cultural capital and the culture in which to utilize it. This maintenance of the social system is one of the mechanisms that enables architecture to remain so white and male, and makes it so difficult to change.

2. As discussed at length above in the section on education, there are several liabilities for black students in architecture school. However, the experience of being in the minority in a predominantly white system does teach future architects some of the skills re-

quired to succeed in the workplace. This does not create a more culturally aware practice, but it does prepare students for the reality of the profession.

3. Donald King, quoted in Susan S. Szenasy, "Designers and Multiculturalism," *Metropolis* 14, no. 3 (October 1994): 114.

4. See Karen Aschaffenburg and Ineke Maas, "Cultural and Educational Careers: The Dynamics of Social Reproduction," *American Sociological Review* 62 (August 1997): 573–87, for a discussion of how early childhood expectations re-create social capital.

5. Vincent J. Roscigno and James W. Ainsworth-Darnell, "Race, Cultural Capital, and Educational Resources: Persistent Inequalities and Achievement Returns," *Sociology of Education* 72 (July 1999): 171. See also Linda Stout, *Bridging the Class Divide and Other Lessons for Grassroots Organizing* (Boston: Beacon, 1996); and George Farkas, Robert P. Grobe, Daniel Sheehan, and Yuan Shuan, "Cultural Resources and School Success: Gender, Ethnicity and Poverty Groups within an Urban School District," *American Sociological Review* 55 (February 1990): 127–42, for useful views on ethnicity, class, and social advancement issues in public schools.

6. Lynne Duke, "Blueprint of a Life," *Washington Post*, July 1, 2004, C4.

7. In May 2001, the AIA held a "Diversity Roundtable" discussion at the national convention. Input was given for the AIA Diversity Committee's strategic plan that included different ways of reaching a wider audience and beginning to expand diversity in the profession. Again, at the 2004 annual convention, a resolution was passed (Resolution 04-2) to "strengthen the demographic diversity of the design profession." They agreed to fund a data collection effort that would reflect the profession over time. While it is easy to second-guess the efforts of others, as one architect said to me, "If the AIA president wanted things to change, they would change."

8. There is an extensive discussion in Stevens on the risk of breaking these rules. An architect such as Frank Gehry, whose technodesigns definitely do not follow the rules, spent his first few years in a kind of exile. Before an architect can head off in a completely new design direction, he or she must already have money, some other store of social capital, or a group of patrons with money. Otherwise, the risk is too great. If a new style does not catch on, it can mean the end of commissions for the architect who has been bold enough to try it. See Stevens, *Favored Circle*.

9. Stevens, *Favored Circle*, 73–77.

10. Jane Holtz Kay, "Invisible Architects: Minority Firms Struggle to Achieve Recognition in a White-Dominated Profession," *Architecture* (April 1991): 106.

11. Throughout this book there are statements from black architects about the ways they continually have to prove their competence. The perception their credentials and experience are less credible than those of white architects is a constant source of pain and anger. See also Joe Feagin and Melvin Sikes, *Living with Racism: The Black Middle-Class Experience* (Boston: Beacon, 1994); and Joe Feagin et al., "The Many Costs of Discrimination: The Case of Middle-Class African-Americans," *Indiana Law Review* 34, no. 4 (2001): 1311–60, for examples of middle-class blacks having to defend their competence in the workplace.

12. Magali Sarfatti Larson, *The Rise of Professionalism* (Berkeley: University of California Press, 1977).

13. Jack Travis, "Architect Jack Travis Explains a Black Aesthetic in Architecture and Design." One Life Incorporated, at www.onelifeinc.org (accessed November 2004).

14. Melvin Mitchell writes: "*Black Architecture* was received by the faculty and professional practice leadership [in the late 1960s] as an *obscenity*. The notion was viewed as unprofessional trashing of the glorious, 'politically innocent, and culturally neutral' western architecture. Architecture, it was felt, was a medium best suited for demonstrating the *parity of black technical competence*. We were socialized to believe that architecture *was not an appropriate medium* for the expression of black culture." Melvin Mitchell, *The Crisis of the African-American Architect: Conflicting Cultures of Architecture and (Black) Power* (Lincoln, NE: Writer's Club, 2001), 105. Also see David Hughes, *Afrocentric Architecture: A Design Primer* (Columbus, OH: Greyden, 1994); and Jack Travis, *African American Architects in Current Practice* (New York: Princeton Architectural Press, 1991).

15. Mitchell, *Crisis of the African-American Architect*, 63.

16. Eduardo Bonilla-Silva, *Racism without Racists: Color-Blind Racism and the Persistence of Racial Inequality in the United States* (Lanham, MD: Rowman & Littlefield, 2003).

17. Duke. "Blueprint of a Life," C4.

18. Dennis Alan Mann, "Making Connections: The African-American Architect," *Journal of the Interfaith Forum on Religion, Art & Architecture* (Fall 1993): 22.

19. See Feagin and Sikes, *Living with Racism*; and Feagin et al., "The Many Costs of Discrimination," for in-depth discussions of the cumulative effect of both daily slights and cumulative, collective memories.

20. At the time, it was easier to get a job with a government agency than it was for a black woman to get a job in a private firm. Although I have been told there are "many" black architects employed in all levels of government, I have been unable to find any data either to substantiate that claim or to provide actual numbers. Only one of the twenty architects interviewed currently works for a government agency; two, or at most three, of the remainder have worked in government at some point in their careers.

21. Historically, racism in the United States has never really been about individual racism. The face of racism, and of Jim Crow laws, was the manifestation of wholesale systemic discrimination. To be sure, individual racism has always existed, but it is fed and nurtured by a larger structural support.

22. Margaret Andersen and Patricia Collins, eds., *Race, Class and Gender: An Anthology* (Belmont, CA: Wadsworth, 1998), 71.

23. See Robert T. Carter, "Is White a Race? Expressions of White Identity," in *Off White: Readings on Race, Power, and Society*, ed. Michelle Fine, Lois Weis, Linda C. Powell, and L. Mun Wong (New York: Routledge, 1997), 200.

24. The most enlightening book I have read on this subject is Ellis Cose's *Rage of a Privileged Class* (New York: Harper Perennial, 1995). The title is brilliant, as it is the most succinct synopsis of the subject.

25. Feagin et al., "The Many Costs of Discrimination," 1343.

26. Feagin et al., "The Many Costs of Discrimination," 1343.

27. For literature specifically about disparities in the profession, see Kathryn H. Anthony, *Designing for Diversity: Gender, Race, and Ethnicity in the Architectural Profession* (Urbana: University of Illinois Press, 2001); Max Bond, "The Black Architect's Experience," *Architectural Record* (June 1992); Holtz Kay, "Invisible Architects"; Larson, *Rise of Professionalism*; and Mitchell, *Crisis of the African-American Architect*.

28. This statement, seemingly an objective observation, has enormous political, economic, and social baggage attached to it. To do it justice, there is extensive literature about structural inequality, community change, community economic development, and transformative education that helps shed light on the struggle. The following is a brief list of what is available in each topic.

See Chester Hartman, ed., *Double Exposure: Poverty and Race in America* (Armonk, NY: Sharpe, 1997); Paul Kivel, *Uprooting Racism: How White People Can Work for Racial Justice* (Philadelphia: New Society, 1996); Manning Marable, *How Capitalism Underdeveloped Black America* (Boston: South End, 1983); Michael Omi and Howard Winant, *Racial Formation in the U.S.* (New York: Routledge & Kegan Paul, 1986); and Cornel West, "Race Matters," in *Race, Class and Gender: An Anthology*, ed. Margaret Andersen and Patricia Collins (Belmont, CA: Wadsworth, 1998), on structural inequality.

See John P. Caskey, "Bank Representation in Low-Income and Minority Urban Communities," *Urban Affairs Quarterly* 29, no. 4 (1994): 617–38; W. E. B. DuBois, *The Souls of Black Folk* (New York: Penguin, 1903/1995); Miles Horton and Paulo Freire, *We Make the Road by Walking* (Philadelphia: Temple University Press, 1990); Daniel P. Immergluck, "Progress Confined: Increases in Black Home Buying and the Persistence of Residential Segregation," *Journal of Urban Affairs* 20, no. 4 (1998): 443–57; Gregory D. Squires, "Community Reinvestment: An Emerging Social Movement," in *From Redlining to Reinvestment: Community Responses to Urban Disinvestment*, ed. Gregory D. Squires, 1–37 (Philadelphia: Temple University Press, 1990), on community change.

See Timothy Bates and William D. Bradford, *Financing Black Economic Development* (New York: Academic, 1979); Timothy Bates and Darrell Williams, "Preferential Procurement Programs and Minority-Owned Business," *Journal of Urban Affairs* 17, no. 1 (1995): 1–17; Caskey, "Bank Representation in Low-Income and Minority Urban Communities"; William D. Bradford, "The Wealth Dynamics of Entrepreneurship for Black and White Families in the U.S." (author's manuscript: Seattle, 2001); Daniel Immergluck and Geoff Smith, "Bigger, Faster . . . But Better? How Changes in the Financial Services Industry Affect Small Business Lending in Urban Areas," Woodstock Institute, 2001, at brookings .edu/cs/urban/publications/immerglucklending.pdf (accessed January 2001), on community economic development.

See Sharon B. Merriam and Rosemary S. Caffarella, *Learning in Adulthood* (San Francisco: Jossey-Bass, 1999); Jack Mezirow, "Transformation Theory of Adult Learning," in *In Defense of the Lifeworld: Critical Perspectives on Adult Learning*, ed. Michael R. Welton (Albany, NY: SUNY Press, 1995); Jack Mezirow et al., ed., *Fostering Critical Reflections in Adulthood: A Guide to Transformative and Emancipatory Learning* (San Francisco: Jossey-Bass,

1990); and Mark Tennant and Philip Pogson, *Learning and Change in the Adult Years: A Developmental Perspective* (San Francisco: Jossey-Bass, 1995), on transformative education.

29. See Frances Fox Piven and Richard A. Cloward, *Poor People's Movements: Why They Succeed, How They Fail* (New York: Vintage, 1979), for an illuminating discussion on the ways leaders of the civil rights movement were co-opted. They stress that apparent conciliation makes repression safer. If the public believes, as so many did in the mid-'60s, real change has been effected, they will more easily tolerate abusing the holdouts. The radicals in the black power movement who saw how much was left to be done were marginalized by federal officials who pointed out the ways new legislation had eliminated racism.

30. Karen E. Hudson, *Paul R. Williams, Architect: A Legacy of Style* (New York: Rizzoli, 1993), 12, 57.

31. See Anthony, *Designing for Diversity*; Jean Barber, "Profile of the Minority Architect" and Roundtable "Today's Minority Architect: A Major Force," Minority Resources Committee of the AIA, July 1990; Bonilla-Silva, *Racism without Racists*; Stephen L. Carter, "The Black Table, the Empty Seat, and the Tie," in *Lure and Loathing: Essays on Race, Identity and the Ambivalence of Assimilation*, ed. Gerald Early (New York: Penguin, 1993); Darell W. Fields, "Diversity Needs a New Mascot," in *20 on 20/20 Vision*, ed. Linda Kiisk (Boston: Boston Society of Architects, 2003), 39–41; Thomas M. Shapiro, *The Hidden Cost of Being African American: How Wealth Perpetuates Inequality* (New York: Oxford University Press, 2004); and Cornel West, *Race Matters* (New York: Vintage, 2001), for different views of how racism has changed and how it has remained the same.

32. See Bonilla-Silva, *Racism without Racists*, among others, for a cogent discussion of this subject.

33. Hudson, *Paul R. Williams, Architect*, 204.

34. Sharon Sutton writes: "With another part of ourselves, we reject the competitive, elitist architectural design mentality that differentiates professionals and clients, professors and practitioners, designers and builders, builders and users. We reject this segmentation because it reflects the segmentation that exists in the larger society between men and women, rich and poor, young and old, white and colored. We reject the dominant voice's 'power over' mentality because it is inappropriate to the 'power with' mentality that is required to bring about social change. We develop the integrity, meaning, and purpose that is so lacking in the mainstream practice of architecture." Sharon E. Sutton, "Finding Our Voice in a Dominant Key," in *African Americans in Current Practice*, ed. Jack Travis, 13–15 (New York: Princeton Architectural Press, 1991), 13.

35. See Cose, *Rage of a Privileged Class*; Joe Feagin, *Racist America: Roots, Current Realities, and Future Reparations* (New York: Routledge, 2001); Feagin et al., "The Many Costs of Discrimination"; and Feagin and Sikes, *Living with Racism*, for more views on the constant battle with racism in the daily lives of blacks. See also Holtz Kay, "Invisible Architects," for a perspective on how minority-owned architecture firms face racism.

36. Duke, "Blueprint of a Life," C4.

37. National Associates Committee, *Diversity in the Architecture Profession*, May 6, 2004, at www.aia.org/siteobjects/files/NACDiversityWhitePaper.pdf.

38. Brian P. Johnson and David D. Horowitz, "Table of Brotherhood: Variety in the Field of Architecture," *Arcade* (Spring 1994): 30.

39. I wish I could take credit for this quote. I have been unable to find a reliable source for it, but it describes what has been a reality in the marketplace for millennia.

40. Peggy McIntosh, "White Privilege and Male Privilege: A Personal Account of Coming to See Correspondences Through Work in Women's Studies," in *Race, Class and Gender: An Anthology*, ed. Margaret Andersen and Patricia H. Collins, 94–105 (Belmont, CA: Wadsworth, 1988).

41. See Bonilla-Silva, *Racism without Racists*, for more on how we whites participate in maintaining systemic racism.

42. Norma M. Sklarek, "Norma Merrick Sklarek," *California Architecture* (January–February 1985): 23.

43. Paul Kivel, *Uprooting Racism: How White People Can Work for Racial Justice* (Philadelphia: New Society, 1996), 19. See also Michelle Fine, "Witnessing Whiteness," in *Off White: Readings on Race, Power and Society*, ed. Michelle Fine, Lois Weis, Linda C. Powell, and L. Mun Wong, 57–65 (New York: Routledge, 1997); and Juanita Tamayo Lott, quoted in Hartman, ed. *Double Exposure: Poverty and Race in America*, for additional discussions on the ways racial and ethnic categories are defined in relation to whiteness.

44. Whitney M. Young Jr., "Man and His Social Conscience: The Keynote Address by the Executive Director of the Urban League," *AIA Journal* (September 1968): 44–49.

45. Whitney M. Young Jr., "Man and His Social Conscience," 46.

46. Although I have been unable to find data on all architects, most African American architects spend at least two hours a week, and many up to ten hours a week, doing "community volunteer work, neighborhood assistance work, or community 'pro bono' work." Dennis A. Mann and Bradford Grant, "African American Architects Survey 1999/2000" (Cincinnati: University of Cincinnati, 2000). See appendix B for complete survey results.

47. Edward Lamont pointed out that, although the Association of Community Design (ACD) states the community design movement started in 1977, it really began in 1964 with black architects and planners. He said, "Once [the CDC movement] got taken over by whites, the history was rewritten."

48. See the discussion in chapter 2 regarding the strikes at Columbia University. See also Robin D. G. Kelley, "Into the Fire: 1970 to the Present," in *To Make Our World Anew: A History of African Americans*, ed. Robin D. G. Kelley and Earl Lewis, 543–613 (Oxford: Oxford University Press, 2000); Dean Kotlowski, "Black Power–Nixon Style: The Nixon Administration and Minority Business Enterprise," *Business History Review* 72, no. 3 (Autumn 1998): 409–445; Piven and Cloward, *Poor People's Movements*; and Robert E. Weems and Lewis A. Randolph, "The National Response to Richard M. Nixon's Black Capitalist Initiative," *Journal of Black Studies* 32, no. 1 (2001): 66–83, for some context.

49. See Lily M. Hoffman, *The Politics of Knowledge: Activist Movements in Medicine and Planning* (Albany: SUNY Press, 1989).

50. This conflict is playing out again in 2006 in the quandary over whether and how to rebuild sections of New Orleans following Hurricane Katrina.

51. Amos Rapoport, "Cross-Cultural Aspects of Environmental Design," in *Human Behavior and Environment: Advances in Theory and Research*, ed. Irwin Altman, Amos Rapoport, and Joachim F. Wohlwill (New York: Plenum, 1980), 7. See also Hughes, *Afrocentric Architecture*.

52. According to Mitchell, there is an "*ironic disconnection* between black culture and modern American architecture. The disconnection is on the minds of black as well as white people—in sharp contrast to the connection that exists between black culture and American music. The joint custody that is acknowledged toward Black America's relationship and ownership of America's musical heritage should pertain to architecture." Mitchell, *Crisis of the African-American Architect*, 70.

53. Stokely Carmichael (later known as Kwame Ture), the man generally credited with coming up with the term "black power," changed the name to Student *Nonviolent* Coordinating Committee.

54. Anthony, *Designing for Diversity*; and Hoffman, *Politics of Knowledge*.

55. See Association for Community Design, at www.communitydesign.org/rex/supportdocs/History.pdf (accessed September 2004).

56. Benjamin Forgey, "First Black Designed Building in Downtown DC," *Washington Post*, March 30, 2002, C5.

57. See Max Bond, "Collaborating with Minority Architects," *Architecture* (June 1994): 43–47; and Holtz Kay, "Invisible Architects," for more information on joint ventures.

58. See Bond, "Collaborating with Minority Architects"; Holtz Kay, "Invisible Architects"; and Mitchell, *Crisis of the African-American Architect*, for discussions on nonmajority firms participating in joint ventures.

59. Mitchell, *Crisis of the African-American Architect*, 82.

60. See Mitchell, *Crisis of the African-American Architect*; and Stevens, *Favored Circle*, for additional information on how the culture of architecture is reproduced.

4

CERTIFIED MINORITY: THE PERCEPTION AND THE REALITY

We can't get the private work. We don't have the connections.

—Thaddeus Collins

During my decade in economic development, every minority-owned business I worked with had questions about the assets and liabilities of being "certified." There were surprisingly few enterprises that could not benefit in some way from participation in government programs, but there were always two sides to be considered. Especially with big jobs and commissions, they had access to a revenue stream and, ideally, profit they would not otherwise be able to receive. On the other hand, the quality of their work on those projects was often perceived to be inferior, whether they did a brilliant job or not. Even so, when marketing plans were being devised, there was usually a plan for including government jobs of one sort or another. In many jurisdictions, businesses have to be "certified" as minority or woman-owned to be eligible for specified government work. Women and Minority-Owned Business Enterprise is the designation the federal government and many state governments use to refer to businesses that are eligible for set-aside programs. Although the designation and the programs have changed over the years, "WMBE" is still a shorthand for any business "certified" by a governmental entity.

Architecture is a competitive profession for everyone, irrespective of skin color, gender, or any other demographic data. In some ways, the intense competition makes it even more difficult for some to reconcile the need for affirmative action. European Americans rarely have to address the reality that privilege, advantage, and access are related to skin color. The legacy of the patronage system is an accepted, and expected, part of doing business.[1] Because the system is so entrenched, it can be difficult for architects of color to break into the private sector. Affirmative action programs have provided projects that otherwise likely would have been unavailable to these firms, but there is always a risk in going after this work. One of the architects from the Midwest talked about his firm's experience:

> Government work is a double-edged sword. When I started the firm in 1982, we had to rely on sheltered markets and set-asides. Most minority businesses were restricted to public work. It hasn't changed a lot in the time I've been practicing.
>
> We trained like our counterparts, we took the same exams, we got the same licenses. We are qualified to do the work, but the set-aside projects the state would consider us for were small. Although, when you look at the alternative, it's not so bad! Having no work doesn't allow you to keep the doors open, but we believed we needed to elevate ourselves out of this level.
>
> We tried to leverage whatever work we got in the set-aside market to show we were capable of doing work. Still, 90 percent of our work in the beginning was public agency work. The private sector said, "You're a minority firm and you don't need our help because you're benefiting from sheltered markets." There was no pressure on them to utilize our services. (Donald Nelson)

This firm was stuck in the double bind of government work. They could not use public projects to grow, because the dollar value of the projects was small. They were battling the perception, mentioned by all the firm owners I interviewed, that they did not "need" private contracts because they were loaded down with government work. Even now that Nelson's firm is large, diverse, and successful, his frustration with the system is clear. The programs ostensibly designed to aid nonmajority firms had the opposite effect.

Some of the bad news in doing this work is about the perceptions created by participation in set-aside programs.[2] Melvin Mitchell tells a story that has an inescapable irony. In a field that is still often characterized as the white gentlemen's profession, this story is emblematic of how hard fought change can be.

> In 1970, with the Home Rule government in Washington, DC, there were new opportunities for African-American architects, . . . tax paying citizens of the neighborhoods and communities slated to receive new facilities should select the architects. Predictably, some members of the white architectural community reacted badly at first. Ironically, a number of prominent white architects felt justified to

bring licensure law charges against black architects for participating in a "crass political process" in order to effect "merit-based" architect selections.[3]

According to Mitchell, the white architectural community was incensed because black architects had a chance to design projects that had previously gone to white architects. Before 1970, the people who would be using new government-built facilities did not have the opportunity to select architects. Presumably, they were selected the old-fashioned way, through connections with people in the City. As Melvin Mitchell says, "the rules of all lucrative games have a strange way of changing when black people figure out a way to get a seat at the table."[4] When black architects were finally in a position to connect to work the same way their white colleagues had always done it, they were punished. One of the many double binds for black architects is they are perceived as not being competent to do the interesting work; when they produce good buildings, they are accused of not playing fair or of receiving special treatment.

Despite the havoc that set-aside programs have brought, black firms are heavily dependent on public-sector work. (See appendix B for a breakdown, by type, of projects in black firms.) Seeking revenue from government jobs is a growth strategy for businesses of color excluded from corporate markets. In architecture, it has been difficult for black-owned firms to develop and retain clients in the private sector. Government work is often the primary revenue source for these firms.[5] Finding profitable work in the private sector takes time, patience, and network-building for all architects. The elite, white-owned firms are considered first when corporate clients seek design services.[6] Jack Travis considered this problem so significant he included it on the first page of his book on African American architects.

> It is evident that racism is still of paramount concern. There is only one [black] firm that has all of its clients from the private sector. All other firms have at least 55 percent (most more than 85 percent) of work from the public sector. . . . Having to rely on public-sector work means riding the economic roller coaster caused by recessions and having to wait long periods of time for payments from agencies unconcerned with aesthetics to any significant degree.[7]

Although the Travis book was written in 1991, things have not changed appreciably. No current data are available on the number of black firms in the country that have an all-black client base, but a few of the architects told me they thought it was likely not more than three or four firms.

The vast majority of black-owned firms continue to rely on clients in government. They realize that public policy can have an immediate impact on the work available to them. While many of us are not conscious of the ways we are affected by changes in the federal budget, black architects are forced to pay attention.

Elections have an impact on our workflow. We had a big government project that made up a substantial portion of our work. Then Nixon froze the budget to the Public Health Service. In two weeks, we went from having a lot of work to nothing. It taught us an important lesson. We no longer specialize in any one building type. We no longer do just housing or housing-related projects. Now we do housing, school work, churches, and planning. Urban design and community design keep us going in lean times. (Thaddeus Collins)

Collins's firm has been in business a long time. He has been through these boom-and-bust cycles enough times that he has learned the hard way about the necessity to diversify the firm's revenue stream. He understands that at any given time the philosophy of the administration in power—both locally and nationally—can have a huge impact on his ability to win bids.

During the civil rights era of the 1960s, black architects made some progress both in training and in practice. The growth of the community design movement, and programs such as the one at Columbia, which enabled larger numbers of students of color to be admitted to Ivy League programs, led to an increase in their numbers. However, the hopes those years created were dashed less than a decade later. In discussing the experience of black architects, Max Bond wrote:

With the Reagan era, the country backed away from earlier progress toward equal rights and opportunity. The withdrawal of federal support to the cities and social programs, coupled with increased spending on the public realm, had a negative impact on poor people and their communities. This situation was immediately reflected in the circumstances of black architects. Black enrollments at schools of architecture decreased as did the impetus to hire black architects.[8]

For those outside the dominant, Eurocentric culture, public policy decisions often result in the creation and reinforcement of institutional racism.[9] Although the Nixon-era minority business programs had problems, they did make more contracts, and thus capital, available for businesses that had formerly been kept out of mainstream markets. The shift in policy implemented by the Reagan administration had a profound negative impact on black architects.

Despite this shift in public policy away from civil rights, the legacy of the policies of the civil rights movement of the 1950s and '60s continues to have an impact.[10] This is most evident in the government programs designed to assist business owners of color. The recent Supreme Court decision in *Gutter v. Bollinger*

(2004), affirming a compelling state interest in maintaining a diverse law school student body and approving the use of admissions criteria to accomplish this, has provided a buffer against attempts to dismantle these programs.

BRIEF HISTORY OF "SET-ASIDE" LEGISLATION

It is useful to understand the history of federal legislation when trying to make sense of the programs that are still in existence.[11] All of the decisions to allocate public resources—economic and other—are the result of "public" policy. The big question in public policy is: Who gets what?[12] The answer to that question depends in part on who is asking, and in part on whether the questioner believes there is a "right answer."[13] Many contend the early legislation passed to assist black business was politically motivated rather than created because of a real desire to make change.[14] The political genesis of the programs explains a lot about why they function the way they do. Although their existence did increase the flow of government contracts to nonmajority enterprises, had the programs actually been established with the purpose of nourishing and strengthening these businesses, they likely would have been developed differently.

For one thing, they would have provided hands-on technical assistance, including a pragmatic exercise in strategic planning. As it is, most programs have a perfunctory process for submitting an annual business plan. One of the applicants to our Fund submitted his annual 8(a) business plan in his application materials; it was not a real business plan, but rather a pro forma exercise that bore no resemblance to his operations.

In addition, there would have been a focus on market and customer development that would enable participating firms to learn how to develop business apart from the programs. Instead, these businesses were left on their own to figure it out, resulting in high business failure rates upon completion of the program.[15]

The bulk of the federal government programs for minority-owned businesses was created in the 1960s. There are two articles in particular that provide useful perspectives on the development of minority enterprise contracting programs. One is Kotlowski's "Black Power—Nixon Style: The Nixon Administration and Minority Business"; the other is Weems and Randolph's "The National Response to Richard M. Nixon's Black Capital Initiative."[16] Nixon's response to civil unrest was to offer leaders of the civil rights movement programs to support black enterprise, something he did more or less successfully. Kotlowski alleges Nixon made this offer to create ways of appeasing a wide swath of America—the black middle class, the white southern voters, and the traditional white, Republican voters who were enthusiastic about both business and keeping their cities calm. "Appealing to whites uneasy over crime, Nixon rejected violence as a protest tactic and pledged to uphold law and order. To heal racial tensions and extend opportunity to ghetto residents, he espoused aid to minority enterprises."[17]

Nixon was interested in fostering the growth of black business for several reasons. The president had an abiding belief in the power of small business to raise people into the middle class; investing in private enterprise was a way for the administration to keep the American dream of economic success alive. By developing programs to aid minority-owned business, he could increase the ranks of the middle class and, he thought, the Republican Party. Kotlowski writes,

> By inviting blacks to acquire a stake in the free market economy, it appeared inclusive without enforcing integration in white schools and neighborhoods. In fact, the president publicized his minority business policies to quell criticism that he was indifferent to civil rights.[18]

Creating the illusion he was doing something to help blacks, Nixon wanted to bring an end to the civil rights movement. He needed a program substantive enough to have the desired effect, but not so substantial it would change the power structure.

Weems and Randolph provide documentation for their contention Nixon created the black capitalist initiative not only to quell radicalism, but also because of a perception that radicalism could be injurious to our capitalist, anti-Communist image abroad. According to the authors, Nixon viewed creating a program to support African American business as less objectionable than letting our Cold War enemies view television footage of American cities in flames.[19]

Nixon hoped the new African American middle class would join the party most concerned with individual rights and developing the economic potential of small business to increase family income.[20] Although in many cases these programs did contribute to black family income, they also created new problems for these businesses.

The black business community had been decimated by the Great Depression. Black businesses did not really recover from the Depression until the '50s and '60s.[21] The development of set-aside programs in the late '60s, designed to help "disadvantaged" businesses, created a second downward spiral. Up to that time, the bulk of black-owned businesses targeted their products and services to inner-city communities.[22] Where they had been able to succeed when they had captive markets in their own neighborhoods, the programs encouraged black-owned businesses to think bigger. Especially in the world of contracting,[23] this meant going out and bidding on much larger jobs than they were accustomed to doing, in markets where the competition, predominantly with white-owned firms, was fierce.[24]

In their 1995 article on preferential procurement programs, Bates and Williams point out:

> MBEs most reliant upon government customers often suffer from this reliance. Involvement in government procurement encourages many small MBEs to overextend themselves and that may result in business failure. MBE preferential procurement programs are often designed and implemented with little thought given to the broader environment that shapes small business viability. Small, young MBEs, for example, are awarded large procurement contracts that they cannot handle.[25]

Edward Lamont reflected on the problem, saying, "Having to hire a minority contractor when you want to hire your brother-in-law makes white contractors resentful and vengeful. Subs have cash-flow problems; they can't come out of pocket to finance a project. It makes it tough to hang onto minority subs." Cash flow is a major problem for businesses that have been operating right at the margin between profit and loss. Taking on larger projects, as so many have been forced to do in order to obtain government jobs, often pushes them farther into the red.

THE 8(A) PROGRAM

The legacy of the Nixon programs lives on in the Small Business Administration (SBA) 8(a) program. The program was established to increase the government procurement opportunities for Small, Disadvantaged Businesses (SDBs). The groundwork for 8(a) was laid in the 1950s in the Eisenhower administration. It provided a vehicle for Nixon to implement his black capital program. According to a General Accounting Office (GAO) report,

> The concept of channeling contracts to small businesses through an intermediate Federal agency was an emergency measure to insure that small businesses were not bypassed in wartime. SBA, however, never used the section 8(a) authority for that purpose. Section 8(a) lay dormant for about 15 years because SBA believed that the efforts to start and operate an 8(a) program would not be worthwhile in terms of developing small business.[26]

In many ways, this was a prophetic statement. The 8(a) program, which was designed as an intermediary between government agencies and SDBs to increase federal procurement dollars flowing to these firms, has had administrative problems since the beginning.[27] There is a lengthy application process that can take months, followed by a humiliating review, and no guarantee of work once a firm has been granted 8(a) status. In what was likely a bit of political grandstanding and a bit of reality, Senator Christopher "Kit" Bond said, in responding to a 2000 GAO study on the 8(a) program, "It's the rich get richer and almost everybody else gets nothing. . . . There are a whole lot of qualified 8(a) firms that don't get anything." About $3.2 billion, or 50 percent of the contracts awarded in fiscal 1998, went to 209 firms. Meanwhile, more than three thousand of the six thousand 8(a) firms didn't get any program contracts at all.[28]

Edward Lamont's firm applied to the 8(a) program in 2002. Although Lamont was not optimistic about whether they would get any work through the program, he said he decided to make the attempt. "I thought it couldn't hurt to go ahead and apply because it seemed like one more way to get a foot in the door. The process was difficult and time-consuming; they make it really difficult for small business."

The programs not only put many black-owned businesses at risk, but they also created resentment, and later lawsuits, from white business owners. White contractors, who have been accustomed to previously existing processes for bidding on government contracts and are concerned about having to compete with a new segment of the market, have shown a lack of understanding about the need for these programs.[29]

The established programs often have difficult application criteria and impossible rules. Black-owned firms are reliant on the revenue from government projects, but the frustration that accompanies them can be overwhelming.

> The bidding process with the state is racist. You can't *get* work from them if you've never *done* work for them. Let's look at the big transportation project we're doing for the City. We found out that one of the best design firms in town wasn't on the roster of bidders, and neither was the most interesting landscape designer. So we did a joint venture with them and got two stations. That's great, but the City took a lot of jobs off the top and gave them to the big firms. Not only did we get penalized for being black, but we got penalized for being small. But we can't get bigger, because we need to already have worked for the state to get any work with the state. (Edward Lamont)

The way the programs are set up, and the resulting frustrations, challenge Lamont's sense of fair play. This is one of the places where his anger at the racism in the system is visible. He has worked so hard to build a successful practice. He has learned the lessons of managing his expectations and his disappointments to keep moving and keep trying. But when he runs into the ridiculous circle of impossibility built into state programs, his anger is more than he can manage. In many ways, the programs where you already have to have experience to get the jobs and cannot get experience without having done the jobs are more of a slap in the face than a way to help WMBE firms grow.

> I went into ODOT [Ohio Department of Transportation] to pursue a project. . . . I went in, and I wanted to do one of those rest areas, and I was competing against a small firm. I needed work. I went through the certification process and filled out all the forms, which was exhausting. I was then called in for a meeting. I was told, "Well, we want to make sure you are a minority." I said, "This is ridiculous." In the meantime, the projects were awarded. I wasn't certified so I lost the opportunity to do the projects, and here it was I was qualified to do the projects. They wouldn't even consider I was like everybody else, because they kept telling me I needed to get certified, so I lost the opportunity to do the projects in order to go through the certification process. My problem was: If I cannot compete on the standard market like everybody else—while I'm waiting for certification—there is something wrong with this system.[30]

The system creates a no-win situation for nonmajority firms. The anger and frustration generated by trying to get work through the systems are responses to the racism, not of the process, but of the culture that made it necessary to create these programs.

THE 8(A) PROGRAM IN THE FIRM

Edward Lamont and I were discussing his prospects for work through the 8(a) program. He was leery, after watching a colleague, one of their construction subs, "fall apart" after graduation from the program. Lamont told me about a conversation he had had with their business opportunities specialist (BOS). The BOS is the person who, ostensibly, provides training and guidance to the 8(a) companies. In all the years I have been observing this program, I have never seen an instance where the BOS provided training or guidance. He told Lamont, "The first two years [on 8(a)] are for learning. Don't expect to get a contract during the first two years." Considering the term of participation is limited to eight years, that means 25 percent of the time is spent waiting. Lamont finds this news both distressing and ridiculous. "We don't *need* to learn how to do this. We've been in business almost twenty years. The people who run these programs have such a condescending attitude."

I shared with Lamont the story of one of the Fund clients who was involved in an 8(a) project. The contracting agency made demands that created serious economic hardships for our client. Among other things, the agency demanded they maintain an office at a remote location, throughout the year, despite the fact the contract was seasonal and they were only expecting to be on-site four months. In addition, once they had done the work and made payrolls averaging $90,000 a week, the agency slowed the paying process and left the company exposed for huge payroll tax deposits.[31] They called on their congressman to see if they could get paid sooner, and if they could get some of the onerous requirements lifted. Although they did eventually get paid, subsequently the agency was hesitant to do business with them because they had involved an elected representative.

A member of Lamont's staff shared with me what seemed to be the view of the staff on firm participation in 8(a):

> The 8(a) program may not be what we want to identify with. It makes the federal government feel good and makes us look like we're accepting handouts. Edward would say we're opportunists, but marketing means planning for success and moving toward that goal. It takes self-determination. 8(a) work is shit work. (Dahlia Morrison)

Some architects are clear 8(a) is not the program for them. They find access to government projects through other, more effective means.

The General Services Administration (GSA) is the federal government's landlord. They own, manage, and develop virtually all government buildings. They are the government's largest client for architectural services. It would seem logical to expect if there were one agency that would be sensitive to hiring black architects, GSA would be the one. According to the architects I interviewed, GSA has never hired a black firm to do a major design project.

> The GSA had their annual award banquet at the National Building Museum, right down the street from our office. The new GSA administrator is black. We still can't get a design job from them. What do I have to do, stand on the table and call people names?
>
> White architects don't really know anything about set-asides. They assume we're doing all the set-aside work. I would've been labeled if I had been 8(a). I do work as a minority firm, but there's a huge stigma associated with doing set-aside work. (Nicholas Rose)

Architects who work inside government face their own battles trying to provide greater visibility for black-owned firms. They have credibility problems inside agencies with trying to shake up the status quo. Interviewees told me the most visible architecture projects are awarded in a process that is highly politicized; black architects do not have the political power to get on the list. The architects working for change have problems with their black colleagues, who are skeptical things will ever be different.

> I did my first GSA job in 1996. We did a day care in California. Now I work for the government. *We* [black architects] hardly know who's out there doing what among black architects, and the white folks have no clue. I think of the way some of my African American colleagues deal with racism as the black bowling ball analogy: white folks are like the bowling pins; the best way to score points is to use force to knock them down. It's as if they're saying "White folks are so guilty, they can't focus on the work, etc." I say, why not set things up to focus on the talent and the work?
>
> I think of my job as a combination of "a picture's worth a thousand words" and "Guess Who's Coming to Dinner?" My job is to mediate between two worlds. I'm in the process of assembling a monograph of the most elite respondents to my request for slides. I want to empower black architects who are practicing and convince students it can be done. I see the monograph as an alternative to the bowling ball. Even though I'm working to help increase their visibility, I do understand black architects aren't waiting for the government to change anytime soon. (Tom Miller)

Among the architects I spoke with, there is very little denial about whether or not government programs were really designed to help them. They all do what they can to find ways to make the programs work for them and to develop other ways to keep business moving when the programs do not serve their needs.

AFFIRMATIVE ACTION

> *President Lyndon B. Johnson signed the Civil Rights Act into law on July 2, 1964. It not only outlawed segregation in public accommodations of every kind throughout the country, but it laid the foundation for federal affirmative action policy. Affirmative action programs were meant to ensure that victims of past discrimination would have greater opportunities to find jobs, earn promotions, and gain admission to colleges and universities.*
>
> —Robin D. G. Kelley, "Into the Fire"

Edward Lamont talked to me about being old enough to have a clear memory of segregation, about life before the civil rights movement. He used his own family history to explain to me his feelings about affirmative action. His great-grandfather's family started out as Pullman porters on the railroad. Between the railroad and jobs at the Ford Motor Car Company, they made good money and managed to put some aside.[32] They lived in Asheville, North Carolina, but he owned some property across the line in Georgia.

> My great-grandfather's brother was light-skinned, and so he was able to "pass" and get by with completing the transaction. He had a white man who collected the rents, but the White Citizen's Council found out he owned the property, and they chased him out of Georgia. Jim Crow laws made the lives of black people very different from the lives of the European immigrants. They could come here and do business, while blacks who were born here weren't allowed to own a business.
>
> They left on the front edge of the "Great Migration" [of African Americans out of the South and into the slightly more tolerant North]. As refugees from the South to the North, my great-grandfather wanted to make sure they wouldn't be trapped again in a bad situation. They moved to Michigan, up by the Canadian border, so they could leave if they had to. They had a different view of America; they had been legally and physically stopped from reaching their potential. We should've been millionaires. My great-grandfather was a very proud man, and they took away everything he had earned and ran him out of town. This is why I can be so clear about affirmative action and other entitlement programs. They're set up with such a condescending attitude. We know that what can be given can be taken away.

This is a source of conflict for many black business owners: knowing their people have been shut out of mainstream markets and believing government programs may be a trap. The availability of government contracts has been a boon to some, while the requirements and structure of the jobs have created economic problems for others. The programs promise business expansion, and the restrictions and bureaucracy make progress difficult.[33]

Despite having an advocate in the bureaucracy, black architects know things will change slowly, if at all. The constant battle to prove their competence, even after many years of professional practice, is infuriating.

> The GSA has never hired a black architect to design anything but very small projects. Even Howard University was slow to hire us. It took twenty years to get the first project there. Twenty years ago, my hometown in Michigan was gearing up to do some economic development. At that point, we had eighteen people in the firm. I was home visiting my family, and I went to talk to someone in the City. They offered us two duplexes to design. Two duplexes, at a time when we were already a

well-established firm and they were getting ready to do major development. That was the last time I went after work in my hometown. (Nicholas Rose)

If a white male architect who was the principal of a mid-sized, well-established firm had met with the City to get information about their economic development projects, he would likely have been shown the whole range of jobs they were considering. Rose understood their offer of two duplexes to be an indication they did not consider the firm capable of doing bigger projects.

The AIA Minority Resources Committee conducted focus groups in 1990 to consider issues and needs of architects of color. Like the data presented in chapter 1, these focus group results are now fifteen years old. It is telling that there has been no update to track whether or not things have changed. Despite the lack of more timely information, based on the interviews and conversations reported on in this book, it seems unlikely the responses would have been much different.

The subject of set-aside programs was advanced, and the list of both problems and suggested solutions made a clear statement about the problems.

Problems with set-aside programs:

- uneven management at state and local levels;
- limited programs;
- inconsistent enforcement;
- difficult and expensive certifications; and
- confusing standards between jurisdictions.

Solutions:

- forming coalitions and putting architects on policy-setting panels;
- lobbying for centralized certification and consistent implementation; and
- providing training on certification and consistent implementation.[34]

These results make it clear why choosing whether or not to participate in government programs can be difficult. The suggestions for solutions, which might have solved some of the problems with these programs, were not implemented. The climate for government set-asides has continued to worsen. The rulings in a series of lawsuits brought by white contractors to stop set-aside programs has seriously limited the number and effectiveness of programs. *Croson* was a suit brought against a local (Richmond, Virginia) affirmative action ordinance that set aside 30 percent of contracting work for minority businesses. The Supreme

Court justices agreed on the doctrinal standard "strict scrutiny" for state and local agencies. *Croson* requires evidence of specific, relevant discrimination to justify affirmative action programs. One way to prove such discrimination is through the use of disparity studies.[35]

Donald Nelson provided a clear example of the impact these suits have had on black firms.

> What changed was the decision in *Croson*. This was the challenge of affirmative action. We saw agencies we were trying to get acquainted with writing new regulations, and we were trying to figure out what they were going to be. After *Croson*, they shut down the programs.
>
> The set-aside programs in the state were looking at 5–10 percent of state purchases of goods and services being available to minority firms. When they categorized the firm as a minority firm for set-asides, it meant you're not going to have larger work, because the large projects were definitely larger than the total 10 percent. The 10 percent was spread over lots of firms, so each firm could only get a small piece. To grow, you have to get larger work. We wanted to put ourselves in the 90–95 percent of the work where there was no size limit. The State was saying no because then they would lose the number of firms they could call on for set-aside work.
>
> The state had two categories of firms: the A list were primes with the capability of doing an entire project, and the B list were WMBEs they could use in association with A firms to participate. That led to two classes of professionals irrespective of qualifications. But we believe we're a prime firm. That was met with resistance. They did away with the A and B lists because of *Croson*.
>
> There's no incentive to have minority firms on big projects; the agencies are satisfied with minority participation rather than leadership. There's a perception they can award a piece of a project to an 8(a) firm and feel like they've taken care of their social obligations. They'll still see participation farther down the line on smaller projects, so they don't feel like they have to worry about it on large projects.
>
> Some agencies had not done affirmative action. They did some when the rules were in place, but after the rules were removed they did none. In any suburban network, where there were neighborhood associations and community groups, etc., there were no minorities. Instead of awarding projects to their network, friends, and neighbors, they needed to award to people other than friends. They had to explain to the communities why they had hired a WMBE. Affirmative action was the excuse for a certain amount of work being awarded to someone besides the same old firms. It was easier to explain the affirmative action requirement than to try to explain someone outside got the job because they were better. After affirmative action went away, there was no longer any pressure to utilize firms other than friends. People do business with people they know, with friends. That's just how it is.

In the last several years, our firm has had two other African American owners. They both left to start their own firms. It's a dilemma for us; because there have been sheltered markets for small firms, there are more opportunities to be helped if you want to stay small. There are six other minority firms in town, five of which came out of our firm. All of them are small. (Donald Nelson)

For firms such as Nelson's that want to continue to grow, it is frustrating to see the ways affirmative action programs were designed to constrain the growth of MBE firms. More frustrating is the understanding that, post-*Croson*, government agencies have limited initiative to hire firms of color.

Appendix C provides an extended discussion of the impact of the ruling in the *Croson* case. It also contains information on three additional cases that had a dramatic impact on affirmative action and set-aside programs.

The goal of black firms, like any other architectural firms, is to get interesting projects that provide enough money to cover the costs and also return a reasonable profit. This is always a difficult juggling act, but many believe it is worse on government contracts. Even with decades of experience doing this kind of work, it often continues to be frustrating and time consuming to manage these jobs. One of the keys to making these projects beneficial for the firm is to try to ensure the first major contract with a government department or agency goes well. A successful first project creates the possibility of additional work that, theoretically, will have a shorter learning curve. It is difficult to know when this investment will pay off and when it will not.

Edward Lamont's firm had a contract with an agency with which it had not previously worked. It took a year to get a contract from this agency from the time the firm won the project. There was a request for a fee proposal it negotiated for three months. There are industry standards for fair fee, but it still took three months. "There's a sense that all architects are the same: they're all hungry. We'll need three or four more jobs like this one to make it up financially, to recoup our up-front costs." The risk is high for new ventures trying to grow on government work; if they are not clear how to do a scope of work, they can lose money if they run into problems. Lamont was obviously frustrated by this project.

It's like the government is trying to trip us up from the beginning. It looks like a scope of work built by committee. It makes me want to toss the 8(a) certificate out the window. Why would we want to do more government jobs, especially the ones that are specifically set-aside for the program? (Edward Lamont).

Many black business owners face the same quandary: there is money to be made, and money to be lost, in government contracts. There is always a risk in taking on new work. However, because black businesses have historically had limited access to the private sector, and continue to have few opportunities in the private sector, the stakes are high to succeed with government work.

Federal jobs are often further complicated by jurisdictional code issues. The staff may be completely conversant with local building codes, but once they get into other geographical locations, it is no longer so easy to look at plans and spot potential problems. There may be parking or set-back requirements that can cause costly redesigns. Even for firms that are well-organized about submitting "change orders" to cover additional costs, there is often an argument with the client about collecting additional fees.

This is always a gamble; if they do not bid on this government work when it comes up, they may never "get into the loop." The long-term payoff could be high if they can get multiple jobs with the same agency. However, if they do the work, there is always a chance they will not get additional work, and they will have spent a lot of time learning the system and then will not be able to use this knowledge again.

> A few years ago, we bid on a big GSA cost-estimating project. We put together a group of the best cost estimators in town and got the job. We did eighty-seven estimates; we were never off more than 2 or 3 percent, which is nothing on this size project, and then we were fired "for convenience."[36]
>
> When we've asked the GSA why they haven't used any black architects, they tell us the same thing we hear from white developers: "We hired a black architect once and it didn't work out." Racism is an irrational act. It's like abortion in that the discussion about it is not logical.
>
> The big, ongoing contracts [such as GSA estimating work] cover payroll. They're task-oriented, they last three or five or ten years. They're good money, but there's no design. We are looking at new projects for the Navy and the FAA. They have hired African American architects. (Nicholas Rose)

As frustrating as it is to have done a good job and then be fired for no apparent reason, it is maddening to have no recourse. Rose knew if he tried to complain, they would never get another one of those contracts.

Edward Lamont voiced concerns about the likelihood of an architectural firm getting federal jobs:

> We're trying to find general contractors we can build relationships with so we can get federal design-build projects. Architectural services alone seem to fall to the bottom of the list. We need to develop a strategy to get good federal work.

The bottom line is how hard it is to do business with the government. When you hear it from the government side, it's as if people are too stupid to figure things out. But they make a mess that's impossible to understand, can't answer questions, and then look at you like you're stupid. The feds have come up with just about the worst combination of things for small business. (Edward Lamont)

It is painful to recognize they are trapped into working within a system that is insulting at least and clearly racist at worst. According to Feagin and others, it is the accumulation of small, daily slights that takes a toll on blacks.[37] Having to work their way through these humiliating obstacles just to get work they would rather not have to do is the worst kind of abuse. Although the government work provides these firms with a revenue stream and, in the beginning, experience, there are seldom opportunities to design, the margins are always tight, and the work can be taken away without cause.

Despite the problems, there is one additional reason affirmative action programs are important to black communities. Access to government contracting dollars enabled black entrepreneurs to build competitive businesses outside of neighborhoods of color and move beyond traditional businesses.

According to the economist Thomas Boston, this expansion of black-owned business has led to an increase in good paying jobs for blacks. "Black-owned firms are about eight times more likely to employ blacks than are firms owned by non-blacks."[38] Additionally, "Eighty-two percent of employees in black-owned businesses are black."[39] The potential for these entrepreneurs to contribute to their communities is quite large. Boston argued the cutting back of, and tight restrictions on, affirmative action programs will have a serious adverse impact on black-owned businesses and communities. Government revenue has provided a source of capital for businesses that had traditionally been left out of capital markets. The disappearance of these sources, without a concomitant decrease in discrimination, is very threatening to the future success of these enterprises.

The big projects we are able to get are always government-sponsored. The money is always not black. We're only 1 percent of the profession. There aren't enough of us. If there were ten times as many of us, you wouldn't be talking to me. It would be easier to push on environmental design. But it's hard enough for black folks just to get by, and to get to the middle class and have a roof over their heads. People don't want to think about how they're marginalized. (Leroy Vaughan)

Vaughan's observation contributes to a better understanding of how difficult it is for black architects to succeed, and what a triumph it is when they do. As many of the architects told me, if they spent their energy being angry or bitter about racism, they would get very little else accomplished. That these firms continue to make contributions to the profession and to their various communities is a testament to the fact they are competent, qualified, and succeeding in spite of the barriers placed in front of them.

STIGMA

> The white contractors and architects believe set-asides are unnecessary. If you're good—competent, qualified, etc.—then you should be able to get the jobs. If you can't get the jobs, then you must not be any good, you must not be "deserving" of the work. (Edward Lamont)

In addition to other problems government programs present for black-owned firms, there is also an issue of the stigma created by utilizing "special" programs. Enlisting in these programs can bring questions from white contractors about the competence and ability of program participants.

> It [minority certification] was a two-edged sword. It was helpful from the standpoint that there were some projects I would not have been able to get close to if there was not a sheltered market program that says, "You're not going to compete against all of the well-established firms starting out. You are going to compete against firms just like yours that may not have had some opportunities." Under that scenario, I have a little better chance. The truth of the matter is, under the sheltered minority programs, or whatever you want to call them, whenever you do a project and you get it done, people look at it and say it was done by a minority architect.[40]

There is always a question about competence. As with many issues of institutional racism, this is a situation that rarely comes up for European American professionals.[41] All of the architects of color I have spoken with complain about the perception of incompetence. They have completed academic programs that provided them with professional training, then served a lengthy internship, and still have to defend their credentials.

> African-American architect Harry L. Overstreet finally gets respect. Thanks to affirmative action, his 40-person firm glows with 20 high-end computer stations plotting designs for San Francisco International Airport's $2.4 billion expansion. "It's to me what the American dream was always about," says Overstreet, overseeing 24

subconsultants designing a $90 million wing to SFO's new international terminal. As a sub on public projects elsewhere, "I would get packed off when decisions were being made. . . . [A]fter I got this project, I was treated like a blond-haired, blue-eyed person."[42]

The City's project manager made an effort to spread the work across the entire community of architects, rather than awarding the whole package to a star design firm. As a result, the participants in this project were all treated equally as designers. For many of the architects of color, it was the first time they had done government work on which they were treated with that kind of respect. Most set-aside programs are not that way. Enlightened leadership led to an experience where the nonmajority architects were treated like professional colleagues, and the City got an airport that reflects more than one design style.

In a design magazine article on diversity, one architect put it this way:

> Problems persist for minorities in architecture. People in this profession fear looking racist, so overt expressions of resentment are rare. Still, whites in the profession—and this is still largely a white male profession—often feel that blacks and other minorities are successful because of affirmative action programs. Consequently, they discount their professional abilities and may even resent their success. The positive opportunities for "partnering" on public work projects are often soured by public agencies' minority participation requirements. This is a sophisticated form of tokenism which victimizes both the majority and minority participants. Indeed, if I have one great remaining professional goal, it would be to reduce the negative impact of this double-edged sword. Blacks and minorities in this profession are often assumed to be less qualified, so they shouldn't mind being sub-consultants, rather than primes.[43]

One of the reasons the San Francisco airport project stands out is the apparent regard the decision makers had for *all* the architects involved. The architects of color were not treated as second-class citizens; they were give true *equal* opportunities to participate in the process. It is rarely the case black-owned firms get to be primes on large projects.

> We did a little building at a big university. It was about a $1 million building. When they were ready to remodel and do a major addition, they hired the biggest white architectural firm. Those guys called us and wanted a copy of my plans. I called the client and asked why they didn't hire me, and they said they were concerned I was overloaded. Can you imagine *them* deciding *I* must be overloaded. I charged the other architects for my plans. (Thaddeus Collins)

The politics of public projects always have to be accounted for. The idea that the university architects would decide a firm was probably too busy to design a building for them is ludicrous. Collins's firm was as capable as any other firm to do the work; clearly, someone on the planning team did not want this firm on the list of potential bidders.

One firm in the West had the most diverse personnel—ethnically and culturally—of any of the firms I visited. Out of curiosity, I spoke with a couple of white architects who work in the firm to get their views on set-aside programs. One of them said that one of the big contractors is looking at them to do some joint projects, specifically because of their minority status.[44] "I hope their young corporate guys have a new view of diversity. Their interest in us might further stigmatize us—'We hired you because you're a minority.' Can we ever move out of that identification?" (Dahlia Morrison).

Another white staff architect told me, "Some clients are pressured to interview a minority firm, even though they have *no* intention of hiring us. It makes you want to expose the situation, and at the same time feel like there's nothing to expose" (Norm Miller). These conversations confirmed what one firm owner had already told me: the white staff members are conscious of the issue and are also baffled by it. For most of them, racism is a very confusing issue. They know it exists: they have witnessed the impact of selection processes that exclude their firms; they have been to interviews they know are just window dressing; they have heard the slights aimed at their bosses—they know it is there, but they do not know what *it* is.

The white architects, like their black employers, were trained in a Eurocentric system. They have a sense of how things should be in the profession. Their education and their lives outside the firm have not prepared them to understand either the reality or the impact of systemic racism. Their experiences with racism leave them confused, not angry; they do not want to believe racism in the profession is as pernicious and omnipresent as it is, but working for a black-owned firm, they encounter it all the time. They are stuck between admission and denial.

THE BAD NEWS AND THE GOOD NEWS

Public-sector work is both problematic and, potentially, lucrative work. Because black firms have trouble gaining access to the private sector, government work can provide opportunities for a firm to gain economic stability and also create visibility with new construction.

When we first started in 1968, we got work white architects didn't want, mostly renovating public housing. It wasn't exciting. Architects talked about being social planners until the community design centers came into being. Housing for low-income families was considered the expertise of black architects. HUD requirements for public housing didn't address the social activities of the CDCs. There was very little opportunity to expand our vision. The budgets were too small, the residents were forgotten. (James Patterson)

Patterson believed these projects were a double insult: the firms were relegated to working on buildings the majority firms "didn't want," and the residents, low-income and often people of color, were not important, either. Almost forty years later, the sense of outrage about public housing continues.

We had a project in the South Bronx that came about because the tenants had organized and asked HUD for an African-American architect. We were working on public-sector housing, so we took the tenants on bus trips to look at how other people live. From that, we came up with design guidelines and a master plan of the work. The tenants were able to get trained and get jobs in the management of a subsequent development.

There's a certain sensibility and distrust by the people who control the purse strings, who are white. If the clients are not vocal, the officials just expect they will adapt to the architecture. When the clients are vocal, that's when we come in.

If it were up to HUD, our firm wouldn't be there; a Republican firm would be there. The major projects—schools, universities, museums—are done by majority firms. You gotta make a little noise, you've got to try to make an impact. (Wendell Marshall)

The politics of government work have not changed since the Nixon years. If the tenants had not organized, and insisted on having a say in the selection of an architect, Marshall's firm would not have gotten the job. The good news about that project is that this firm is devoted to empowering low-income residents in the community. HUD's actions notwithstanding, both the firm and the people living in the project benefited from the arrangement. These contracts do not always have such a happy ending.

We were negotiating on a project that included public and private funds. We were trying to make sure that minority contractors would be adequately represented in the construction process *and* in the process of managing the building. We were relying on the black banker to negotiate the whole package. He's a good politician, and we knew the people with the money would trust him. He opposed the idea of trying to make sure there would always be jobs for minorities associated with this building.

We didn't want minority participation *just* during construction. One of the participants in the process, when he discovered the banker's opposition, said, "He means well." We get put in a position where it's very difficult to speak out about racism. (Thaddeus Collins)

Black architects are well aware of their responsibility to make change. Although each generation finds a different approach, the architects I spoke with all mentioned the ways they continue to make the struggle against institutional racism more visible.

Because these projects are often fraught with frustrations, when they work well for everyone involved it is a real triumph. Though they are few and far between, there *are* positive stories about productive, respectful processes with government entities.

The Veteran's Administration gave us an opportunity to express design concepts and what I thought buildings should be about. We did a blind and low-vision center in Palo Alto. I got to play with color. Then we did a 120-bed extended-care facility. It taught me how to go in and research a building. We did interviews with users, and it helped me understand what to do with the interviews, so I was able to design to the needs. It taught me how to take the logic of their program and design to it. It helped me justify building past the normal government standards.

The Palo Alto project gave us a prototype of a nursing station based on what would make their jobs easier. I needed to have a way to justify the design. The VA hospital is there to serve the veterans, and we got the opportunity to design for the users. It was a great project, and also kind of depressing because that kind of thoughtful design process happens so seldom in public work. (James Patterson)

Several architects told me about their frustrations with doing government work. A project such as the VA hospital is rare because budgets, and not aesthetic or functional issues, dictate the jobs. Additionally, with rare exceptions, these are not buildings that are publishable. They are not the kind of high-end design that gets featured in national architecture magazines; they contribute to the financial stability of a firm, and they employ people, but they are rarely able to be used for public relations. As discussed above, government work is a mainstay for black-owned firms, but it creates almost as many problems as it solves.

NOTES

1. See Max Bond, "The Black Architect's Experience," *Architectural Record* (June 1992); Andrew E. Brimmer, "A Croson to Bear," *Black Enterprise* 22, no. 10 (1992): 43; Magali Sar-

fatti Larson, *The Rise of Professionalism* (Berkeley: University of California Press, 1977); Melvin Mitchell, *The Crisis of the African-American Architect: Conflicting Cultures of Architecture and (Black) Power* (Lincoln, NE: Writer's Club, 2001); and Jack Travis, ed., *African American Architects in Current Practice* (New York: Princeton Architectural Press, 1991), for a broader view of the subject of patronage.

2. Set-asides are programs in which certain federal contracts are available only to certified businesses involved in specific public programs. Portions of the contract are set aside and reserved for "disadvantaged" businesses. The definition of eligibility has changed over time. Broadly speaking, businesses owned by people of color, women, and people with disabilities are currently included. This can vary significantly across jurisdictions.

3. Mitchell, *Crisis of the African-American Architect*, 122–23.

4. Mitchell, *Crisis of the African-American Architect*, 142.

5. See Kathryn H. Anthony, *Designing for Diversity: Gender, Race, and Ethnicity in the Architectural Profession* (Urbana: University of Illinois Press, 2001); Bond, "Black Architect's Experience"; Mitchell, *Crisis of the African-American* Architect; and Travis, *African American Architects in Current Practice*.

6. See Anthony, *Designing for Diversity*; Bond, "Black Architect's Experience"; Benjamin Forgey, "First Black Designed Building in Downtown DC," *Washington Post*, March 30, 2002, Style C1, C5; Jane Holtz Kay, "Invisible Architects: Minority Firms Struggle to Achieve Recognition in a White-Dominated Profession," *Architecture* (April 1991), 106–113; and Mitchell, *Crisis of the African-American Architect*.

7. Travis, *African American Architects in Current Practice*, 1.

8. Bond, "Black Architect's Experience," 60.

9. Foucault taught that part of what makes the ruling ideology so successful at remaining dominant is its omnipresence. When successful, the ruling ideology is so embedded in a culture it is extremely difficult to discern. The tacit ideology is insidious precisely because it *is* tacit. Colin Gordon, ed., *Power/Knowledge: Selected Interviews and Other Writing by Michel Foucault* (New York: Pantheon, 1980).

The changes in public policy appear to support the contention that the ruling ideology is designed to maintain itself. Louis Althusser, "Ideology and Ideological State Apparatuses: Notes Towards an Investigation," in *Lenin and Philosophy and Other Essays* (New York: Monthly Review Press, 1971), 127–86.

10. Robin D. G. Kelley, "Into the Fire: 1970 to the Present," in *To Make Our World Anew: A History of African Americans*, ed. Robin D. G. Kelley and Earl Lewis, 543–613 (Oxford: Oxford University Press, 2000); and Frances Fox Piven and Richard A. Cloward, *Poor People's Movements: Why They Succeed, How They Fail* (New York: Vintage, 1979.

11. Over the years, my knowing some of the history has created bemusement and wonder that the programs function as well as they do. This has been a big improvement over the fury my clients' problems used to evoke.

12. See B. Guy Peters, *American Public Policy: Promise and Performance* (New York: Seven Bridges, 1999), for an elucidation of the politics in public policy.

---

13. See Mark Rushefsky, *Public Policy in the U.S.: Toward the 21st Century* (Belmont, CA: Wadsworth, 1996); and Dvora Yanow, *How Does a Policy Mean: Interpreting Policy and Organizational Actions* (Washington, DC: Georgetown University Press, 1996), for discussions on the public policy process.

14. See Dean Kotlowski, "Black Power–Nixon Style: The Nixon Administration and Minority Business Enterprise," *Business History Review* 72, no. 3 (Autumn 1998): 409–445; Manning Marable, *How Capitalism Underdeveloped Black America* (Boston: South End, 1983); and Robert E. Weems and Lewis A. Randolph, "The National Response to Richard M. Nixon's Black Capitalist Initiative," *Journal of Black Studies* 32, no. 1 (2001): 66–83, for perspectives on the politics of set-aside legislation.

15. See Joyce Jones, "Graduation Day from 8(a)," *Black Enterprise* 28 (February 1998): 161–66, for information and numbers on postprogram failure rates.

16. Kotlowski, "Black Power–Nixon Style," and Weems and Randolph, "National Response to Richard M. Nixon's Black Capitalist Initiative."

17. Kotlowski, "Black Power–Nixon Style," 3.

18. Kotlowski, "Black Power–Nixon Style." Also see Piven and Cloward, *Poor People's Movements*, for an illuminating discussion on the ways leaders of the civil rights movement were co-opted. They stress that apparent conciliation makes repression safer. If the public believes, as so many did in the mid-'60s, real change has been effected, they will more easily tolerate abusing the holdouts. The radicals in the black power movement who saw how much was left to be done were marginalized by federal officials who pointed out the ways new legislation had eliminated racism.

19. Weems and Randolph, "National Response to Richard M. Nixon's Black Capitalist Initiative."

20. Kotlowski, "Black Power–Nixon Style"; and Weems and Randolph, "National Response to Richard M. Nixon's Black Capitalist Initiative."

21. Marable, *How Capitalism Underdeveloped Black America*.

22. See Timothy Bates, *Race, Self-Employment and Upward Mobility: An Illusive American Dream* (Washington, DC: Woodrow Wilson Center Press, 1997); Timothy Bates and William D. Bradford, *Financing Black Economic Development* (New York: Academic, 1979); Timothy Bates and Darrell Williams, "Preferential Procurement Programs and Minority-Owned Business," *Journal of Urban Affairs* 17, no. 1 (1995): 1–17; and Marable, *How Capitalism Underdeveloped Black America*. The discussion of the changes in the character of black-owned business in the first half of the twentieth century is about race and public policy, and about the impact of cultural change. While important, the subject has not been explored in depth, specifically with respect to architecture.

23. I am using the terms *contracting* and *contractor* to mean firms engaged in the development and construction of real estate projects. There are architects, black and white, who will argue with this use of the terms. In general, architects do not include their profession in the category of contractors. Given both the history of the split between designers and builders, and the years of education and apprenticeship they have to complete to

become architects, I can appreciate their disapproval. In the language of doing business with the government, however, architects are "contractors."

24. Peter Behr, "Contract Woes for Small Firms: 'Bundling' Found to Undermine Minority-Owned Companies," *Washington Post*, July 20, 2000, A23.

25. Bates and Williams, "Preferential Procurement Programs and Minority-Owned Business," 2.

26. General Accounting Office, "Questionable Effectiveness of the 8(a) Procurement Program," Report to the Congress (Washington, DC: 1975), 1.

27. General Accounting Office, "Questionable Effectiveness of the 8(a) Procurement Program," Report to the Congress (Washington, DC: 1975); General Accounting Office, "The SBA 8(a) Procurement Program—A Promise Unfulfilled," Report (Washington, DC: 1981); General Accounting Office, "Problems Continue with SBA's Minority Business Development Program," Report to the Chairman, Committee on Small Business, House of Representatives (Washington, DC: 1993).

28. Eleena DeLisser, "SBA Program Falls Short on Helping Firms Win Jobs," *Wall Street Journal*, August 1, 2000, A2.

29. See Thomas D. Boston, *Affirmative Action and Black Entrepreneurship* (New York: Routledge, 1999); and Brimmer, "Croson to Bear."

30. Mitchel R. Levitt, "Flying with Eagles: An Interview with Curtis J. Moody, FAIA," *SMPS Marketer* (October 2002): 5–6.

31. If it had not been for their access to capital from the Fund, the business would have gone under. There are very few 8(a) companies that have access to that kind of funding.

32. At that time, the railroads were completely segregated. The only blacks allowed in the sleeping cars were the porters and the servants who accompanied white travelers. Lamont pointed out that working on the railroad, even under oppressive conditions, gave his great-grandfather the opportunity to travel and see new things and new places. It also enabled his great-grandfather to become bicultural, which made life easier when they moved north.

33. See Bates, *Race, Self-Employment and Upward Mobility*; Bates and Williams, "Preferential Procurement Programs and Minority-Owned Business"; and Boston, *Affirmative Action and Black Entrepreneurship*, for more information on the impact of government programs on minority-owned businesses.

34. Jean Barber, "Profile of the Minority Architect" and Roundtable "Today's Minority Architect: A Major Force," Minority Resources Committee of the AIA, July 1990, 1. Although the focus group was conducted fifteen years ago, little has changed. If anything, things have gotten worse. Funding for set-aside programs has been cut, and access has been broadened to the point where the programs, never spectacularly successful, are all but meaningless. The AIA continues to struggle with effective ways to address the "diversity" problems in the profession. The current attempt is yet the latest in a long series of projects to increase the number of people of color in architecture. As one of the architects said, "If the AIA wanted things to change, they would find a way to make it work."

35. See Boston, *Affirmative Action and Black Entrepreneurship*; Brimmer, "Croson to Bear"; Richard A. Epstein. "A Rational Basis for Affirmative Action: A Shaky But Classical Liberal Defense," *Michigan Law Review* 100, no. 18 (2002): 2036–62; and Paul J. Mishkin, "Foreword: The Making of a Turning Point—*Metro* and *Adarand*," *California Law Review* 84, no. 4 (1996): 875–85.

Andrew Brimmer, in the above-cited article in *Black Enterprise*, made the point that disparity in hiring minority contractors is based on racial discrimination. In his view, Croson showed the need to continue and enlarge race-conscious programs in the construction industry. "Racial discrimination is widespread and deeply rooted in the construction industry. . . . Common threads, such as apprenticeship systems and trade unions, help connect the construction industry. Moreover, there is the old-boy network composed entirely of white males." Brimmer, "Croson to Bear," 43–44. Both in the research for this book and my decade of working with businesses of color, I have been made aware of the truth of this statement. I also am clear most European Americans do not perceive the ways the system works to their advantage.

36. "For convenience" is a contractual mechanism the government uses to get out of a contract without having to provide a reason other than it is not convenient for it to continue the contract. One of the Fund clients had a large, profitable contract terminated for convenience; the firm tried to fight it, but quickly determined it would take more time and money than it was worth.

37. See Ellis Cose, *Rage of a Privileged Class* (New York: Harper Perennial, 1995); Joe Feagin and Melvin Sikes, *Living with Racism: The Black Middle-Class Experience* (Boston: Beacon, 1994); and Joe Feagin, Kevin E. Early, and Karyn D. McKinney, "The Many Costs of Discrimination: The Case of Middle-Class African-Americans," *Indiana Law Review* 34, no. 4 (2001): 1311–60, among others for examples of the impact of the accumulation of racist slights over time.

38. Boston, *Affirmative Action and Black Entrepreneurship*, 26. Unfortunately, I have been unable to get statistics on the ethnicity of employees in architecture firms—black *or* white. Twenty years of working with small businesses leads me to believe black-owned firms hire a much higher percentage of people of color than do white-owned firms.

39. Boston, *Affirmative Action and Black Entrepreneurship*, 50.

40. Levitt, "Flying with Eagles," 5.

41. See Bond, "Black Architect's Experience"; Stephen L. Carter, "The Black Table, the Empty Seat, and the Tie," in *Lure and Loathing: Essays on Race, Identity and the Ambivalence of Assimilation*, ed. Gerald Early (New York: Penguin, 1993); Cose, *Rage of a Privileged Class*; Feagin and Sikes, *Living with Racism*; bell hooks, *Killing Rage: Ending Racism* (New York: Holt, 1995); Peggy McIntosh, "White Privilege and Male Privilege: A Personal Account of Coming to See Correspondences Through Work in Women's Studies," in *Race, Class and Gender: An Anthology*, ed. Margaret Andersen and Patricia H. Collins, 94–105 (Belmont, CA: Wadsworth, 1988); and Norma Merrick Sklarek, "Norma Merrick Sklarek," *California Architecture* (January–February 1985), for a variety of views on the connections between systemic racism and the questions of professional competence.

42. David B. Rosenbaum, "Expanding the American Dream: For Its $2.4 Billion Airport Expansion, San Francisco 'Spread out the Work as Much as Possible' for Designers, CMs," *ENR New York* 240, no. 25 (1998): 32.

43. Brian P. Johnson and David D. Horowitz, "Table of Brotherhood: Variety in the Field of Architecture," *Arcade* (Spring 1994): 14.

44. Often federal projects will have a requirement for a certain percentage of the work to be done by subcontractors of color.

5

CRAZY-MAKING: RUNNING A BUSINESS

Being an architect will make you crazy!

—James Patterson

Owning a business can be a rewarding, remunerative way of life, but it is a daunting challenge under the best of circumstances. Entrepreneurs of color face challenges above and beyond those faced by "nonminority" business owners. Given the toll this culture takes on African Americans, it is greatly to be admired and celebrated when black-owned businesses are able to thrive.[1]

Most business owners start their enterprises because they know how to do something—dressmaking, security services, and so on—and they either hate their job, have family members who have loved their barbecue sauce recipe or computer repair, want the perceived freedom of being their own boss, or are unemployed. I cannot think of one example of a person who loved management and thought she could excel at running her own business. Architects are no exception. Many said they started firms because they wanted to practice architecture. Now they have employees, and have less and less time to practice.

Unlike the other black business owners I have known, most black architects are clear about needing to be bicultural. It takes a lot of energy and savvy to be able to navigate well in both the dominant, European American culture and the African American culture. For many, it takes a toll—on health, on friendships—but black architects are tired of being an endangered species. They do what they have to in order to create and maintain thriving firms, and make a point of mentoring architects of color along the way.

> I was a sophomore before I saw the ideas my classmates were getting from the professional magazines, and I had missed them in the library. But the thing that registered with me most was the fact that there were no minorities represented in the magazines. There were none showcased as great designers, as great marketing people, as great businessmen. There was just no reference.[2]

Once they became architects, several figured out the only way they would ever get to do what they wanted was to start a firm. As discussed in chapter 3, they always knew what they wanted to do, and figured out what it would take to do it. A lot of them started a business so they could really be architects.

CONTEXT FOR BLACK BUSINESS

In the United States, success in business is measured in economic terms, with returns to the shareholder being one of the primary, motivating forces. Absent personal wealth, there has to be enough capital to cover the operating expenses and support the required assets. Among the community of people who provide business counseling, there is agreement that sometimes the best advice for those wanting to start a business is "Don't do it." For those who will not be deterred, there are ways to evaluate, and potentially mitigate, the risks. Management experience, preexisting connections to the market, and money to put into the business are factors that influence potential funders.

The predictors of success for entrepreneurs of color are remarkably similar to those for any other entrepreneurs: education, management experience, access to capital, and social capital (for example, social networks, club membership, and mentors).[3] That said, the reality is black business owners have to address the social, political, and financial contexts in ways their white colleagues do not. The focus on prior experience and financial and social wherewithal overlooks the reality of the effect of institutional racism in the business sector. Although many black-owned businesses fit the success profile, there are more left out using that formula.

The cultural assumptions built into those predictors presume that all entrepreneurs have equal opportunity to acquire education, experience, and capital. Institutional racism has a broad influence; the environment for black business owners is difficult across all socioeconomic levels.[4] The environment consists of many facets, but the most important have an impact on access to capital, which often determines whether the potential of these entrepreneurs can be realized.

LACK OF MANAGEMENT TRAINING

We do not usually think of professional services firms as "businesses." This is underscored by the fact that most professional training programs, especially in architecture, offer no management training. When I was in graduate school in business, I got a job as the receptionist for a small architecture firm. It was immediately clear to me they needed a business manager. I took over the budgeting and accounting, and struggled to help them get control of their cash flow. They were borrowing money for payroll at the same time they had hundreds of thousands of dollars of receivables due from clients who were developers. When I told them they were making a big mistake not to try harder to collect some of the money they were owed, they told me, "You just don't understand this industry." I understand it much better now, and I still wonder how any firm manages to stay afloat.

I thought the architects I worked for were just not gifted in management; I was unaware they got no business training in architecture school. Until I started doing research in the field, I did not really understand the magnitude of the impact of that omission. Edward Lamont said, "What is firm management about? We got no training in architecture school for running a business. There's all the juggling of staff needs, and then there are always too many meetings. I started my own firm because I wanted to have the freedom to really practice architecture, and now I'm a manager."

For an architect of color, that lack of management training compounds the other problems of firm ownership. This lack of training is more of a challenge for black architects than it is for their white counterparts; they have fewer management role models they can turn to in their families, and they have less support in the business community.

Good management is often as important to the survival of a firm as access to capital. In architecture, though, power and money are closely allied.

FINANCE

Insufficient capital is a primary cause of the problems of *all* small businesses. Data presented by the authors cited in this chapter add up to compelling evidence this problem is exacerbated for black entrepreneurs.

Many believe institutional racism is the foundation for this reluctance to lend to black entrepreneurs.[5] There is a clear connection between segregation in housing and the economics of funding small business. Even in situations where the business owner has a good credit score,[6] a prospective lender will require the applicant to display her belief in the business by putting a certain amount of her own capital at risk. The more risk the lender perceives, the more the borrower will have to contribute, and the more it will cost to finance the remainder.[7]

One of the primary sources of start-up capital is home equity. Historically, blacks have been kept out of the housing markets with the most potential for equity appreciation.[8] Residential segregation results in limitations on the availability of investment capital, which means blacks are less able to use home equity as a source of start-up capital. Ultimately, they have less access to debt to fund business start-up and expansion.

Finally, there are considerably more data available on mortgage lending than on business lending. It is telling that this is the case. There are pragmatic reasons for the paucity of data, but it often seems like an indication of information that is either not important or so important it is vital to keep it a secret. Caskey, Denton, Immergluck and Smith, and Squires have all suggested the use of residential lending data as a proxy.[9] The crux of the issue with both residential and commercial lending is that bias in the system limits the wealth, and therefore the range of economic and social options, of those who are unable to get funding.

Controlling cash flow is always an issue in business. It is more of a problem in the world of architecture. In part because the capital requirements are large, and there are usually layers of management involved in getting paid, the lag times between billing and payment can be long. In the meantime, payrolls must be paid, and payroll taxes must be deposited. Wendell Marshall addressed the problem when he said,

> We try to make projects something more than architecture. On occasion, we're blacklisted. A developer approached us to work on a project (developers occasionally *do* advocate for us), but the difficult thing about working with developers is:
>
> - there's an antiquated fee structure;
> - they often don't pay for two or three years after the work is done;
> - you can get blacklisted if you try to get paid sooner; and
> - you have to pay interest on a line of credit, but these projects don't pay us interest!
>
> I subsidized the firm in the beginning. As the owner/principal, I made and continue to make a lot of sacrifices. You get paid last from the crumbs that are left. If there

are more crumbs, then I get slices. I live with it all the time. It's not a career, it's a lifestyle. I sacrifice for it, and do whatever it takes to make it work. I've tried to make sure every aspect of the work was not detrimental to the business. There were parts I didn't enjoy, but I had to do them anyway. I finally decided to delegate those and just focus on the parts I enjoy, with the hope and belief that we could grow even further. (Wendell Marshall)

Although firm ownership means additional risk and responsibility, it also brings a degree of control not available to architects employed by others. The majority of the architects I spoke with are firm owners. They were all clear about their reasons for starting a firm. They felt they had something new to offer in the way of design and/or social mission, believed they would have more control over the process on their own, and believed in their abilities to succeed financially. They also recognized firm ownership is not for everyone.

Most people don't want to take the responsibility to own a business. You're the last to be paid. You've got to put up your house, your personal possessions. If the firm revenue is not in the seven- to eight-digit category, a lot of people don't want to take the risk. Banks don't provide money or lines of credit. Corporate industry is not going to go out and hire black architects. Black architects have to feed off the public trough. White architects can balance private and public involvement. A lot of people don't want to invest in that, or they invest in white-owned firms. (James Patterson)

Like any small businesses, architecture firms have limited resources to devote to firm growth. The downside to this is not being able to take advantage of new opportunities. The advantage of having to live with limited financial capital is it forces firms to get creative about increasing professional and cultural capital.

Another difficult thing about running a small firm is the research and development aspect. As a small firm, we don't have an R&D budget. So we learn it in the field as we develop the buildings. We learn from the past and, blending new and old technologies, we're constantly learning how we present things and how we speak architecture and how we work with people who help in making architecture, the consultants, who are an extension of the firm. Bigger firms have the luxury of not having to learn as much in the field. (Wendell Marshall)

Marshall went on to talk about the value of learning by doing. His firm looks forward to the time when it can spend more time and money doing research and development in advance of projects, but he is also clear about the value of lessons learned "on the ground." It takes a lot of confidence, and a real love of architecture, to keep a firm alive.

Some architects decide it is not worth the aggravation and the liability to be a firm owner. While owners have more control over all aspects of the firm, they also have to make the decisions and bear both the professional and financial consequences. In an online biography of Norma Sklarek, she is quoted about her reasons for leaving firm ownership.

> In 1985, Sklarek became a principal in a firm headed by three women, Siegel-Sklarek-Diamond, one of the largest all-female owned architectural practices in the United States. The projects that her architectural firm was able to obtain commissions on were of a smaller nature than Sklarek was used to doing. In addition, she says, "I was not happy with the possibility of being personally financially liable for anything which might go wrong during construction. For those reasons I left the firm."[10]

One of the firm owners I interviewed established an executive committee to oversee marketing, management, and planning. The executive committee members are in an interesting position; they all have opinions about the best course of action, but none of them has a financial investment in the firm. This is not unusual for black-owned firms.[11] It is useful to have additional input into the planning process; it is often easier for people without a financial interest to think more broadly and more creatively about future plans and directions. The process of business planning is complicated by a devotion many black architects have to maintaining their ties and their responsibilities to their communities.

There are differences in both attitude and the potential for sustainable community work between firms in cities with large black populations and those in cities with fewer blacks. On the East Coast, in cities with large black communities, there is work available for those firms that want to work in the community. The biggest risk comes from the white architect and development firms moving into communities of color as those neighborhoods begin to be "gentrified."

> I've never thought of competition as an issue. I decided to stay here in the community to serve the community. There is a lot of work for everyone. We do a lot of work with black churches; we fell into that niche. There was an architect who died in a plane crash. He was doing government housing and churches. When he died, his staff was young, and his clients had to look for new architects. That's how we got the churches. There's enough work for everyone in this milieu. Some downtown firms, white firms, are now working in this community. We've been marginalized by our economic and financial capabilities. (Wendell Marshall)

The cash cycle for architects, the time between billing a client and receipt of the funds, can be quite long. This is exacerbated by the difficulties firms, particularly smaller firms, have borrowing working capital. All businesses, and all architecture firms, have to address their cash requirements, but the situation for black firms requires them to do ongoing effective budgeting. An East Coast architect in a well-established, black-owned firm said,

> One of the partners decided to retire in 1998. At the time, we had two offices. We struggled to keep our second office open. We eventually closed it, but now we're looking at reestablishing that office. We have two people here and two in the reopened office. We need to hire one more experienced person, and we need to project work nine months out. The question is, can we afford to hire another person? (Thad Collins)

Although Collins has tried to diversify his client base enough to smooth out the up-and-down cycles of different types of work, it remains difficult to rely on budgeted revenue turning into cash on a timely basis. The culture of the profession is to hire employees in good times and lay them off in lean times, but it is difficult to maintain a firm without consistent personnel.

For those architects who got their training in bigger firms and had the opportunity to learn management and marketing before they started their own practice, things can be very different. Even with good management training, there can still be surprises. The most important component of good management is being able to respond to those events you cannot control.

> I wanted to structure my practice on what I'd already been doing for fourteen years. I wanted to do bigger work. I wrote a detailed business plan and secured a line of credit. Other black firms complain because they can't get funding; I went to six banks and got offers from all of them. People already knew me, and I had a solid business plan.
>
> In 1990, when I started the firm, the economy looked good. When it blew up shortly after we started, I figured "no woe is me." As I said before, I'm an optimist, so I tried to figure out where's the upside. I had to be very careful and very deliberate in what I did with the firm. We got into good business habits because we had to. There were excellent people available, because the job market was so bad. We had a noncompete, so we couldn't hire people from the old firm, but that didn't stop us from finding excellent employees. (Rob Green)

Like Wendell Marshall, Rob Green learned important lessons about how to manage his firm when his projections suddenly bore little relation to reality. Despite the immediate chaos, he learned from that time the importance of tight budgeting and good cash management.

When I worked as a corporate financial analyst, the first thing my new colleagues impressed upon me was the supremacy of cash. I was recently out of school, and they all had a lot of corporate experience and were generous with their advice. When they told me never to forget "Cash is cash," I thought they were crazy. Once I started working with small businesses, I was grateful to them for the lesson. For businesses giant and small, being able to pay the bills every month is one of the most difficult tasks.

> The biggest challenge is the cash planning. We have to plan for two years; we're always marketing for a constant level of work, but work that is enjoyable enough, and challenging enough that people can be excited about what we're doing with no doldrums and no complacency. Those things translate to the building. This business has been connected to the past, the present, and the future. (Wendell Marshall)

The exhilaration and the terror of owning a firm keeps architects focused on planning for the future while integrating the lessons of the past. It is a constant balancing act that requires confidence, critical thinking, and nerves of steel.

INDUSTRY ASSOCIATIONS

Industry associations can be useful for a variety of reasons. They are a good way to build social networks; often they serve as a source of referrals and information. Over years of membership, friendships are made, partnerships are built, and deals are done. The most successful architects and business owners perform service to the community; this provides a way of giving back, widening social networks, and also a way to demonstrate publicly the values of a firm.

American Institute of Architects

The mission statement of the AIA says:

> The American Institute of Architects is the voice of the architecture profession dedicated to:
> Serving its members
> Advancing their value
> Improving the quality of the built environment[12]

The AIA, with over 75,000 members—50,000 registered architects and plus or minus 25,000 associates and affiliate members—is the primary industry association in architecture. Black architects make up approximately 1 percent of the AIA membership.[13] Among the architects I have known over the years, and also among the architects I have interviewed for this book, there is a kind of love-hate relationship with the AIA. The dues are high, the national conventions crowded, and the marketing opportunities limited, and the architects all believe it is tantamount to professional suicide not to belong. For black architects, there is the additional assessment that AIA membership is one more way for them to gain credibility in a profession where their competence is questioned on a regular basis. Although they all belong, and many have been elected to the College of Fellows, there is a consensus about the impotence of the AIA as a political force, and about the racism in the organization. In contrast to many industries, architecture receives little support from the AIA. There is no national political agenda to support public policy that might be useful for *all* architects, much less black architects. In part because it is still perceived as the gentlemen's profession, there has been a hesitance to get political.[14]

> We [black architects] don't have the political clout, the voice. The AIA can't get elected officials to call us back because we have no PAC [political action committee] money. As a profession, we don't have a political agenda. As a profession, we've been marginalized. September 11th changed that in New York City. The community has turned to architects to be public advocates for public design. The City has looked to architects to respond and design the future. However, the mayor is about *big* business. We get the crumbs after the big businesses get theirs. This election, we have to be more politicized about what we do. (Wendell Marshall)

There is considerable disaffection with the AIA. In an era when political action committees and lobbyists are active at all levels of government, the AIA is perceived to be missing in action.

Membership in the AIA is general membership. Although the dues structure is established by category—licensed architect, associate (working toward licensing), student, and professional affiliate—there are no membership distinctions regarding specialty. Unlike other professional organizations, there are no sections based on specific types of work. There is talk in the organization about establishing certification by specialty. Black architects, generally excluded from corporate and other private commissions, feel this process would further preclude opportunities for growth. There is concern it would work against them the same way other certification programs have worked against them: firms that have not already completed certain building types would likely not get chosen for those projects.

> In the 1970s, I worked for the national AIA as the government affairs liaison. I was hired *not* to address black issues. There's a black cultural influence everywhere but architecture. Seventy-five percent of the firms in America have fewer than ten people. All certification would do is keep me off the short list. We are not invited to the table.
>
> The leadership at AIA is responsible for making change. There are other African American members, so when *we're* discriminated against, AIA members are being discriminated against. If there's no work [for black architects], there's no demand for architects to be members. The GSA hires more architects than any other agency. They have never hired a black architect to design a building. It's like asking why aren't there more black rabbis? The demand just simply isn't there. (Nicholas Rose)

When Rose worked at the AIA, he was actively discouraged from discussing race issues in the course of developing relationships with government agencies. He was hired as the government liaison, representing the AIA, and his supervisor made it clear that his job was not about discussing racism. Thirty years later, he is still incredulous that architecture in general, and the AIA in particular, is so impervious to the influence of black culture.

National Organization of Minority Architects

The mission statement of NOMA says:

> NOMA, which thrives only when voluntary members contribute their time and resources, has as its mission the building of a strong national organization, strong chapters and strong members for the purpose of minimizing the effect of racism in our profession.
>
> Strength in NOMA is built through unity in the cause that created the organization. Our impact is felt when our organization wrestles with the dilemmas that face this nation, particularly as they affect our profession. There is strength in numbers. By increasing the number of people in this organization, we add strength to the voice with which we can speak against apathy, bigotry, intolerance and ignorance; against abuse of the natural environment; and for the un-empowered, the marginalized and the disenfranchised.
>
> By building a strong organization, we develop a showcase for the excellence and creativity which have been ignored for so long. Through our publications and conferences, we are able to inform the world that minority professionals have the talent and capabilities to perform in design and construction with any other group.

By building strong chapters of design professionals whose sensibilities and interests include promotion of urban communities, we are able to respond to the concerns that affect marginalized communities and people. Our goals are to increase the level of participation in the social, political and economic benefits afforded the citizens of this nation and to tear down the barriers that make full participation unattainable. Chapters give members a base from which to be involved in politics, to visit schools and reach out to children, to conduct community and civic forums and to responsibly practice in our professional capacities.

The difference in the mission statements of these two industry associations provides a clear explanation for the following section. Although professional strategic planners may quibble with the brevity of the first and the length of the second, the statements speak loudly about the distinctions in the organizational cultures of the two institutions.

Over thirty years ago, a group of black architects got together at an AIA national convention and decided they needed an alternative to the overwhelmingly white AIA. NOMA's fortunes have risen and fallen over the years, but the current officers have made a renewed commitment to bring some energy back to this organization. In a newsletter of the AIA National Associates Committee, Jack Travis wrote this history:

In 1970, in Detroit at the AIA National Convention, seven Black architects met in one of the hotel lounges, to organize the National Organization of Black Architects [NOBA].

In 1971, a total of 22 members met at Nassau, Bahamas, and drafted the first charter for the organization. Thus the National Organization of Minority Architects was born. The group, now made up of mostly Black members (85 percent or higher), just recently celebrated its 31st year of existence and is still a vital working force.

It is important to note that the name change from NOBA to NOMA came primarily as a result to align with the AIA to receive funding. Using the word "Black," or any reference to a specific race or group, in a title excluded an organization from receiving not-for-profit status and/or government assistance.[15]

Among the architects I met, there is a fondness and a sense of belonging engendered by NOMA. Although not all are active members, all acknowledged the importance of an organization that recognizes and validates architects of color.

NYCOBA [the New York Coalition of Black Architects] became a NOMA chapter. When I first joined, there were no other women. I just kept showing up anyway. My first meeting was in Atlanta in 1992. I felt like a stranger. Everybody seemed to be so friendly to each other, like they really wanted to make people a part of things. It's good to be around folks who have the same kind of issues and you don't have to explain The [race] Issue. It's a lot like "Waiting to Exhale."

You can talk openly, not so much at the conference per se, but there were all these people in business. I could ask them questions. If you just kept your ears open, you heard things relevant to you. Black architects in different cities have different experiences. If you live in a city where the politics favor you working, you work, cities like Atlanta, Chicago, DC, and places in North Carolina. New York City is a no. Even when we had a black mayor, it was worse. He thought he already had black votes in his pocket, and then blacks didn't go out and vote.

I was president of NOMA in the '90s. The students are all ethnicities, across the board. Feeling like you're being treated like a minority, you joined NOMA. There are a lot of people who feel marginalized. People are on the outside; we're not part of the in crowd. It's hard to distinguish between racism and sexism. In the end, it's not what you call yourself, it's what you do. In NOMA, you can be who you are. (Sharon Young)

NOMA provides a meeting place where black architects can speak frankly about firm management, design issues, and race in the profession. There is a sense of community they do not feel inside the AIA.

I feel much more connected to NOMA than to the AIA. There's a spark about NOMA that's very different from how I feel about AIA. It's difficult to define, but I think it's because at a NOMA meeting it always feels like family. You don't feel like you need to be guarded all the time, like you need to be protecting yourself. (Wendell Marshall)

Although all these architects belong to AIA, it is clear they get a kind of reinforcement and validation from belonging to NOMA they do not get from AIA. Given the demographics of the AIA, this is not surprising. There are not many places in architecture, or in higher education outside the HBCUs, where students and practitioners can go to a meeting and be surrounded by other architects of color.

I was introduced to NOMA during college. Two principals from [the firm] RAW came and lectured on architecture and mentioned NOMA. The first conference I went to was at Harvard. There were so many people of color doing architecture; I was blown away. I came back to school and started a NOMA student chapter. This was sometime between 1990 and 1992. There were about eight of us. We started to bring in more speakers. We had lots of energy. We also had an AIA student chapter [AIAS], but I didn't connect as much to AIA as to NOMA. It's the same thing with the seminars at events. I'm an Associate member of AIA, but I'm not as bonded to AIA. (Danelle Graham)

These conversations about NOMA make clear the need for a place where black architects can gather with others who share their professional status *and* their understanding of the struggles in the profession. The fondness these architects express for this organization is, in part, about the relief of being in workshops and meeting rooms with people who look like them. As Marshall said, of not having to be on guard.

Some architects I met are second-generation NOMA members. They share the fondness for the organization. Tom Miller knew that the architects he met over the years in NOMA provided him with role models who convinced him he could thrive in the profession.

My father is an architect and, as a child, I went to NOMA and played a role with the community and the stories. The differences between generations in the way we all look at the race issue is not necessarily age-driven. Success examples are *really important*. That's one of the things we get from NOMA. If we can't get success one way, we'll get it the bootstrap, self-determination way. My firm is angry, too, but we couldn't wait, so we went and got. Knowing there were black architects with successful firms made it easier for us to believe we could succeed. (Tom Miller)

MARKETING

> *I think any organization that doesn't put a high priority on marketing is destined for failure.*
>
> —Mitchel R. Levitt, "Flying with Eagles"

"Marketing" is the catch-all phrase used in business to describe the comprehensive effort that goes into earning revenue. It comprises such activities as advertising, public relations and social network development, and product design and definition. To build an effective marketing plan, it is important to ask: What is your product or service? Who is likely to buy it? How will you go about finding them, and how will you tell them about what you do?

The public relations aspect of marketing is one of the most important for architects. As discussed elsewhere in this book, the hiring process for professional services is often based on personal relationships and social networks. Institutional racism creates barriers to black architects being able to develop the same kinds of contacts as their white counterparts. As all the architects I interviewed pointed out, "When the playing field is level, we can compete and we can win. It just doesn't happen very often."

Marketing is one of the functions within a firm through which inequality of opportunity stifles the degree of economic, professional, and aesthetic success black architects can attain. "To get recognized as an architect, one has to be able to bring in the business. It's difficult for blacks to get projects" (Olivia Tucker).

It is easy to be glib about the fact it is cheaper to get more revenue from existing clients than cultivating new ones. Getting new clients is often difficult, not only for all architects, but for all business owners. However, more than in other professions, selling architectural services is about visibility and cachet. Since black firms are rarely awarded "glitter" projects, they are also rarely featured in the "glossies"—the high-end architecture publications—which makes it harder for them to show off their design work. Their invisibility makes marketing more important and more challenging. As people who are both creative and visual, blacks develop imaginative ways to address the problem. This is an old problem for these firms. Hudson quotes Paul Williams's reflections:

> "The weight of my racial handicap forced me, willy-nilly, to develop salesmanship. The average well-established white architect, secure in his social connections, might be able to rest his hopes on his final plans; I, on the contrary, had to devote as much thought and ingenuity to winning an adequate first hearing as to the execution of the detailed drawings."

Hudson continues:

> Williams' difficulty in expanding into the larger scale of public and commercial projects was shared by most of the smaller firms in the LA area. . . . Williams had by the end of the '20s established a reputation as a skilled and sophisticated designer of houses for the upper middle class and the wealthy. These Southern California practitioners could not move easily from the world of residential design to that of business and government. But Williams alone suffered the continual presence of racial prejudice.[16]

The owner of a large firm learned his marketing lessons working in someone else's large firm before he started his own firm.[17] In all small businesses, there is a problem finding the time to do marketing, let alone a problem making the time and space to develop an effective marketing plan. As with knowing when to hire additional employees, there is always a judgment call about when to hire either an independent contractor or an employee to focus on the marketing. Small and medium architecture firms—black *and* white—are further challenged in this effort by the fact they usually have limited photographic evidence of their design abilities. In addition, most architects have not had much opportunity to get experience with marketing.

> Architects have no sense of entrepreneurship. It can't be done on the basis of architecture culture. We're not taught about promoting ourselves. In order to run a successful business, you have to paint the picture differently. To increase the number of black architects requires an increase in black wealth. You can't expect people to take a vow of poverty, and we're not taught how to run a business.
>
> Black architects like to complain about rich blacks hiring white architects. It's not just a case of black people not being interested in black architects—black architects have to find ways to reinvent themselves and become visible. There's an education that has to go on. (Nelson Norton)

Norton does not think black architects take an active enough role in marketing their firms. He believes as a group they need to get up to date on how marketing works, and how best to get their names out to the public. He would like to see group advertising in publications targeted at black audiences, and he wants black architects to take the initiative to learn more about firm management. On one hand, he is very clear about institutional racism; he knows the barriers these firms face when looking for work. On the other hand, he sees some as not connecting to the expanding market for architectural services in black communities.

The architecture education system, and the gestalt of practice in the United States, focus on design as the source of success. As I have talked to nonarchitects around the country about this book, one of the first questions about the interviewees is, "Oh, what buildings would I know that they've designed?" It confirms what I have been told about the skewed perceptions of architecture.

> I think the teaching in college programs does that. The whole curriculum is built around an individual being able to showcase their talents. And when you look at all your professional magazines, the superstars are who you see all the time. So the mentality of most individuals is: If you are good enough, then you are going to be hired, so why do you need to market?[18]

Given how much time we in this culture spend inside buildings, it is a great irony those who create them are so invisible. Outside of the real estate industry, their families and friends, few Americans consider how amazing it is that most of our buildings are safe and secure. The marketing effort to sell architectural services often requires educating the prospective client. For black architects, there is a sense that the health of each firm is also tied to the health of all firms.

There is a constant clash between the Eurocentric culture of architecture and the cultural realities of architects of color. Whether or not Black Architecture exists, all architects bring a cultural heritage to their work. Nelson Norton is adamant about taking those cultural realities into account.

> "The black community doesn't have repeat work." It's a simplistic statement and presupposes the black economic structure is the same as the white economic structure. It just can't be approached traditionally. How do you get the architects who get this to a critical mass?
>
> Blacks have to understand that it's all about culture. We were trained to be worried about being as proficient technically as white architects. There was *no* emphasis on culture. You'd have to be crazy not to notice the Euronationalistic implications of Corbusier and Frank Lloyd Wright. (Nelson Norton)

For the majority of black architects, this conflict between the architecture of their training and the feeling of their culture is not easily resolved; it is a constant struggle to find a balance. One of the East Coast architects who is focused on Afrocentric architecture, and who has been successful with black clients, talked about how difficult it is to do marketing, to try to be mindful of your black heritage, and to keep the business going.

> We don't know where we're from and we've not been taught it. Look at the Jews; their history exists. Ours is unknown. But more importantly, our potential clients don't see there's a need for understanding history. It's hard enough just to get by; people don't think about how marginalized they are. Clients don't know black architects.
>
> If I see a need, I just do. I'm working now on an apartment building in Harlem. It's about every place, every surface. It may not be form and space, but we can start. The cultural void has to be filled. It's all about doing something special that you offer that fills a void, that makes other people's lives better. (Leroy Vaughan)

Vaughan and others would disagree with Norton's assessment of their marketing prowess. Three of the architects I spoke with have very deliberate strategies to market their services in communities of color, and all three have been successful in that endeavor.

All the architects interviewed for this book are sophisticated and diligent in their marketing efforts. Most work in both majority communities and communities of color. The struggles to get work "downtown" are an indication of the extent to which racism is a reality for black architects. They do everything they can to get new work outside "the community," and their efforts are stymied by preconceived notions. When they *do* find allies among corporate decision makers, they deliver.

> We've done corporate renovation projects, but not a plum, but not a plum project. The chair of the board on our big project wanted *us*. The project manager, who was white, wanted the white-owned interior design firm to take over the building design, but the chairman wouldn't hear of it. It's not about money, it's about design. We use money to value the design, but it's not about money.
>
> Most of my clients don't run private corporations or government agencies. They're HBCUs, churches, schools, or St. Georges County. (Nicholas Rose)

Rose and his associates are pragmatic in their approach to marketing. They take good care of the existing clients who are loyal to them, and they work very hard to create relationships with corporate decision makers. From time to time, those efforts pay off. In the case of Rose's big downtown project, professional colleagues tried to edge them out of the design work, but the corporate decision maker specifically wanted Rose's firm to do the work. The chairman made the decision, and the chairman was in a position to make sure it was implemented. The frustration comes from the near impossibility of building those connections.

The generational differences among this group of architects is nowhere more apparent than in their approach to marketing. The younger architects' attitude toward racism is to acknowledge its existence, and then do what they can to develop a collaborative way to overcome it, or at least end around it.

> The strategies successful firms have used translate to black firms? In our firm, good public relations overcame race. We very deliberately came up with a strategy and stuck to it. Good PR can mean having a black architect at the table is a *good* thing. (Tom Miller)

The philosophy for Miller's West Coast firm was successful in part because it was relentless in showing up, and also because it was in a diverse city where corporations had more experience doing business with professionals of color.

The larger firms have more opportunities for marketing because they have more people creating visibility for them. One of the owners of a large firm is clear about the importance of spreading the marketing task across the entire firm. Not only does it result in a more effective effort, but it also provides training and exposure for every member of the firm.

Everyone [in the firm] is accountable. Everyone markets, and we have a marketing team. A designated marketing team backed up by the marketing staff, backed up by the principals, and the fact of the matter is, we're set up as lines of business. Health care is a line of business. Sports architecture is a line of business. Civil engineering, interior design, general architecture. Then we go to branch offices, Nashville and Cincinnati, and they have regional issues.

From a marketing standpoint, each has a marketing lead. . . . A principal, in each case, is head of that area. They are supported by marketing people and other staff who are called upon to meet the needs of the project we are pursuing.[19]

While there are liabilities to running a large firm, one luxury is being able to organize the management structure to support effective marketing. This firm, with 130 employees, is able to afford the staff and the training to ensure its marketing efforts are in line with its business plan *and* are being implemented. In small firms, where everyone is already stretched to the limit by trying to get the work done, marketing often becomes a low priority. This is the usual state of affairs for small businesses of all kinds, and it creates a vicious circle. At the point where large projects are winding down, there should already be new projects on the horizon. Better training in what marketing really is, and how to do it effectively, would be useful for small firms. Despite the resource crunch, there are many ways to go about marketing that do not take large blocks of time and can pay off in the long run.

When black-owned firms do get work downtown, they often have to spend time and energy on PR in ways comparable white firms do not have to do. The clients want to know the owner is paying attention. Except on very big, visible projects, this is rarely the case at bigger and European American–owned firms. In those cases, the project owner is satisfied conducting business with a project manager or other associate. I asked a white staff member in a black-owned firm, "Why is it your boss has to show up to so many meetings? What would happen if he just said no?" The staffer replied,

Look at our last big project we did for the City. They insisted he show up for City Council meetings. It's the BA syndrome: they want to see his Black Ass. The other side of that is when we mess up people tend to say, "We shouldn't have hired them anyway. See, I told you so." It's exhilarating, and there's a lot of terror. It keeps you just mad enough to play well. It gives you the drive to keep going. Kinda' like the LA Lakers! It makes you think, "Look what I've been through. I can do anything." (Norm Miller)

The need to see the owner at meetings stems in part from the perception this firm is not as competent as white-owned firms. It is a subtle impact of institutional racism rarely visible to whites.[20] It is difficult for all architects to market their services and manage their projects, but there is an additional layer for black-owned firms. They continually have to prove they can do the work. They want to be invited to present for corporate projects, but even after decades, their networks are not wide enough. It is frustrating for them because they are not able to be assertive with clients regarding design until they have proven themselves to be good designers; they cannot prove themselves unless they get the jobs.

PRODUCTS OR SERVICES?

There is a wide range of opinions about whether architecture provides a service or a product—or both. The answer makes a difference in the kind of marketing a firm needs to do and the ways it relates to clients. Where a firm comes down on this subject is a function of the way it views its mission, and the decisions it has made about the kinds of projects it will and will not do.

One of the reasons there are so few African American architects is the historical lack of economic power. This subject came up repeatedly: outside of community design, black architects have not been visible in communities of color. Edward Lamont believes that is one reason for the lack of understanding about architectural services on the part of people in the community. He has a lot of frustration about this:

> I have a theory. As a people, we haven't had the economic power to be builders. We've only been stuck with adaptive reuse, that is, what you collect in the neighborhood you move into. Black architects weren't there. Outside of community design, they weren't even visible. As Melvin Mitchell says, there wasn't a critical mass, which naturally meant a lack of community support for African American architects.
>
> Mitchell talks about the intimacy of architectural services.[21] There are a lot of people who would buy *products* from a black supplier, but wouldn't buy *services* from a black person. It's a great irony—black folks don't mind asking us for help, but a lot of them don't understand they're really looking for services. (Edward Lamont)

Having now talked to several architects about this conflict between products and services, I find it is another area where black architects are likely more sensitive to the differences than either their clients or their white counterparts. The idea that blacks can only provide services to other blacks is a remnant of the Jim Crow laws. Personal services such as barbershops, beauty salons, and mortuaries were provided by members of the community to members of the community. As with many aspects of systemic racism, black architects learn to move past their anger over mistaken perceptions. They are pragmatic, knowing that creating successful firms is the best revenge.

The owner of a large firm takes the long view about developing and maintaining clients. The kind of relationship he is interested in developing reflects a concern for providing a service to clients who will ultimately pay for products.

> The more information you can obtain on the client the better. Has the client ever hired architects, engineers, and/or interior designers before? If so, what was involved? What did they like/dislike about the firms? What are the client's hot buttons? What are the real needs of the project? We like to feel we market a client versus a project. Projects come and go, but a client you hope to maintain for life. So, if you market a client, a strategy must be developed for not just getting the project—it needs to be a strategy for getting and keeping the client.[22]

We find a different approach from one of the East Coast architects. This firm has a commitment to work in communities of color, and the firm owner views the end users, rather than the building owner, as the real clients. His clarity about the issue of products and services facilitates the development of a marketing strategy that will put the firm in a position to do fulfilling work in the community.

> We need to make the product the goal. If you hire us again, we can produce the product; services lead up to the end product. We inject the services that go with the product, like at the big housing project we did. It has thirty-eight six-story buildings with a total of 1,240 families. The clients, who in this case were the tenants, were vocal, which is how we got involved.
>
> We don't want to compromise the aesthetic qualities of the building, but we have to make it affordable and sustainable. Part of our job is to help find money for our clients.
>
> The church projects' funding is self-induced, but desires to expand mean the funding becomes an issue even once the drawings are done and the approvals are in.
>
> I've never looked at our firm as a firm that can *only* do work in the "'hood." I'd prefer to only work in the 'hood because it would make it a Place and empower all the people in the community to be first class citizens. We haven't marketed for corporate work. We have enough work with what we're doing. We have a sociological philosophy to empower the people who use the building.
>
> When we do corporate work, our philosophy is the same. We did a small office building for a corporation that funds organizations that do development in urban

areas. We wanted anyone who walked in the building to feel they were part of the city. The modulated views we built into the building empower both the workers and the clients. It makes them feel they are part of the environment. We hope to do more corporate work; it will give us the opportunity to bring our philosophy to that work. (Wendell Marshall)

For Marshall, the operating philosophy guides the marketing and management. They have a consistent design approach they use with all their clients: the people who will be using the building are the focus of their efforts. In some practices, the social mission helps define the particular niche a firm will occupy. In the case of a large southern firm, the provision of services enables the creation of a profitable product.

Our mission is to benefit the larger society. Given that, it's preferable for us to do public-sector work. There are things we specifically don't do. We don't do prisons. It doesn't match up with our vision. We would rather work upstream, for example, doing schools. We feel there's more value there. Besides which, doing your specialty makes the best sense economically and it's more fulfilling. (Rob Green)

The "star" architects do not have to address this question of products versus services. Since they are the ones who are visible, they are the model for what the general public thinks about architects (when and if they do!). This makes the issue even more important for the remainder of the profession.

What the broader group doesn't understand is that you are talking about 3 to 5% of the profession. The other 95% of us have to differentiate our services. What I believe, and what I teach my staff, is marketing is the first essential, not second, third, or fourth. A lot of people say, "No, no, architecture is first." You don't do architecture without having the project. So no matter what your talents are, your first goal is to get the work. That's something we really push around here.[23]

HUMAN RESOURCE MANAGEMENT

Human resources (HR) is the most difficult task for most business owners. It is the one place where entrepreneurs are confident in their abilities, and it is the task that, if done badly, can get them in the most trouble.[24] In small to medium firms, the difficulty and expense of finding effective supervisors can leave principals afraid to delegate.

I've had my own practice for several years. It's been really difficult to find the right employees. I didn't take any time off for years, because I was afraid what would happen if I wasn't there. If I left for three days to go to an AIA meeting, I would always come back to chaos. I finally fired most of my employees and started over. I have a great group of architects now, and I have a managing principal who is doing a great job of keeping things straight. Now I can go to national conferences and get out and do some marketing and not be worried the work we've already got is going to spin out of control.

I realize now how exhausted I was, and how ineffective, too. I was trying to manage an office full of people who either didn't want to be there or had no experience that would help them manage themselves. (Daryl Johnson)

This story reflects a worst-case scenario of a firm owner afraid to leave the building. It is not that unusual for a business owner to be reluctant to give up control. Almost all of these architects started their firms in order to get control; it makes sense they would be loathe to let that go. Some owners delegate other functions and retain the role of personnel manager, but it is an acquired taste.

I enjoy doing design, the marketing interaction with people, and reviewing the construction and the end product. You sacrifice what you enjoy to do the things you don't enjoy, like the human resources aspect. I actually figured out HR from teaching college and from knowing how to deal with people. I see the firm as a group.

Like a band, each person has to do their part well; each one has to have a sense of camaraderie not only onstage but offstage as well, which is much more difficult. As creative people, your mind is so caught up in the work you can have an "attitude" and forget your colleagues. This is a professional family, and I am the referee. (Wendell Marshall)

Whether it is the band analogy or the family analogy, architecture firms are made up of creative people who need to learn to negotiate ways to work well together. Many owners spoke of feeling like a parent, always having to monitor attitude and mediate between squabbling colleagues. Adding cultural diversity to the mix only makes it more complex.

I spoke with one of the firm owners on the East Coast about maintaining diversity on the staff. Of the architects who employ staff (professional and administrative), just under half employ only people of color. The rest are clear that diversity is an important factor in hiring, but it can be difficult to maintain a high degree of ethnic diversity. It requires a very deliberate effort.

As I've matured in the profession, I realize things are not as easy and clear-cut as you think they are. We have four principals—two whites, one Japanese American, and one African American. We're 51 percent minority owned. We've recently downsized from fifteen to ten. I'm guilty. We were unable to replace some people, but we have a responsibility to practice what we preach. The economics of architecture often drive one's ability to do the right thing.

The easy way out is to say there's not a critical mass, but in part it's a question of comfort level. We had a diverse staff, but people left through attrition. The critical mass issue shouldn't let people off the hook. As far as comfort level goes, you hire who you know, you hire within your network. This is a tough profession no matter what color you are, but the cards are really stacked against you if you don't have that social network. (Roland Davis)

It was refreshing to hear that kind of candor on the subject of hiring architects of color. It was a reminder that even for some black architects, the hiring process requires a conscious, deliberate decision to establish and maintain a multicultural office. Most of the owners I spoke with have made a definitive choice about the value of hiring and mentoring architects of color; they know it broadens the range of projects they can deliver, and they also know it is a way to increase the numbers of nonwhite architects. The owner of a bigger firm is clear about the ways staff diversity is an asset to the firm. An ethnically diverse firm makes a statement about values of the firm and also provides a broader range of experience to bring to projects.[25]

I started the firm in 1990. Although I still hold 85 percent of the stock, I am not the sole owner. There are two other shareholders, and we're about to add two more. We have twenty black employees, Asian Americans, foreign nationals from Nigeria, India, and Indonesia. Women are prominent and hold leadership roles in the firm. Our diversity is intentional; we believe it's a real strength. Increasingly, the client teams, both public and private, are diverse. We're able to mirror their makeup. Given the percentage of black architects out of the total, if we weren't deliberate about this we would be expected to have half a black person! It definitely helps inform our work to have diverse perspectives on the team.

I suddenly understood that saying, "it's lonely at the top." I'm good at delegating, but it's taken years for me to be able to do it. I want to hire people who are better than I am. We have an excellent leadership team because we're all different and so we complement each other; I am *not* the operations manager. I'm good at marketing and design. You have to give those good folks in your firm an opportunity or they'll leave and you'll be competing with them. (Rob Green)

Rob has learned the importance of valuing employees and providing ongoing opportunities for them to grow and contribute. He has been successful, in part, because he defined his HR strategy and stuck to it. He has also done well by knowing his strengths and his limitations, and delegating tasks to people with talents that differ from his.

Even in big firms, the owner continues to have responsibility for the employees. It is important to continue to mentor and acknowledge the employees; good management creates good morale, and keeping in touch with the employees is part of good management. Since the pool of good midlevel architects, especially architects of color, is so small, paying attention to the existing employees also helps ensure they will recommend the firm to their colleagues.

> We do have a human resources person, but I still deal with individuals on a range of different levels. Diversity is a cornerstone of the business. There's a limited supply of minority architects, and we have the largest share in the region. The way we're organized, the progression is from associate to senior associate, to associate principal, and then principal. We have a number of good senior associates, but we're lacking associates. It's always a challenge to hire good employees. Our minority architects are always being called by headhunters; we're a good recruiting source. Sometimes they are being attracted by offers that really pay more than the positions should pay.
>
> Of course when you have this many employees, there are always personality issues. I lead the design studio. The core design team of five is made up of one African American, one Korean, one Hispanic, and two nonminorities. As a studio, we cover more diversity than any other firm in the region. We don't have trouble finding good entry-level people. It's a lot harder to find people with five years of experience. (Donald Nelson)

Of the six architects who talked about this issue, they all sympathized with Nelson's quandary. For those who are committed to maintaining a diverse firm, it is difficult to find experienced architects of color. There is a small pool of them, and the competition to hire them is intense. Once they are hired, it is often difficult to convince them to stay. Although this problem varies by location, maintaining a diverse workforce can be a struggle.

GROWING THE FIRM

The allure of growth is almost irresistible to business owners. The opportunity to do one big, noteworthy job or add a new line of service is usually just what an entrepreneur thinks would be the ticket to more revenue. What many fail to understand is the increased expenses required to support additional income. The start-up costs for a large project can put a firm out of business; the combination of increased payroll and acquisition of required assets stretches the cash requirements for even the best strategic planners.

Managing growth in an architecture firm means maintaining a delicate balance between having enough people to complete the projects and paying employees to look out the window: "It's hard to know whether to hire someone for a new project until we have the project, but if we get the project we won't have anyone to work on it." Temporary layoffs are a fact of life in the industry; effectively matching staff expertise with project requirements given such variability is an art. The range of stories about firm growth spans decades and generations, both chronologically and philosophically.

Many businesses start in the owner's home. In an essay in the Travis book about African American–owned firms, Harry Overstreet writes, "By 1966, the African-American architect emerged from the spare bedroom, converted garage, or corner of his living room. . . . The African-American architect was an invisible person, with no friends in high places."[26] The social costs of expansion can be as burdensome as the economic costs. Edward Lamont, who practices in a city with a small black population, said explaining to members of the community the need for a black-owned firm to be downtown and well designed can get complicated.

The firm seems to go in five-year cycles. The first five years I was working out of my home. When I started adding employees, they were all single. When those original employees started leaving, three left to follow their wives, women who had moved to take jobs. After about five years, as they either got divorced or started having children, they came back. Now there are five people who have returned.

In the beginning, I did project management jobs for other offices to get money into the firm. From 1985 to 1990, I lived in the back bedroom and had two people working in the front bedroom, two people working in the dining room. They used the kitchen as a staff lounge.

We moved to an office for eight on Capitol Hill. I felt serious and grown-up. Someone in the community said to me, "You've got an office that looks like a white person's office." Some of my black business friends think we spend a lot on facilities. They don't understand the symbolism of being downtown and making a design statement. Their lack of understanding leads to questions about why we're spending so much money to be in this location.

The new space will make a statement.[27] This place where we are now is just a work space. People don't understand how big the wealth gap is; I have one foot in both cultures. I'm able to hear both sides in The Great Myths. I'm still trying to decide how many of the great myths are real. The theory about how deals get done is true. The thing that's scary is our biggest problem is we're stuck in a six-person management style. We've grown faster than we can put the procedures in place. (Edward Lamont)

Successfully growing a business requires a delicate balancing act. It is important to build an operating plan that will reflect the needs of a larger organization and at the same time continue to manage the ongoing work. Even for professionals such as architects who are trained in the art of planning, it can be challenging to take time out to develop a new business plan. As Lamont's firm grew, it became obvious the old ways of doing business were not going to meet the firm's new needs. The requirements of growing a firm—capital, personnel, and operations—may be one reason the overwhelming majority of firms remain very small. Only 13 percent of AIA firms have more than twenty employees.[28]

Some firm owners began as employees and over time became owners. It takes stamina and courage to stay on alone after older partners have passed away or retired. While changes can provide opportunities for new endeavors, the kinds of decisions once made by committee are now made alone. There is no one else to take the blame or get the glory. Architects are risk-takers by nature, or they would never be able to endure the iterative process required to complete projects. They are professionally prepared to accept there is no one right way to proceed with a project, so they need to be decisive—and prepared to make mistakes. When it comes to management, a mistaken judgment call can be costly.

From 1968 to 1985, I worked with a senior partner. We had a 50–50 corporation. He retired in 1984. There are pros and cons of sole ownership. At fifty, I was in for a shock. Before that, I always had my partner. We had the chance to take on a job that was about ten times the size of anything we had done. It meant visibility for the firm, and a chance to Design. I learned my lesson the hard way. I expanded faster than I should have. I'm still glad we did that job—I'm proud of that building—but it has taken us a long time to bounce back. (James Patterson)

Firm growth, or the successful growth of any business, requires a steady hand and a good grasp of management principles. The lack of management training in professional schools leaves practitioners at a disadvantage in times of crisis.

The skills required to start a firm, or any business, are not the same as those required for growth. An owner needs to be able to understand the tasks required for an expanded firm and, more importantly, be able to gauge whether the required expertise is available. It is often painful to acknowledge the need for new personnel—or the need to let go of current employees. Some firm owners are fortunate to have gotten on-the-job training in preparation for growing a firm.

I worked for other people the first fourteen years. I always had a feeling about what I did and didn't want to do. The seven years prior to starting this firm, I worked for the same firm. In that time, they went from 40 employees to 140. I was the youngest partner in the firm. I saw a lot of growth and was part of the dynamic/static, happy/sad, clear/murky, the up and down of rapid growth. I did a lot of design work there; my work in that firm informed what I wanted to do. (Rob Green)

At the other end of the spectrum, there are firms that have grown by availing themselves of the latest technology to manage their growth. By operating globally, they have a variety of problems that do not exist for local or even national firms, but they also circumvent some of the specific cultural issues black-owned domestic firms face.

Our firm is a modern, technology-driven partnership. I started with them in 1997 from New York. The partners had moved from Boston to Hawaii years ago. They wanted to work around the Pacific Rim. Now the managing principal is in Hawaii, and one principal is in Manila. We do conference calls on the computer. We have three people in Manila and four in Washington. Essentially we're a twenty-four-hour shop now. (Roland Davis)

Davis's partners were confident enough in their management abilities to create a new model for how to grow the firm internationally. The problems they encounter are more about coordinating scheduling and less about the traditional growth issues. That said, this firm still struggles with knowing when, how, and where to add staff. The workload is expanding, and the firm's analysis for how to manage a larger office is complicated by the need to manage time, distance, and technology.

In the end, the ability to grow a firm comes down to a combination of management skill, the economics of the industry, good planning, and old-fashioned tenacity. The owner of a big firm describes it this way:

A lot of it has to do with the personality of the individual. When I was in elementary school, I knew I wanted to design buildings, but I was a C student and I was also an athlete. My coach asked me what I wanted to do. I told him, and he suggested I talk to my counselor. My counselor said, "How many black architects have you seen? There aren't many, so I think you should be a draftsman. I cannot advise you to be an architect. You need to be smarter and know math and have better grades to be an architect."

She told my coach he needed to talk to me because I could never become an architect. He sat me down and told me I needed to learn math, and pointed out I had a C average, and had gotten bad grades in math. I told him I intended to get an A in math the next term. I got a 97 in algebra the next term. It all depends on what you want. Once I knew I wanted to be an architect, I took control and made sure it would happen.

When people tell me, "You can't do this," my response is, "You're not the one who gets to decide what I can or cannot do." (Donald Nelson)

NOTES

1. See Stephen L. Carter, "The Black Table, the Empty Seat, and the Tie," in *Lure and Loathing: Essays on Race, Identity and the Ambivalence of Assimilation*, ed. Gerald Early (New York: Penguin, 1993); Ellis Cose, *Rage of a Privileged Class* (New York: Harper Perennial, 1995); Joe Feagin and Melvin Sikes, *Living with Racism: The Black Middle-Class Experience* (Boston: Beacon, 1994); and bell hooks, *Killing Rage: Ending Racism* (New York: Holt, 1995), among others for lucid discussions of the cumulative effect of daily encounters with racism in the United States.

2. Mitchel R. Levitt., "Flying with Eagles: An Interview with Curtis J. Moody, FAIA," *SMPS Marketer* (October 2002): 5.

3. See Timothy Bates and William D. Bradford, *Financing Black Economic Development* (New York: Academic, 1979), and Pierre Bourdieu and Loic Wacquant, *An Invitation to Reflexive Sociology* (Chicago: University of Chicago Press, 1992). Bates and Bradford's study was focused on the risks of equity investing in black-owned businesses. Although the world of equity investing is fraught with uncertainty, some of that risk can be mitigated by going with likely "winners," as defined by Bates and Bradford.

4. For relevant discussions on institutional racism, see Eduardo Bonilla-Silva, *Racism without Racists: Color-Blind Racism and the Persistence of Racial Inequality in the United States* (Lanham, MD: Rowman & Littlefield, 2003); Carter, "Black Table, the Empty Seat, and the Tie"; John P. Caskey, "Bank Representation in Low-Income and Minority Urban Communities," *Urban Affairs Quarterly* 29, no. 4 (1994): 617–38; Cose, *Rage of a Privileged Class*; and Daniel P. Immergluck and Geoff Smith, "Bigger, Faster . . . But Better? How Changes in the Financial Services Industry Affect Small Business Lending in Urban Areas," Woodstock Institute, at brookings.edu/cs/urban/publications/immerglucklending.pdf (accessed January 2001), among many others.

5. See Phyllis Craig-Taylor, "To Be Free: Liberty, Citizenship, Property, Race," *Harvard Blackletter Law Journal* 14 (Spring 1998): 45–90; Fred Galves, "The Discriminatory Impact of Traditional Lending Criteria: An Economic and Moral Critique," *Seton Hall Law Review* 29, no. 4 (1999): 1467–87; Benjamin Forgey, "First Black Designed Building in Downtown DC," *Washington Post*, March 30, 2002, C1, C5; Daniel P. Immergluck, "Progress Confined: Increases in Black Home Buying and the Persistence of Residential Segregation," *Journal*

of Urban Affairs 20, no. 4 (1998): 443–57; Daniel P. Immergluck and Erin Mullen, "New Small Business Data Show Loans Going to Higher-Income Neighborhoods in Chicago Area," Woodstock Institute Reinvestment Alert, no. 11, November 1997, at www .woodstockinst.org/document/allert11.pdf (accessed 7 April 2002); Gregory D. Squires, *From Redlining to Reinvestment: Community Responses to Urban Disinvestment*, ed. Gregory D. Squires, 1–37 (Philadelphia: Temple University Press, 1992); and Gregory D. Squires, *Capital and Communities in Black and White* (Albany: State University of New York Press, 1994), for discussions about the relationship between lending and institutional racism.

6. Credit scoring itself is a process that has been criticized for a propensity to discriminate against applicants on the basis of both race and class. See Immergluck and Smith, "Bigger, Faster . . . But Better?" for more on credit scoring.

7. The community development finance industry grew up, in part, in response to this conundrum. See the websites for the National Community Capital Association (NCCA), www.communitycapital.org, and the Community Development Financial Institution Coalition, www.cdfi.org, for more information on the industry.

8. There is a considerable amount of literature on the subject of discrimination in housing markets. See, for example, Galves, "Discriminatory Impact of Traditional Lending Criteria"; Immergluck, "Progress Confined"; Alex Schwartz, "Bank Lending to Minority and Low-Income Households and Neighborhoods: Do Community Reinvestment Agreements Make A Difference?" *Journal of Urban Affairs* 20, no. 3 (1998): 269–301; and Thomas M. Shapiro, *The Hidden Cost of Being African American: How Wealth Perpetuates Inequality* (New York: Oxford University Press, 2004).

9. See Caskey, "Bank Representation in Low-Income and Minority Urban Communities"; Nancy A. Denton, "The Role of Residential Segregation in Promoting and Managing Inequality in Wealth and Property," *Indiana Law Review* 34, no. 4 (2001): 1199–1211; Immergluck and Smith, "Bigger, Faster . . . But Better?"; and Squires, *Capital and Communities in Black and White*.

10. "Norma Sklarek," Essortment: Information You Want to Know, at ni.essortment .com/normasklarek_rqbo.htm.

11. See appendix B, Dennis A. Mann and Bradford Grant, "African American Architects Survey 1999/2000" (Cincinnati: University of Cincinnati, 2000).

12. "The AIA: Advocacy, Community, Knowledge," American Institute of Architects, at www.aia.org/about_default.

13. Dennis Alan Mann, "Making Connections: The African-American Architect," *Journal of the Interfaith Forum on Religion, Art & Architecture* (Fall 1993).

14. See Mark A. Branch, "Chicken Little Critics," *Progressive Architecture* 75, no. 6 (June 1994): 25; and Michael J. Crosbie, "AIA: Worth the Price of Admission?" *Progressive Architecture* 75, no. 4 (April 1994): 60–65, 100–102.

15. Jack Travis, "Hidden in Plain View," *National Associates Committee Quarterly* (Spring 2003): 4.

16. Karen E. Hudson, *Paul R. Williams, Architect: A Legacy of Style* (New York: Rizzoli, 1993), 12, 22.

17. In architecture, any firm with over fifty employees is considered a large firm.

18. Levitt, "Flying with Eagles," 7.

19. Levitt, "Flying with Eagles," 6.

20. See Carter, "Black Table"; Cose, *Rage of a Privileged Class*; Feagin and Sikes, *Living with Racism*; Michelle Fine, "Witnessing Whiteness," in *Off White: Readings on Race, Power, and Society*, ed. Michelle Fine, Lois Weis, Linda C. Powell, and L. Mun Wong, 57–65 (New York: Routledge, 1997); Paul Kivel, *Uprooting Racism: How White People Can Work for Racial Justice* (Philadelphia: New Society, 1996); and Peggy McIntosh, "White Privilege and Male Privilege: A Personal Account of Coming to See Correspondences Through Work in Women's Studies," in *Race, Class and Gender: An Anthology*, ed. Margaret Andersen and Patricia H. Collins, 94–105 (Belmont, CA: Wadsworth, 1988).

21. Melvin Mitchell, *The Crisis of the African-American Architect: Conflicting Cultures of Architecture and (Black) Power* (Lincoln, NE: Writer's Club, 2001).

22. Levitt, "Flying with Eagles," 14

23. Levitt, "Flying with Eagles," 7.

24. Employment problems are second only to payroll tax deposits in disaster potential. See Victoria Kaplan and Robert Kunreuther, *The A to Z of Managing People* (New York: Berkley, 1996), for examples of how bad human resource management decisions can cause managers to run amok.

25. This is the case the AIA National Associates Committee, Kathryn Anthony, and Melvin Mitchell make for increasing the numbers of architectural students (and, presumably, architects) of color.

26. Harry L. Overstreet, "The Bastion of Hope," in *African American Architects in Current Practice*, ed. Jack Travis, 12 (New York: Princeton Architectural Press, 1991).

27. Edward Lamont had just signed a lease on a new, much larger space. He is concerned about making the commitment. He will be fifty-seven soon, and by fifty-seven both of his parents had passed away.

28. American Institute of Architects, *AIA Firm Survey, 2000/2002* (Washington, DC: American Institute of Architects, 2000).

IT'S WHO YOU KNOW: THE IMPORTANCE OF SOCIAL NETWORKS

African American architects must understand themselves to be cultural agents rather than merely technically oriented business persons.

—Melvin Mitchell,
The Crisis of the African-American Architect

THE RULES

The connections we have to others define our social networks. Family ties, educational experience, and social and business acquaintances come together to create a web of relationships. Those affiliations serve as links to other networks. If your networks are working and are getting you what you need, you rarely think about their existence. That is, you can take them for granted precisely because they are functioning.

The contacts we make through our networks provide us access to capital. There are various kinds, or species, of capital—cultural, social, economic, environmental, and so forth—each of which has value in certain situations. According to Pierre Bourdieu, a French philosopher–sociologist, these species can be exchanged for one another. Bourdieu defined social capital as "the sum of the resources, actual or virtual, that accrue to an individual or a group by virtue of possessing a durable network of more or less institutionalized relationships of mutual acquaintance and recognition."[1] In commercial settings, social capital is very often the key to increased economic capital.

The ability to get customers, obtain funding, and have access to professional services and clients is often dependent on both behavior and connections; competence is relevant only if you do not have it, or if, on the basis of ethnicity, you are *perceived* not to have it. Appropriate behavior, or what Aschaffenburg and Maas refer to as being able to "decode the implicit 'rules of the game,'" can often be invested in other ways.[2] Cultural capital can be used to gain social capital, and social capital can be exchanged for economic capital. Knowing and abiding by the rules often results in more invitations to play.[3]

This country confers assets on whites that are not automatically given to people of color; further, whites are free to invest those assets, with the realistic expectation of getting a positive return.[4] Those most likely to be the recipients of the dominant culture are those who, as a result of birth and upbringing, have already acquired the cultural capital to receive it.[5] Or as Langston says: "the middle class way of doing things is the standard—they're always right, just by being themselves. . . . If you're other than white middle class, you have to become bilingual to succeed in the educational system. If you're white middle class, you need only the language and writing skills you were raised with, since they're the standard."[6] The capital assets—economic, social, and cultural—may get you in the door, but unless you are white, they are usually not enough to get you a seat at the table.

In architecture, *cultural* capital is especially important. Franklin defined cultural capital as "the financial advantages that accrue to certain social classes due to their higher levels of education and their ability to influence popular styles and tastes in the artistic and cultural arenas."[7] As every architect I interviewed pointed out, they have the same education and the same credentials as all other architects, yet they do *not* have the influence on style and taste their white colleagues possess. The pedigreed star architects define style and taste. Those outside the "favored circle" are hard-pressed to redefine the existing norms.[8]

We don't express enough that we're out there. Most of our firms are doing government work. There's not one black-designed tract house community in America. There's not one black-owned car company. Atlanta's the only place in the country with middle-class black housing tracts. We need to get the word out about our work.

I've had some of my interior design work published in magazines, and I've done a lot of work on high-end residences. But a lot of people, blacks included, just don't know that black architects can design. That, and because of racism, white people don't feel comfortable talking about bedrooms and bathrooms with a black architect. The combination of the lack of visibility and the racism means we don't get to do a lot of the work we would be good at. (Leroy Vaughan)

It is problematic for all architects to market their services and manage their projects, but there is an additional layer for black-owned firms. They are continually having to prove they can do the work. Most of them want to be invited to present for corporate projects, but even after decades in practice, their networks are not wide enough. It is frustrating for them because they are not able to be assertive with clients regarding design until they have proven themselves to be good designers; they cannot prove themselves unless they get the jobs. Even when they get the jobs, they cannot leverage the experience the same way white architects can.

> The white star architect who worked on the huge municipal project we were a part of could parlay this work to get similar jobs all over the world. Black architects catch hell practicing in their own backyard. We can't parlay the work into another project like this. They don't believe I can see; they don't believe I have the vision. (James Patterson)

Expectations play an important role in who will accept any given cultural and social capital. Not unlike foreign currency, it can only be used in places where it is accepted. The idea that black architects have no vision becomes a real professional barrier. These cultural perceptions begin early.[9] In school, the micropolitical climate is often established by the teachers; they act as gatekeepers. Even in "integrated" schools, there is still tracking—that is, assignment to differing achievement levels based on perceptions that are culturally bound—at the classroom level.[10] Often irrespective of actual academic achievement or capability, children of color are expected to be less accomplished students. This expectation can lead to internalized oppression, which creates self-fulfilling prophecies and limits their ability to perform.[11]

On occasion, these expectations on the part of educators can be so annoying they serve as motivation. One of the women architects said:

> I went to first through sixth grade in Harlem. They didn't want me to be the best student; they didn't expect a black girl to excel. So my parents moved me to a school in Central Park. My father got me in by giving a false address. I went through junior high in an all-white school. The only other people of color were the offspring of maids and janitors.
>
> Taking algebra, I learned if you really try and keep working at something you can succeed. I took the test to get into the magnet school. It was all engineering and

math. I got a 99 on the test, the highest math grade. The homeroom teacher was mad that I had gotten such a high grade. I was too shy to say anything to her, but I knew I could get the highest grade. (Olivia Tucker)

The assumption of underperformance continues to be reality for African American entrepreneurs. Based on that assumption, bankers, vendors, and customers serve as gatekeepers, based on an expectation black businesses are not as good.[12] There is consistent commentary across a range of disciplines, from sociology to finance, that African Americans have to be twice as good as European Americans to produce equivalent results in business.[13] In architecture, the more profitable and interesting work generally goes to those firms who are already known and are a part of the industry power structure.[14]

When I got out of school, my title was different than my classmates. When I graduated, I found out that I was a minority architect. I wasn't in school to be a minority architect: I was in school to be an architect. And then the industry said, "If you start a firm, you are a minority architectural firm," and that's a given, then I need to be able to find a way to change some things. Because minority architects, as I knew them, were thought of as someone who was going to be added to a team, not leading a team. And I thought, "Somehow, I've got to change that."

Some of the greatest challenges we still have in front of us are the challenges to rise to the top of our respective field without the connotation, "They're only an African American–owned firm or minority firm." I find that to be a restriction. I don't have a problem at all with being identified as an African American firm as long as it is with the understanding that I am first of all an architect.

Hopefully, people will say I'm a good architect. Also, my goal is for our firm to be known as a great architectural firm, and then have the minority African American part come into play. The challenge is the opinions of people outside of our firm. Convincing new clients they should not allow their past understanding of what an African American firm is all about to be the judge of my firm's character. I find in most cases people have predetermined that a minority or African American–owned firm is not of the caliber of others. Because my firm falls into the category of African American firm, I find I am being thought about in that vein even before I have a chance to present my qualifications. The challenge continues to be changing the attitudes of those we deal with. Each opportunity we get to do a project is an opportunity that allows us to showcase our skills so we can show the positive attributes of a minority-owned firm.[15]

What are the ways business owners of color have to accommodate Eurocultural capital when they're trying to build "mainstream" businesses?[16] What kind of capital is required to buy your way into doing business downtown, and what kind of family culture provides an economic advantage to entrepreneurs? As with Bell's theory of Afrocentric learning styles, Stevenson and Renard present a picture of black family culture. Quoting Boykin and Toms, they suggest nine aspects of African American culture: spirituality, harmony, movement, verve, affect, communalism, expressive individualism, orality, and social time perspective. Particularly in a business context, many of these aspects are distinct from the European American culture of rationalism/cognition, competition, fitting in, and respect for time. Trying to fit into both is stressful for black entrepreneurs. And yet, in order to succeed, it is often necessary to try to fulfill both the role of the family and the role of the business owner. Admittedly, it is difficult for any business owner trying to maintain some semblance of family life while growing a business, but it is doubly difficult when the family culture is, in many ways, in opposition to the business culture.[17]

> Architecture is a little different. It's even an elitist profession for working-class white folks. I believe it's more about class than about race in the profession. Class is very important in architecture. The worst thing that happens to young African Americans is to think it's all about racism. The Bush presidency epitomizes that. (Thaddeus Collins)

Class remains one of the great hidden variables that lead to success in the United States.[18] As discussed by Roscigno and Ainsworth-Darnel, both social and cultural capital can be inherited.[19] They can also be earned, a process which often starts as soon as attendance in school begins. However, not unlike economic capital, it is difficult to earn cultural capital if you do not already have it. Family background is extremely important as a source of this capital. While it is possible to earn your own social capital, it is a difficult undertaking.[20] As we get older, the influence of our parents diminishes, but family ties and culture continue to influence how far we can get. Blacks continue to be at a disadvantage for amassing cultural and social capital.

Capital can be spent only in very narrowly defined settings; like with foreign currency, we can spend it only in places where it is accepted. The economic structure of this country is built on the premise of privilege, which plays out in racial terms. "Racial classification systems reflect prevailing views of race, thereby establishing groups that are presumed to be 'natural.' These constructed racial categories then serve as the basis for allocating resources. . . . Wealth is significant because it provides a cumulative advantage to those who have it."[21] We like to think we live in a classless society, but the additional social and cultural capital earned in families with more education provides a powerful model that is assimilated and carried into adulthood. Seeing it is possible to do what you want to do can mean the difference between professional success and just getting by.

One of the owners of a large firm in the South told me,

My father was a great guy. He was a business person, a sales guy who rose to the top in a corporate setting. He lived in Paris for ten years. Because of him, I could see it was possible for me. My mother was a teacher, and later an educational administrator. My family has been college-educated for four generations, so I have been taught to value education and excellence. (Rob Green)

Social learning theory, advanced by Bandura in the 1970s, teaches that all behavior is learned, and it is learned most effectively by observation of others.[22] This is obvious in the stories successful architects tell about their parents. Although all the architects in this book have created successful careers, those who grew up in families with a higher socioeconomic status—more economic assets, better-educated parents, higher income neighborhoods—went into the profession with a raised expectation about the prospects for their own success.

A genial man who is both genteel and informal in his manner, [Max] Bond has thrived as an architect, he says, because of "a lot of luck." But it is clear that mediocrity of any kind was unacceptable in the Bond family, where his father, an educator and university president, pushed him hard to achieve.

"We had a funny relationship," Bond says of his late father. "It was a good relationship particularly in terms of these high expectations. . . . But the difficult side is you're always expected to do better."

The Bonds, it seems, had made a tradition of plowing right through obstacles. At a time of deep segregation and racism, J. Max Bond Sr., for instance, earned his doctorate in sociology and economics in 1934 from the University of Southern California. And Bond's mother, Ruth Clement Bond (who turned 100 in May), majored in literature during undergraduate work at Northwestern University in Illinois.[23]

On a more contemporary note, a young East Coast architect told a story about how he learned the importance of networking. Because he learned the process as a child, it has been easier for him to put into practice in his own firm.

A lot of the institutions in DC support black professionals. Howard was a breeding ground for top black intellectuals. My parents both went to Dunbar High School. There were four colored high schools, and there were limited opportunities at the time. There were concentrated pockets of black professionals. Because there is a long tradition of support for black professionals, there is fertile ground here for me as an architect.

My father graduated in the '50s from a prestigious private law school and went to the Midwest. He did what was necessary to expand his social network. He would start every day with exactly twenty business cards, so at the end of the day he would know how many new contacts he made. He joined organizations like the NAACP and the Urban League. He became the chair of the state civil rights commission. In 1978, Jimmy Carter made him a federal judge.

You need to join organizations and hit the pavement. Pretty soon, phone calls start to come back to you. You have to establish relationships rather than chasing individual projects. To build a practice, you have to develop a long-term strategy and stick with it. (Roland Davis)

Davis learned from his father's experience that he would have to spend a lot of energy building social networks and getting his firm's name known. It was easier for him in Washington because he already felt connected in ways that he could not accomplish in New York.

The environment and the curriculum of architectural training present difficult challenges for black students, who represent such a small minority of the student population. However, those who went into school and into practice with more social capital possess a wider variety of options for dealing with the institutional disparities. They were armed with both examples and knowledge from their family cultures that enabled them to see what success could look like for them; they had obtained the social and cultural capital that enabled them to use that knowledge in building a career.

I did my undergrad at a state university and my master's at MIT. My grandfather was a painter and an educator, and I was always creative. I discovered architecture at fourteen or fifteen in drafting and design classes in high school. I never met an architect until college.

I am involved in community organizations and on boards and things. I'm on the board of the Chamber of Commerce, and on the statewide Chamber; I've served on the Arts Council and the board of the Center for Visual Arts. Politically, I've been involved with candidates who are involved in the selection of public works projects. Being in the South and on the East Coast, there is good black representation across the board. (Rob Green)

There is a huge difference between believing you can be successful and having spent your childhood being told you cannot. All of the architects who talked about their educational experiences mentioned a champion; for some it was an art teacher, or a school counselor; for others it was a parent. That support person brought connections to additional social networks.

Mitchell provides an interesting commentary on the contribution family socioeconomic status can make to an architect's practice. When he speaks of mothers, he is speaking literally about the families of some of the best-known architects.

> Black architects instinctively know the importance of early commissions from "mother" as the starting point for establishing "design" personas and getting noticed. So they are inclined to suspect that white or Jewish architects have an infinitely better chance at starting out with "mother" type commissions. . . . Black architects spawned from the still evolving and financially marginal black lower middle-to-middle classes rarely have such "mothers." Black "mothers" are rarely capable of commissioning retreat houses on budgets that allow for publishable quality "delight" architecture.[24]

Many white architects also did not have wealthy mothers and may believe they have had the same struggles as black architects. It is true that most architects, irrespective of ethnicity, do not have a shot at becoming stars.[25] However, the fact remains *none* of the most celebrated architects in the United States is black.

Nelson Norton put it this way:

> We're one of the only ethnic groups in this profession who have gone so long without specific champions. *Architectural Digest* did a spread on twenty-five deans of American architecture. There wasn't one black face in the group. No one knows us; African American names don't appear; we're not recognized to any degree. They're building an African American museum in Washington, DC. No African American name has been mentioned as the architect—everyone downtown will be fine if an African American *participates*.
>
> We have design talents that sometimes aren't showcased in our firms. We do good work and try to make a living, but we didn't have the parents and the support to do the high-end design. There wasn't the kind of money or exposure in our communities to do the glamorous work.
>
> The industry thinks we don't have it, but we do. (Nelson Norton)

The great frustration for black architects is that they can never get around the systemic racism in the profession. They will never have enough social or cultural capital to be asked to "join the club." They have business savvy and design prowess, and they are still overlooked for prize commissions. Given that reality, they use what they have and put their talents, experience, and networks to use for their firms.

Knowing the impact of family role models on the ability of entrepreneurs to succeed, I asked Edward Lamont whether he knew any business owners when he was growing up. At first he said no, but as he took a minute to think about it, he broke into a grin and said, "Uncle Skinny."

> My father worked as a presser in the cleaners. He left when I was five. Ulysses James, my Uncle Skinny, my aunt's first husband, owned a pool hall/barber shop/candy shop. I hung out there after school. There were little card games in the back and a boarding house upstairs. Uncle Skinny owned the building. I was a "latchkey" kid, so I would go there after school. I would sweep the floor, rack the balls, and fill the soda machine. He paid me twenty-five cents. I'd give it back to him for ice cream. I guess I really did learn something from Uncle Skinny about running a business.
>
> My aunt's second husband, Uncle Henry, was the political boss of southwest Detroit. He was in the UAW [United Automobile Workers]. He was the godfather in southwest Detroit. On New Year's, we'd all be together, the six of us and my cousins. The five of us all went to college, and my five cousins all went to college. Some of the kids we went to school with died of drug overdoses; some died in Vietnam. The ones who came back all had PTSD [post-traumatic stress disorder]. A few of those kids stayed and worked at GM or Pontiac or Miller Brass and did okay, or else they left. It reminds me how important my family was in keeping us focused and on the right track. (Edward Lamont)

Having successful role models and family expectations of success propelled Lamont and his siblings and cousins to academic and, later, professional accomplishment. The importance of the family influence has remained with Lamont.

Although role models make a difference in how well we can envision our success, for black architects, the fact of structural inequality in the profession remains a barrier. All the architects I talked to told me the reason they do not get private projects is their lack of connections to corporate decision makers. The social and cultural capital earned in college and in the process of getting licensed is never enough to overcome the constraints of ethnicity. Twenty-first century racism is powerful because the bar is invisible to those whose way is not blocked. The inability to see the restraints enables whites to believe our race problems are behind us. That view absolves whites of any responsibility for making change; it is a sophisticated kind of oppression that allows for a simplistic view by those seemingly unaffected. In the meantime, we are missing out on a cultural and visual richness that could be had if there were more diversity in our built environment.

NETWORKS IN THE PROFESSION

A lot of architects provide referrals to other architects. It is one more way black architects are kept out of the most innovative design jobs. The jobs that garner the most public attention, or the covers of monthly architecture magazines, are not awarded to black firms. However, despite their lack of access to private work, these firms still need to rely on networks for commissions. They learn early to rely on each other as much as they can.

> The founders of this firm were part of the original cadre of new firms in the early '60s. They got started doing public work, or they had friends working in public works, people they'd gone to school with, who let them know about new jobs. (Thaddeus Collins)

The importance of social networks is borne out by the following stories of what can happen if a firm loses an important connection. Even though they are still equally capable of doing exactly the same kind of work they may have just completed, when their personal connections are severed, so are their opportunities for repeat work.

> We did a headquarters building for a big corporate client in Virginia. A black woman I had known twenty-five years earlier helped put us in touch with the decision makers. After the building was done, she moved out of the construction department. After she moved, we didn't even get asked to submit; we couldn't even make it to the short list. We came in $3 million under budget and on time, and then we couldn't even make it to the short list. We need an advocate at the table. That building was the only major corporate headquarters building designed by black architects. The development community in DC know they're not hiring black architects. (Nicholas Rose)

Occasionally, black firms do get corporate work, but it tends to be small, low-risk projects. It is difficult to counter the perception that black firms are not capable of completing major projects.

> Clients want me to be involved, but they don't realize what it takes to manage a project. We worked for one of the big downtown banks for a while, but it only lasted as long as the vice chairman who hired us was there. Corporate clients were giving the firm small projects that left the clients at no risk from hiring a black-owned firm—like they thought we wouldn't be able to do the work. The firm has the ongoing need to get past the ethnic community in terms of projects. (Edward Lamont)

The profession is volatile for all firms. Work flow is uncertain and hard to plan, and getting new work is always an arduous task. Because black architects do not get chosen for highly visible projects, it can be even more challenging for them to prove they are capable of a broader range.

I've been twenty years in this firm. Right now I have a lot of work. It's not always this busy. Sometimes we have no work. Right now, there are thirteen of us; usually it's between eight and ten. We still do some health facilities. We also do residential work. We did a renovation of an apartment/hotel building. The next five projects were like the first. That's what people can see, so that's what they identify you with. It makes it hard to get new kinds of work. (Sharon Young)

It is frustrating, annoying, and marginalizing to know a firm is capable and innovative and still unable to get new and different work. Black architects understand the power the AIA has in the profession. They also know how little support they have received from the organization to make change.

Nothing's changed. The AIA doesn't want it to change. We're busy but it's not the work we want to do. It's not about me, it's about opening the door. There are a lot of talented architects who will never have a chance. I don't like it that I don't get hired because of how I look. What if GSA had never hired a Jewish architect? We don't have political clout, and neither does our community. (Nicholas Rose)

The fact that the AIA is working on a member survey with the express intention of addressing diversity issues is a hopeful sign. It is possible that the demographic shifts across the country will encourage the organization to do more in the near future to create a more multicultural profession. In the meantime, blacks and other architects of color are doing what they can to increase their markets.

Sometimes the social networks black architects have are useful in unexpected ways. Thad Collins graduated from Columbia and had access to a useful network of successful firms. That and his abilities got him an interview, but his mother's contacts with the airline baggage handlers got his interview materials to the meeting on time.

I had just graduated and was starting to look for a job. I wanted to live in San Francisco or New Orleans. Ida Karmie was an Israeli architect and an instructor at Columbia. She recommended me to Moshe Safdie.[26] At that time, he was spending two weeks a month in Montreal and two weeks in Israel. I found out at the last minute that he was coming through town, so we set up a meeting. I interviewed in a coffee shop at Kennedy Airport. My mother shipped my portfolio to Kennedy with the baggage folks, who were friends of the family.

He hired me to work on the Cold Stream New Town in Baltimore and work with the community. I worked for eighteen months with Safdie in Baltimore. He was totally personable; it was a great job. (Thaddeus Collins)

Collins's experience provides an important reminder about the nature of social networks. We each have a unique set of connections to other people; we can never know exactly when or how those connections will serve our needs. One of the frustrating issues for black architects is that although their personal networks may be broad, their store of social capital is often not the right denomination for engendering commissions.

As Sharon Sutton wrote:

Most of us [black architects] receive little mentoring or social support, but carry a large burden to participate in mentoring and a variety of other community service activities. Most of us overachieve in the hopes of being accepted while managing daily situations in which we are unduly scrutinized, treated as inferior, or openly harassed.[27]

In social networks, perception is of paramount importance. Within architecture, where design is so highly prized, being able to publicize your design prowess is one measure of success.[28] Not having publishable work is seen as an impediment to firms being able to get their work seen by a broad spectrum of both peers and potential clients.

It's a matter of how we're perceived. We're not recognized for the talent we have. If your peer group hasn't recognized you, you're just another firm in a pile of firms with qualifications. There are lots of good firms. We're not on the magazine covers, so our architect peers don't recognize our design talent. (Donald Nelson)

Nelson's observations clarify the importance of networks within the profession. Clients and architects often rely on other architects to provide referrals for joint venturing and for specific types of projects. If black architects are not able to provide their colleagues with examples of their work, they are unlikely to come to mind when those same people are called on to make recommendations for project architects.

Our work is not publishable; we don't have access to publications. We started to design an award-winning school, and the school district wouldn't let us. The district has this cookie-cutter approach to schools. Sixty-five percent of the students in this school district are minority students, so they figure it doesn't matter what the schools are like. The secret is not in doing the work, it's in getting the commissions. (James Patterson)

All the architects I talked to told me when they can get the work, they can do it. The problem over and over again is being visible enough to be chosen, or even being visible enough to learn of projects that weren't being bid competitively.

One reason I left New York City was that all you had to do was look to see who was getting the significant projects. The same group of fifteen to twenty was always on the short list. It has something to do with talent, but more to do with relationships. Coming to DC enabled me to be a bigger fish in a smaller pond. After a few months, it was easier to establish an identity. Washington, DC, has a significant percentage of professional African Americans. It's unlike Boston, Philadelphia, New York City, etc. It was not founded on industry; it was always a white-collar place. In DC, "loft" apartments are not really lofts. (Roland Davis)

WORK DOWNTOWN: MAKING CONNECTIONS

The tenacity that gets people to and through architecture school has to be retained and nourished to get work. Client development requires establishing relationships with developers and others who hire architects. It is most successful when approached as a long-term process apart from specific projects. However, it is difficult for black-owned firms to get people in their networks to make the "right" professional connections. Even when they have made connections downtown, they are rarely in touch with the decision makers.

"We've heard such good things about your firm." That's what the corporate folks say to us when we try to get business from them. They never follow up and come through with jobs. So we've learned you just need to be in people's faces. (Edward Lamont)

Other social theorists have emphasized cultural capital in the form of educational credentials possessed by members of the upper and middle classes, which become economic resources for individual economic advancement. Clearly there are class issues involved in the profession of architecture. By its very nature, architectural plans would never be executed without the requisite capital. Even given the theories on the intergenerational transfer of social and cultural capital,[29] whether a black architect is the first member of the family to graduate from college or the fourth generation of college graduates, the struggles are often the same.

At one firm, I asked a lot of questions about the kind of work they were doing and how they went through the process of deciding what jobs to bid. As they talked about their work and the jobs they were thinking of bidding, it was clear it is very difficult for them to get jobs without having connections, and that means maintaining connections in the community[30] and downtown. The competition for architectural services is intense, especially in what remains a relatively depressed economy. Even though black-owned firms are unlikely to get premiere design jobs, being connected to the decision makers, both downtown and in the community, can make the difference between being "short-listed" or not.[31]

The professional networks that create and connect to work downtown are generally closed to black architects. Even after years of doing all the appropriate business development activities—serving on boards, donating to philanthropic organizations, and playing in celebrity golf tournaments—the work is not theirs.

In her *Washington Post* article about Devrouax and Purnell, a firm in Washington, DC, Maryann Haggerty writes:

> In the fat '80s, when there were "cranes on every corner," he [Paul Devrouax] recalled, "We tried to position ourselves as a competent design firm that can do architecture for clients. Period. Not as an African American firm."
>
> He said, "We went to the parties, we tried to network as much as we could. We knew the same developers—we served on the boards with them."
>
> Purnell picked up the conversation. "We still do those things, although it hasn't resulted in doing work for those people. . . . I couldn't understand, and I still can't. I look at K Street, and I look at the handful of architects responsible. There's nothing there that impresses me, that says you had to go to certain firms."
>
> Said Devrouax, "It's difficult to put a finger on it, to say this is it. But the fact is, we all had to go to school, we all had to pass that architect's exam. If you look at it, there could be some maybe inherent racism in the profession."[32]

Given the reality of the profession, and the overwhelming evidence of racism in the form of blatant exclusion, Devrouax's comment seems the height of diplomacy. One of the issues I have considered throughout the process of doing this research is what happens to the black-owned firms that are not at the top of their game. The majority of the professionals I interviewed have been elected to the College of Fellows of the AIA, one of the highest honors the profession bestows, and they still have these stories.

The impact of corporate exclusion varies with geography. In parts of the South, particularly in cities with black mayors past or present, black architects often have better access to municipal and regional administrators. Around the country, there are cities, such as Chicago and Boston, where black-owned firms are more visible and have a higher probability of getting work downtown than in cities with small black populations such as Wichita or Seattle.

The lack of access to visible projects, both corporate and civic, is due in part to the inherent structure of the profession, and in part to institutional racism. The entrenchment of money and power is nowhere more apparent than in architecture. The economic system that facilitates great concentrations of wealth, coupled with the influences provided by social networks, leaves black architects with limited entry to projects downtown. Some readers will, no doubt, argue this is a problem for small white-owned firms, too. That is true, and it is one of the issues that make it hard for white architects to appreciate the impact of racism in the profession.

Despite the frustration of lacking access to decision makers downtown, black architects continue to strive to build as broad a network as possible. Even given the geographic differences, one way to attempt to dismantle the barriers is to become visible: volunteering on committees and getting to know decision makers; serving on boards and representing the organization at functions downtown; and getting active in trade associations such as the AIA. It takes a lot of discipline to maintain this level of activity, especially when the returns are so long in coming. The fact that architects love the profession seems to make all this effort worthwhile.

However, frustrations and rebuffs remain. Even in Washington, DC, with its large middle-class black population, black architects are unable to land large commissions.

There's nothing we've done we can photograph. A big part of the problem is in corporate America. If you look at the Fortune 1000, 100, or 50, who makes the decisions about building? It happens in the board room. New buildings, new factories—the design decisions are made so far in advance of any middle management decisions. The names of architects get passed around in the boardroom, but there's nobody to speak for us in the boardroom. The architects who get chosen are the ones who play golf with the chair or the board members, or if he gets enough publicity in the popular press, like an article in the style section. There's no one to speak for us on the golf course. We have the same issues with government. Think about it.

Let me explain it this way. Let's pretend you're a white architect. You got your bachelor's degree from a state school, and you got your M.Arch. from the same school, or maybe you even got your advanced degree from an Ivy League school.

You're licensed to practice in the state where you live, and you're also licensed in one or two other states, places where you have family, or places you like to play golf. All the other licensed architects in your office are licensed in more than one state. You've even had the opportunity to do some work in other places. Of course, most of it was government work, you know, schools, a sewage substation, maybe a remodel of a small office building.

There's a big project you really want that's coming up in your hometown. It will be a large, profitable commission, very prestigious, and will get a lot of attention from the local community and the regional press. You know your firm can do the job, and you know you're going to have to get political and develop a strategy for how to win the competition.

You know it would be useful if you could find a way to play golf with the developer. He's a great guy, and he belongs to a club with the best course in town. You're pragmatic enough to know that's probably not going to happen, so you try to figure out if there's another way to get his attention—the United Way dinner, maybe, or the Chamber of Commerce cocktail party.

There are two meetings you have to attend to find out how to get on the list of firms that will be asked to compete. The first meeting is a joint meeting with the city council, the developer, and five or six other architects. You try to get as much information about the project—funding, siting, schedule—as you can before you walk into the meeting. No one is really talking much about it, but you're able to pick up a few details you hope will come in handy.

It's the day of the first meeting. You've left calls for everyone you can think of who might be associated with the project. A couple of them called you back, but they did that mostly because they've known you so many years it would be embarrassing if they didn't at least return the call. They didn't really give you any useful information.

You walk into the meeting and find a place to sit towards the front of the room. By the way, everyone on the city council is black. The developer and his senior management, who are sitting in front of you, they're black, too. Oh, and the contracting agent for the city planning office, she's also black.

Everyone is polite and says hello and asks about your partners or your wife or something to indicate they recognize you. As you look around the room, you know they've all been playing golf together, and you can imagine that when they're on the back nine they're laughing because they've all gotten calls from you, and you were behaving like you really thought you had any chance to get this project.

As you look around the room, it becomes completely clear to you that you are not going to get this job, and the primary reason you're not going to get it is because of how you look. Simply put, you're not black. How does that make you feel? (Nicholas Rose)

Rose went on to talk about how it makes him feel to know most of the downtown projects his firm wants will go to white firms. He stays active in the downtown community because he knows at some point it will pay off. In the meantime, he is clear that they do not get the opportunities to live up to their potential.

It is slightly easier for bigger firms to get some visibility and credibility downtown, but they have different issues. The owner of a large firm in the Midwest emphasized the importance of connections. Volunteer work in his community has benefited the firm, but they work nationally; it is much more difficult for this firm to make useful connections outside their community.

Social networks are essential. There's an interesting dynamic around social networks. I am involved as part of the community, particularly in the broader community. I serve on nonprofit boards, business boards, university boards, and alumni boards. I do those things for two reasons: I want to support my alma mater and the business community and certain social issues I want to support, *and* there are people I might associate with on those boards who have positions elsewhere in the community. Often they are important decision makers. I support both political parties, and my church, and other organizations.

Our profile in the community is strengthened by me working on those boards. The difficulty is across the nation, going to a region in which they haven't seen a firm like us. A lot of decision makers perceive African American firms as 15 percent participants to meet diversity goals, and not necessarily because they're the best at the project.

The most difficult thing for a minority business is this: if you're looking to do small community projects, your network is fine the way it is. Given time, those connections will produce relationships that will be good for business. When it comes to bigger commissions—the classroom buildings, the courthouse, the big public buildings—your network needs to be broader. There's a lack of minorities in that broader network.

With a neighborhood park, or a new development in the black community, you'll have a peppering of minority individuals as part of the decision-making team. But on bigger projects, my competition may have a stronger network in that community than I do. In other words, in the places where I have solid connections, there are other minorities. In the places I want the firm to be, there aren't enough minorities involved to influence decisions. We need more minorities to impact how the big projects move ahead. (Donald Nelson)

It is discouraging, and not particularly surprising, to realize the struggle for corporate work has gone on unchanged for a very long time.[33] The design of a high-rise building was elusive even for Paul Williams. His practice brought him fame and prosperity, but even he could not count on his networks to deliver a significant, downtown commission.

As was the case throughout the country from the late 19th century on, however, and certainly in Los Angeles, it was the large, well-established architectural firms with close ties to the business community that almost always generated the large, lucrative commissions. Though Williams did obtain a number of smaller commercial and public commissions from the mid-twenties on, it was not until the late thirties that he began to receive an increasing number of commercial and government commissions. Then, after World War II, his firm continued to obtain business and government commissions, although he never received one for any of Los Angeles's major high-rise buildings.[34]

Small to medium-sized architecture firms of all ethnicities, and even large black-owned firms, have trouble competing for high-end work. What Stephens refers to as the "Favored Circle" is a microcosm of the larger culture. The white gentlemen's profession continues to reward white men.[35] In an article about the rare exception, when a black firm *was* selected to do a corporate headquarters building, the feelings expressed are justifiably mixed. When faced with the reality of doing *one* corporate project, why should competent, highly trained professionals be expected to celebrate? Their skills are of the highest caliber, whether or not they receive corporate commissions. As I read and heard the same stories, repeatedly, from all black architects, I was even more respectful of their tenacity in managing not only their firms, but also, for the most part, their attitudes. Cognitively, I understand perfectly well energy directed toward anger uses energy that could more productively be used elsewhere, but emotionally I find it difficult to imagine the cumulative effect of career development repressed because of skin color.[36]

Maryann Haggerty describes the architect selection process for a prized corporate commission:

> The firm was among about two dozen interviewed to design the two buildings. "We made sure that we included women-owned firms and minority-owned firms," said Stokes [the construction manager for the agency–owner], an African American who has known Purnell for years. "We saw this as an opportunity for us to expand our horizons and be very inclusive. . . . It could only be a better project if we were more inclusive, looking at all types of firms rather than the top five or Famous Five."
>
> Devrouax and Purnell say that they try to give clients more work than they expect, and did so to get the . . . job. They even put together a computer-assisted-design presentation that showed what their building would look like from all angles, including from a helicopter and from the . . . road.
>
> "It was a great presentation," Stokes said. The firm brought not only its computer models, but also at least 20 team members, she said. "We picked them because they had the breadth of experience over many other companies," she said.

Purnell said, "We had to compete, but we knew the playing field was level. If the playing field is level, we can produce, and the building is a testament to that."

Charles I. Bryant, a principal in Bryant & Bryant, another prominent D.C. African American architecture firm, places much of the blame on how clients pick architects. "Good architecture opportunities are few and far between," he said. "Whenever a good commission comes along, that commission is heavily sought after. All the linkages of the most capable parties come into play, social linkages, business linkages. It can be a tremendous advantage to belong to the same club as an important client."[37]

WORK IN THE 'HOOD: HOW COMMUNITY WORK ENHANCES AND RESTRAINS GROWTH

While many black architects bemoan the fact they do not have access to wealthy, white clients, there is another view of how black architects need to be networking. The focus on commissions downtown is understandable for architects who have been trained in the Eurocentric tradition, but it can also be seen as a putdown of black communities. Nelson Norton is clear that continuing to face the frustration of trying to do design work for the majority community is not the best use of resources—economic or emotional. He believes black architects have overlooked the potential of black America to provide ample connections and commissions.

> The crisis in black architecture comes from their disconnection from black America. They don't do the networking with black America, they don't understand how to leverage the power it will give you. They don't understand that's how Max Bond did it. Max is civil rights royalty. It's no accident he's successful. It's a result of connections to black America, using political connections to black America. He's not some disconnected guy. When he got out of school, and white firms were closing the door in his face, he went to Ghana and worked for the new Nkrumah government.
>
> Black architects have to learn this lesson and how to utilize it. What's happening to Max today is evolutionary. Blacks can't just sit on the sidelines and complain. (Nelson Norton)

A discussion about black architects working in the community is both a thoroughly straightforward and an extremely complex proposition. In the economic development world, working in communities of color generally means doing projects in distressed, often forgotten neighborhoods where searching for funding is part of the project. In architecture, working in the 'hood usually means commissions from cash-strapped not-for-profits, but may mean black-owned businesses or developers in Prince Georges County, Chicago, Atlanta, or other metropolitan areas. Most of the stories in this section refer to work in low-income communities of color.

In these neighborhoods, there is little exposure to architecture. The firms working there have the job of education *and* project development. They must help communities overcome the sense of helplessness that often pervades neighborhoods overlooked on one hand and exploited on the other.

In black communities, there is little sense that residents have any influence over the long-range planning of their built environment. Lacking political or economic power, these communities tend to view the built environment as a fact of life beyond their influence, controlled by government or outside developers and profiteers.[38] Architects who work in the 'hood are mindful of both the challenges and the opportunities for making change and empowering residents. The architects who work in these communities experience both gratification and frustrations.

Like the struggles over government work, doing projects in the community presents its own set of challenges. Black architects recognize the importance of doing work that is appropriate for the community. This is always a goal in architectural projects, but the work in low-income communities presents a particular set of considerations. In terms of design and construction, the reality of scarce resources for long-term maintenance dictates many of the parameters.[39]

> The biggest problem working with poor clients is they expect architects to be a whiz on codes. They can't fathom the importance of design. The question becomes how to build it well with low maintenance. This is the key to infrastructure in low-income communities. They don't have money for upkeep. Even though condos and co-ops cost less to buy initially than other kinds of housing, a lot of people still can't afford them. It makes it tough for people to become homeowners. (Leroy Vaughan)

There is a certain irony in the relationship between black architects and work in the community. On one hand, these design professionals are clear how little exposure residents of low-income communities and communities of color have to architecture. Many of them serve as mentors for black youth and are involved in school activities to give the profession a face in these neighborhoods. On the other hand, there is a kind of exasperation with the lack of understanding of the value—aesthetic, emotional, and economic—of good design.

Inner-city kids have utilitarian buildings. We need to introduce a vision of other kinds of spaces. Our people have no exposure to architecture; they have no concept.

Even when people mature and start businesses in black communities, there is no value placed on design. They're not aware of whether the plastic laminate matches the walls, etc. People with no vision have no appreciation of what makes a great space. It doesn't take a lot of money. Great architecture doesn't have to have a huge budget. It's knowing how to put things together. (Lewis Thomas)

Many architects believe the inaccessibility of design in low-income communities and communities of color is a civil rights issue. "Knowing how to put things together" is what design has come to be about in the United States. It is not a lack of will that precludes aesthetic considerations in these neighborhoods, but a lack of knowledge, time, and resources. A long history of residential segregation, lower property values, and therefore, diminished access to capital keeps poor people from "good" design.[40]

There's a duality between African and American. We move between the irony and the exaltation of the duality, the amorphic form versus the rectilinear. The actual space/form/interior design/interior decoration starts with an education of us and then of the client. The client program and budget have to come together to make it work. Cultural capital needs to be more completely developed. The struggle for civil rights continues in the form of both environmental and aesthetic justice. (Leroy Vaughan)

W. E. B. Du Bois first described the duality of being African American. There is a "twoness" about being black and being American that is keenly felt by black architects. Trained in a Eurocentric academy, they are left to find ways to reconcile their culture of origin with their education.[41]

Gentrification is the term used to describe a particular demographic shift in central-city neighborhoods. It is caused by an influx of more affluent, generally white, buyers looking for close-in property at reasonable prices. The forces of institutional racism have left these areas with lower property values than surrounding neighborhoods. The process results in long-time residents, usually people of color and often low-income, being slowly pushed out by rising real estate values and increasing taxes.

The issues of gentrification further widen the gap between design and not-design. The changes in black communities can have adverse impacts on black architects; the social networks that existed in the old neighborhood shifted dramatically when long-time residents were priced out of their homes. When black architects did projects in the community, the work was discounted by the profession and got no attention. Work in the same neighborhoods, when done by white architects in the process of gentrification, suddenly became trendy and "important."

> The Harlem Renaissance [the period from the end of World War I to the mid-1930s] led to the creation of the HUDC, the Harlem Urban Development Corporation. This community has gone from a bedroom, transient, absentee-owner, no-services community to a neighborhood with homeowning middle-class residents that would attract services. The change enabled some people to be part of the system. It put the area back on the map as a safe place, a decent place. After all, planning is driven by demand. HUDC made sure black contractors, architects, etc. were involved. When HUDC's power was usurped, majority firms moved in and black firms were marginalized.
>
> The sacrifice of doing community work is that there's an economic trade-off. You can't publish this stuff. The people who get invited are the people who do the sexy work. As a result, we're getting stereotyped as architects who aren't capable of doing the publishable work. On the other hand, the churches are as high end as possible. (Wendell Marshall)

In some ways, it would be a relief if the difficulty of finding design in the 'hood occurred just because the residents were not interested. It becomes a civil rights issue precisely as a result of that lack of choice. It falls to black architects to create opportunities for exposure to design. Edward Lamont talked to me about his experience with the lack of understanding that the profession has no real presence in most black communities:

> When I was at the AIA Fellows reception in San Francisco, the black mayor, Willie Brown, came up and asked me, "What building did you do downtown?" When he found out I hadn't done a hotel, he was disappointed. He's the *mayor*, and he doesn't have a clue. The idea that architects do high rises—there's not a lot of understanding about what architects do, and very little in the black community. Black architects need to be a dark-skinned white person. (Edward Lamont)

In a place with a small black population, it can be time consuming to stay connected to the community and continue to seek to broaden firm ties to people downtown. One of the ways Lamont connects to the community is through volunteering with one of the black men's service groups. He feels this is an important activity for him to maintain; it keeps him tied to the community, and he believes the organization provides a good mentoring opportunity for the younger black business owners.

Black men are programmed to self-destruct. It's so hard to get black men to work together. It's more visible here because the community is smaller, and so problems are more visible. The big guys don't want to be associated with this organization—the big real estate developers, car dealers, and professional services firms. Their attitude seems to be "Don't let those people grab onto your coattails. They'll just drag you down." The black culture is a culture of community, which makes it tough for black businesses. Those successful businesses that are willing to stick around are expected to support the community. It's like the overcrowded lifeboat. The way to make that work in a small community is to increase the number of black businesses. Many black entrepreneurs just move to the suburbs and don't look back. It's like the movie *Barbershop*: "can't you just give me a free haircut?" (Edward Lamont)

Black culture is focused on community and extended family. Nonminority-owned businesses are also faced with tough management and project decisions: Should I hire my brother-in-law? Can I afford to donate to the local school? How much volunteer time can I allow my employees during working hours? And so on. The fallout from these decisions somehow does not seem to spread as far as it does for black-owned businesses. Especially in a small community, the support, or lack of support, by a business can mean the difference between getting jobs in the community and being snubbed.

One of the ways black architects can get visible is by doing volunteer work. Developing contacts can be an effective long-term strategy for business development and is an important part of a good marketing strategy. Often, however, black architects find they are inordinately reliant on network-building to get new work, and also kept out of networks where decisions about hiring architects are made.

I do the marketing, and we have someone who's being hired to do some outside marketing. We're signing up with agencies, and we get some pro bono work. I'm on the board of the AIA, and I go on site reviews. We're just in the process of developing a marketing effort; we're working on a couple developers.

The more everyone [black firms] grows, the more we grow. Our constituents come to us because they feel whatever we do will benefit them from a cultural, financial, and economic standpoint, and also from a realistic standpoint. The black network has relied on itself, from slavery to today. (Wendell Marshall)

Despite the difficulties of continuing to do work in black neighborhoods, those whose early training included community work continue to be involved. They learned the lessons of staying connected to the community. Since his early training in the CDCs, working on design projects in the community has been vital to

Edward Lamont. The fact the black community where he lives is small is both advantageous and a liability for the firm; everyone knows everyone, and a lot of them are related.[42]

Ignoring a request for architectural assistance, or even charitable contributions, is simply not an option. These requests can cost us time and money, and occasionally they may lead to contracts, but usually we have to do it anyway. Currently we're working in a couple different locations for one of the evangelical churches; they have thirteen churches in the region. Urban renewal is encroaching on the big urban churches, and they need master plans; they need to figure out what they are going to do with their property. We were hired to help with the process.

We're also doing a day-care project for one of the other churches. My wife went to school with one of the daughters of the day-care folks, so it was relatively easy for us to get the job. Our day-care consultant was already a known quantity, so the clients expected a good relationship. When we've got the connections, we get the jobs. (Edward Lamont)

The black churches, which are an integral part of the community, are an excellent source of commissions for black architects. One of the unintended consequences of the Jim Crow laws was the development of black churches as the center of African American life. They continue to provide connections to the community, and often allow black architecture firms opportunities to design in ways they otherwise cannot.

One of our specialties is churches, almost all African American. The work is sexy because it allows us, from a social standpoint, to experiment with form and function. These churches are community centers that have a great impact on social and spiritual balance and impact on the people they serve. We are advocates for the challenges they have with city officials, like parking, height, and bulk. Some of these buildings were inherited and some were built by congregations; now they need meeting rooms, work rooms, etc. They've grown because they serve the community. They are very complex little cities on their own. Finding churches that appreciate our services is very important. We do this kind of work all over New York City and into the suburban counties.

The advantage of working on churches is, because of programmatic needs, you can work closely with them to get a project, as opposed to agencies that already have a defined program. The financial relationships are good, but they're also going through what we're going through because they don't have pools of funds. They have big needs, but it takes the churches a long time to raise money. They have to do it exogenously. Commercial and housing projects have funding already in place. The churches don't have the experience they need to find capital. (Wendell Marshall)

Black firms rely on and delight in these community connections. The networks they develop in communities of color serve them well as a source of commissions and cultural gratification. Some prominent black institutions, however, have been less sensitive about connecting with black architects. Given the importance of social networks, and the visibility of major institutions in the community, the politics of hiring can raise the hackles of black architects. They are reliant on those organizations; when they are shut out of places they would expect to find friends, it can be frustrating and provocative.

> The president of Howard University came from SUNY-Buffalo. He brought a couple people with him from SUNY. He had a guy from SUNY doing facilities. He was a white guy, and he brought in his white friends to do the new law library at Howard. After they hired a white architect, they went and got a small black firm to do a little piece.
> There are more black architects in DC than anywhere else in the world. My network, the folks who hire me, wouldn't consider hiring SOM. (Nicholas Rose)[43]

Rose said he would expect the administration of the premier black educational institution to understand the importance of hiring professional service providers from their own community. His fury was exacerbated by the fact that 36 percent of the licensed black architects in 2005 had degrees from the Howard architecture school.[44]

Farther north, I was told about another example of an institution that is located in a black community, but has maintained almost total independence from the residents. There are many communities, especially in the Northeast, where prestigious educational institutions situated alongside or in the middle of black communities remain aloof. Politically, these neighborhoods do not have enough power to confront the institutions in any effective ways. Leroy Vaughan has put considerable effort into trying to build relationships between the university and the community.

> The City needs to do a lot more to support poor people and provide housing. The university's having to come out of their shell because they need to expand to the north. The community will have more say while they're making the transition. The administration will probably make one or two significant gestures. After 250 years, they've never connected to the community, so it's not in their best interest to start now. We've been holding their hand and trying to get them to do more for the community, even though everybody knows they don't need to do anything.
> I have developed a black aesthetic. One hundred percent of my clients are black. I've decided to investigate on a personal level realizing a black aesthetic. It's about

three things: design, education, and culture. I now have eleven years of focus on the black aesthetic. There's a legacy of built work in that environment. With black architecture, I believe it's important just to do it rather than making it an academic pursuit. African American architects need to work in African American communities. If they did, there would be plenty of work for all of us. (Leroy Vaughan)

The owner of a large firm in the South focuses on the community as a source of expanded social networks. It is a clear strategy that has worked well for the firm. Social networks are vital to the continuing development of an architectural practice; making a contribution to the community and making contacts at the same time is an efficient use of resources.

I'm involved in the black communities, not so much because of the projects but because there are African American elected officials involved. We [African Americans] are represented broadly across the community. We all know each other, and help each other, and socialize with each other. I'm involved in fraternal organizations, church, and civic groups. I'm a member of 100 Black Men of America, mentoring young African American males at risk. I'm in contact with other black men at the same time. Networking is one general concept that works in both [black and white] arenas. I'm involved in organizations that are African American and others that have African Americans involved in them, and sometimes I'm the only one who's African American. (Rob Green)

There are parts of the country where this strategy is viable, and many more where it is not. The presence of a substantial number of black elected officials, especially over time, can make a difference in both the character of the black community and the resources that flow to it. In places, especially in the South, where there are large black populations *and* large numbers of black elected officials, black architects are more able to capitalize on networks in the neighborhood.

David Hughes, in his book on Afrocentric architecture, provides a useful description of how culture influences the built environment:

The nucleus of a society and culture is the family. While Western society is based on the nuclear family that shapes individualistic acquisition and possession, African society embraces the extended/pluralistic family that shapes a communal culture of joint acquisition and shared possession.

This family/societal base also shapes the basic perception of space, its use and design in African society. Distinct attributes include the "outside/inside" relationship of the compound (entire dwelling area) and the unitary cells (private/functions space). . . . Thus, traditional family origins can shape attitudes towards the design and use of space in contemporary public buildings giving Africa a distinct contribution in this area of design.[45]

The following is a tale of the joy of being in the 'hood. It reflects the reality of Hughes's observations. Sylvia's is a landmark restaurant in the heart of Harlem that drew Leroy Vaughan into the scene. Telling me this story, he taught me a lesson about the connection between black communities and black culture, and why it is important to maintain contact with that heritage.

In 1990, I came up to Sylvia's and there was so much activity. I knew I had to be up here. I've observed a lot about front space and rear space. People behave differently in different spaces—and there are big cultural differences between how different groups of people behave in different spaces. The way black people behave goes back to the village. The village was built in a circle, but the circle was never perfect; it was natural and amorphic.

Slave quarters were built so people could be out in front, so the master could see them. In the late 1880s, shotgun houses began to be built.[46] They have the porches on the short end. We wanted, and continue to want, to be seen and be heard. We were the last ones with telephones. To see the cars, and see who was going by, we had to be outside. To know what was going on, we had to be out on the porch.

We have a boldness in color, texture, and pattern. We also have a different sense of intensity and how we use space. You have to calm it down to go downtown. Not all of us live in the ghetto, but we all came *from* it. (Leroy Vaughan)

This story is one of the very few where the practice of architecture is about connecting the built environment to the culture of the people who inhabit the space. Vaughan does all he can to connect the Afrocentric heritage to contemporary architecture.

DEPENDENCE ON THIS WORK

This profession is full of contradictions for blacks. They are forced to make economic sacrifices to maintain their cultural identity. In order to do business with people who look like them, they often have to accept projects that use up scarce resources, with minimal economic return. Holtz Kay and others have written about how difficult it is for black architects to get high-profit projects, *even in their own communities*.[47] There is a price to be paid for cultivating and retaining cultural ties.

We are having trouble overcoming the perception that a small multicultural firm with over 50 percent women can design just as well as the larger, Euro-American corporate firms. Even though our portfolio is growing, we're still having trouble breaking into the downtown market. Not only is there a belief we're not capable of doing corporate work, the lessons we've learned working in the community are constantly discounted. (Edward Lamont)

For an architect who came up in the community design tradition, it is the ultimate insult. Just as there is a stigma associated with doing government work, the experience firms gain doing projects in communities of color is not transferable to corporate projects. They are dependent on this work; ironically, these commissions often require more attention to detail and more skill in relating to the client, but they are not given credit for developing these skills.

There is a certain set of qualifications that you gain as an architect in doing community work, and those are regrettably devalued and dismissed by the profession. . . . They figure it's the bottom-end of the professional practice. But working with communities and their needs is harder and much more rewarding than they realize. It's a two-way education, and it's a wonderful thing.[48]

NOTES

1. Pierre Bourdieu and Loic Wacquant, *An Invitation to Reflexive Sociology* (Chicago: University of Chicago Press, 1992), 199.

2. See Karen Aschaffenburg and Ineke Maas, "Cultural and Educational Careers: The Dynamics of Social Reproduction," *American Sociological Review* 62 (August 1997): 573–87, for more on knowing the rules.

3. "How difficult it is to make audible the voice of oppression in a choir where privilege controls the resources and accepted tonalities of seeing, knowing and being." Sharon E. Sutton, "Finding Our Voice in a Dominant Key," in *African American Architects in Current Practice*, ed. Jack Travis, 13–15 (New York: Princeton Architectural Press, 1991), 13.

4. See Stephen L. Carter, "The Black Table, the Empty Seat, and the Tie," in *Lure and Loathing: Essays on Race, Identity and the Ambivalence of Assimilation*, ed. Gerald Early (New York: Penguin, 1993); Joe Feagin, Kevin E. Early, and Karyn D. McKinney, "The Many Costs of Discrimination: The Case of Middle-Class African-Americans," *Indiana Law Review* 34, no. 4 (2001): 1311–60; bell hooks, *Killing Rage: Ending Racism* (New York: Holt, 1995); Paul Kivel, *Uprooting Racism: How White People Can Work for Racial Justice* (Philadelphia: New Society, 1996); and Peggy McIntosh, "White Privilege and Male Privilege: A Personal Account of Coming to See Correspondences Through Work in Women's

Studies," in *Race, Class and Gender: An Anthology*, ed. Margaret Andersen and Patricia H. Collins, 94–105 (Belmont, CA: Wadsworth, 1988).

5. Peter Jarvis, "Meaningful and Meaningless Experience: Toward an Analysis of Learning from Life," *Adult Education Quarterly* 73, no. 3 (1987): 164–72.

6. Donna Langston, "Tired of Playing Monopoly?" in *Race, Class and Gender: An Anthology*, ed. Margaret Andersen and Patricia Collins, 126–35 (Belmont, CA: Wadsworth, 1998), 129, 131.

7. Vincent P. Franklin, "Introduction: Cultural Capital and African-American Education," *Journal of African-American History* 87 (Spring 2002): 176.

8. Garry Stevens, *The Favored Circle: The Social Foundations of Architectural Distinction* (Cambridge, MA: MIT Press, 1998).

9. According to Louis Althusser, "Ideology and Ideological State Apparatuses: Notes Towards an Investigation," in *Lenin and Philosophy and Other Essays* (New York: Monthly Review Press, 1971), 127–86, the intergenerational transmission of cultural mores is precisely the role of modern education.

10. See Aschaffenburg and Maas, "Cultural and Educational Careers"; George Farkas, Robert P. Grobe, Daniel Sheehan, and Yuan Shuan, "Cultural Resources and School Success: Gender, Ethnicity and Poverty Groups within an Urban School District," *American Sociological Review* 55 (February 1990): 127–42; Franklin, "Introduction: Cultural Capital and African-American Education"; Matthijs Kalmijn and Gerbert Kraaykamp, "Race, Cultural Capital and Schooling: An Analysis of Trends in the United States," *Sociology of Education* 69 (January 1996): 22–34; and Vincent J. Roscigno and James W. Ainsworth-Darnell, "Race, Cultural Capital, and Educational Resources: Persistent Inequalities and Achievement Returns," *Sociology of Education* 72 (July 1999): 158–78.

11. hooks, *Killing Rage*; and Linda Stout, *Bridging the Class Divide and Other Lessons for Grassroots Organizing* (Boston: Beacon, 1996), both talk at length about internalized oppression. If you are told long enough, and in enough different ways, that you do not measure up to the "standard," there is a high probability you will begin to believe it. The toxicity of internalized oppression is in the way the oppression continues, even in the absence of an identifiable oppressor.

12. For more on the function of gatekeepers in commerce, see John P. Caskey, "Bank Representation in Low-Income and Minority Urban Communities," *Urban Affairs Quarterly* 29, no. 4 (1994): 617–38; Daniel P. Immergluck and Erin Mullen, "New Small Business Data Show Loans Going to Higher-Income Neighborhoods in Chicago Area," Woodstock Institute Reinvestment Alert no. 11, November 1997, at www.woodstockinst.org/document/allert11.pdf (accessed 7 April 2002); Daniel Immergluck and Geoff Smith "Bigger, Faster . . . But Better? How Changes in the Financial Services Industry Affect Small Business Lending in Urban Areas," Woodstock Institute, at brookings.edu/cs/urban/publications/immergklucklending.pdf (accessed January 21, 2001); and Gregory D. Squires, *Capital and Communities in Black and White* (Albany: State University of New York Press, 1994).

13. The ongoing complaint from black architects that their competence is always questioned makes sense once one has perused the literature. This is a problem across the

board for blacks in the United States. See Kathryn H. Anthony, *Designing for Diversity: Gender, Race, and Ethnicity in the Architectural Profession* (Urbana: University of Illinois Press, 2001); Max Bond, "The Black Architect's Experience," *Architectural Record* (June 1992); Thomas D. Boston, *Affirmative Action and Black Entrepreneurship* (New York: Routledge, 1999); Carter, "Black Table"; Ellis Cose, *Rage of a Privileged Class* (New York: Harper Perennial, 1995); Patricia Dawson, *Forged by the Knife: The Experience of Surgical Residency from the Perspective of a Woman of Color* (Seattle: Open Hand, 1999); Joe Feagin and Melvin Sikes, *Living with Racism: The Black Middle-Class Experience* (Boston: Beacon, 1994); James I. Herbert, *Black Male Entrepreneurs and Adult Development* (New York: Praeger, 1989); Manning Marable, *How Capitalism Underdeveloped Black America* (Boston: South End, 1983); and Jennifer Reese, "Paul Williams, An Architect," *Via* (September–October 1999), 52–55, among many others.

14. See Anthony, *Designing for Diversity*; Bond, "Black Architect's Experience"; Jane Holtz Kay, "Invisible Architects: Minority Firms Struggle to Achieve Recognition in a White-Dominated Profession," *Architecture* (April 1991), 106–113; Magali Sarfatti Larson, *The Rise of Professionalism* (Berkeley: University of California Press, 1977); Melvin Mitchell, *The Crisis of the African-American Architect: Conflicting Cultures of Architecture and (Black) Power* (Lincoln, NE: Writer's Club, 2001); and Stevens, *Favored Circle*. This phenomenon is what the social network analysts describe as "the rich get richer." The people who are already connected to decision makers (a) are *already* connected and (b) bring their friends to the network. The people who have already met at church or on the golf course, or who have reason to believe a friend of a friend can be a useful contact, are more likely to continue to utilize existing contacts. See Albert-Laszlo Barabasi, *Linked: How Everything Is Connected to Everything Else and What It Means for Business, Science and Everyday Life* (New York: Penguin, 2003); Mark Buchanan, *Nexus: Small Worlds and the Groundbreaking Science of Networks* (New York: Norton, 2002); Ronald S. Burt, *Structural Holes* (Cambridge, MA: Harvard University Press, 1992); Malcolm Gladwell, *The Tipping Point: How Little Things Can Make a Big Difference* (Boston: Back Bay; Little, Brown, 2002); and Duncan J. Watts, *Six Degrees: The Science of a Connected Age* (New York: Norton, 2003), for an introduction to social network analysis.

15. Mitchel R. Levitt, "Flying with Eagles: An Interview with Curtis J. Moody, FAIA," *SMPS Marketer* (October 2002): 5, 15.

16. See Carter, "Black Table"; Cose, *Rage of a Privileged Class*; Feagin and Sikes, *Living with Racism*; and Herbert, *Black Male Entrepreneurs and Adult Development*.

17. Howard C. Stevenson and Gary Renard, "Trusting Ole' Wise Owls: Therapeutic Use of Cultural Strengths in African-American Families," *Professional Psychology: Research and Practice* 24, no. 4 (1993): 433–42.

18. See Dalton Conley, *Being Black, Living in the Red: Race, Wealth, and Social Policy in America* (Berkeley: University of California Press, 1999); Cose, *Rage of a Privileged Class*; bell hooks, *Where We Stand: Class Matters* (New York: Routledge, 2000); Melvin Oliver and Thomas Shapiro, *Black Wealth/White Wealth: A New Perspective on Racial Inequality* (New York: Routledge, 1997); and Thomas M. Shapiro, *The Hidden Cost of Being African Ameri-*

can: How Wealth Perpetuates Inequality (New York: Oxford University Press, 2004), for insights into class issues.

19. Vincent J. Roscigno and James W. Ainsworth-Darnell, "Race, Cultural Capital, and Educational Resources: Persistent Inequalities and Achievement Returns," *Sociology of Education* 72 (July 1999): 158–78.

20. See Aschaffenburg and Maas, "Cultural and Educational Careers"; and Kalmijn and Kraaykamp, "Race, Cultural Capital and Schooling," on the reproduction of social capital and the possibilities for earning it.

21. Margaret Andersen and Patricia H. Collins, eds., *Race, Class and Gender: An Anthology* (Belmont, CA: Wadsworth, 1998), 74–77.

22. Albert Bandura, *Social Learning Theory* (Englewood Cliffs, NJ: Prentice-Hall, 1977).

23. Lynne Duke, "Blueprint of a Life," *Washington Post*, July 1, 2004, C4. Dalton Conley found that the educational level of parents was the single greatest predictor of the educational accomplishments for the subsequent generation, and second only to parental net worth in predicting their economic status. See Conley, *Being Black, Living in the Red*.

24. Mitchell, *Crisis of the African-American Architect*, 81.

25. See Stevens, *Favored Circle*, for a greater understanding of how the star system is perpetuated in architecture.

26. Safdie is an Israeli architect who has worked all over the world and is known for innovative design.

27. Sutton, "Finding Our Voice in a Dominant Key," 12.

28. See Magali Sarfatti Larson, *Behind the Postmodern Facade: Architectural Change in Late Twentieth-Century America* (Berkeley: University of California Press, 1993); Magali Sarfatti Larson, "Patronage and Power," in *Reflections on Architectural Practices in the Nineties*, ed. William S. Saunders, 130–43 (Princeton, NJ: Princeton Architectural Press, 1996); and Stevens, *Favored Circle*.

29. See Aschaffenburg and Maas, "Cultural and Educational Careers," for a discussion on the intergenerational transfer of social capital, which leads to what they refer to as "social reproduction."

30. Unless otherwise indicated, I use *the community* to refer broadly to the black community. In many places in this country, it is debatable whether there is *a* black community, but in this context it is defined in contrast to the "downtown, white business community." It is a useful shorthand so both the reader and the writer can continue without having to explain with each use of the term what is meant. However, this explanation begs the question: Why would we think there is, or should be, *a* black community when there is no one white community?

31. Competitively bid projects often elicit fifteen to twenty responses. The "short list" is the list of finalists.

32. Maryann Haggerty, "Behind the Design of a New Headquarters: High-Profile Freddie Mac Contract a Bittersweet Victory for Devrouax & Purnell," *Washington Post*, June 19, 1995, F5.

33. Not surprising because, the civil rights movement notwithstanding, capital and power continue to be the provenance of the dominant, white culture.

34. Karen E. Hudson, *Paul R. Williams, Architect: A Legacy of Style* (New York: Rizzoli, 1993), 22.

35. This view is supported by John Morris Dixon, "A White Gentlemen's Profession?" *Progressive Architecture* 75, no. 11 (November 1994): 55–61; Holtz Kay, "Invisible Architects"; Larson, "Patronage and Power"; Shapiro, *Hidden Cost of Being African American*; and Stevens, *Favored Circle*.

36. In both Feagin and Sikes, *Living with Racism*, and Feagin et al., "Many Costs of Discrimination," there are frank discussions with middle-class blacks about the cumulative effect of a lifetime of small slights. Very little documentation exists on the incidence of post-traumatic stress disorder among blacks, but there is conjecture the rates are high. There is evidence that the paucity of data may be attributable to racism in the health care system. Blacks are less likely to receive mental health care; when they do, they are likely to encounter mental health professionals who are not trained in cross-cultural therapy, and therefore the diagnoses are often based on a "normative" white behavior description. See Eve Bender, "Complex Factors Keep Many Blacks from MH System," *Psychiatric News* 39, no. 21 (2004): 14; and Hyoun K. Kim and Patrick C. McKenry, "Social Networks and Support: A Comparison of African Americans, Asian Americans, Caucasians, and Hispanics," *Journal of Comparative Family Studies* 29, no. 2 (1998): 313–34.

37. Haggerty, "Behind the Design of a New Headquarters," F5.

38. Lee D. Mitgang, "Saving the Soul of an Architectural Education: Four Critical Challenges Face Today's Architecture Schools," *Architectural Record* (May 1997): 124. See also Lily M. Hoffman, *The Politics of Knowledge: Activist Movements in Medicine and Planning* (Albany: SUNY Press, 1989), for another view of the political relationships between low-income communities and outside development professionals.

39. The concerns about property maintenance in low-income communities have been an issue since at least the late 1930s. The Federal Housing Administration was, at best, complicit in the collapse of some inner-city communities. Because of their relatively liberal underwriting criteria, people were able to buy houses with much less equity capital than they could with conventional financing. Low- and moderate-income families, as well as minority home buyers, were likely to be pointed in the direction of older housing stock. They got into these houses, then found they needed extensive maintenance and repair. The default rate on these loans went up, and the developers were able to buy them for taxes. See Nancy A. Denton, "The Role of Residential Segregation in Promoting and Managing Inequality in Wealth and Property," *Indiana Law Review* 34, no. 4 (2001): 1199–1211; Alex Schwartz, "Bank Lending to Minority and Low-Income Households and Neighborhoods: Do Community Reinvestment Agreements Make A Difference?" *Journal of Urban Affairs* 20, no. 3 (1998): 269–301; and Squires, *Capital and Communities in Black and White*.

40. See Angela G. Blackwell, "Promoting Equitable Development," *Indiana Law Review* 34, no. 4 (2001): 1273–90; Conley, *Being Black, Living in the Red*; Denton, "Role of Resi-

dential Segregation in Promoting and Managing Inequality in Wealth and Property";
Oliver and Shapiro, *Black Wealth/White Wealth*; and Shapiro, *Hidden Cost of Being African
American*, for additional commentary on the relationships between residential segrega-
tion, discrimination, and family wealth.

41. W. E. B. Du Bois, *The Souls of Black Folk* (New York: Penguin, 1903/1995).

42. Carol B. Stack, *All Our Kin* (New York: Harper Colophone, 1974), refers to systems
of "fictive kin" in the black community. Calling someone "cousin" can be an indication of
blood relations or of close friendship.

43. In the Southeast, the community of black architects got started at Tuskegee, a historically black college. There was consensus among the architects I interviewed that there
are some clients they should be able to count on to hire them. HBCUs are on that list.
African American museums are also on the list. Not all architects agree with that assessment. See Fred A. Bernstein, "For African-Americans, a Chance to Draft History," *New
York Times*, June 24, 2004, F1, F8, for opposing opinions.

44. Appendix A has the complete breakdown of graduation data by school.

45. David Hughes, *Afrocentric Architecture: A Design Primer* (Columbus, OH: Greyden,
1994), 59.

46. In an article in the *Seattle Times* about New Orleans, Peter H. King provided a definition of shotgun houses: "century-and-a-half-old shotgun houses—wooden structures so
narrow that, it's said, a shotgun blast through the front door would exit through the back
and blow a hole in every room—that are an architectural presence in some flooded neighborhoods. Peter H. King, "Putting Away New Orleans," *Seattle Times*, October 9, 2005, A2.

47. See Anthony, *Designing for Diversity*; Holtz Kay, "Invisible Architects"; and Susan S.
Szenasy, "Designers and Multiculturalism," *Metropolis* 14, no. 3 (October 1994): 110–15.

48. Silja J. A. Talvi, "No Dreams Deferred: Donald King Builds Community through Diverse Architecture," *ColorsNW* 3 (September 2003): 16.

7

SUMMARY AND RECOMMENDATIONS

Why do whites spend so much time discussing how hard it is to talk about racism? People like you, who do this antiracist work—you're the ones in the dominant culture who understand racism the best. Don't get me wrong, I'm glad you're doing the work. It gets lonely out here, but I don't understand what's so hard about it. My life—as a black man in the United States—*that's* hard. But what's so hard about telling people what you know about racism? (Black attendee at a white privilege conference)

After years of thinking about that question, I have come to an understanding of what makes it so difficult for whites to talk about racism. We all bring our own cultural assumptions to any endeavor. Talking about race, or reading this book, is no exception. Particularly as twenty-first-century European Americans, we have very little explicit understanding of our cultural assumptions. The institutions we interact with on a daily basis—political, economic, educational, and so forth—all reflect our image. We do not talk about racism because it makes people uncomfortable; it is hard to talk about because inequality is not "the American way."[1]

We make faulty assumptions about economic and social disparity because the models we have for considering inequality are based in the dominant culture. We like to believe our "troubles with race" are behind us. We trust that our beliefs are valid, so we do not seek out additional information. We accept the notion that people who do not thrive in this culture are not working hard enough; we rarely stop to consider the possibility our institutions, those places where our cultural mores are defined and defended, are designed to maintain white dominance.

As I have traveled around the country doing the research for this book, I have had many conversations, in airplanes, hotel lobbies, and restaurants, about my work. Almost without fail, the people I have talked to have had the same response: "Black architects? I never thought about that." The notion of blacks, or one would guess, any people of color, in architecture often shocks people into considering what the content of such a book might be.

I have used the profession of architecture as a lens through which to evaluate some of the institutions referred to above. Although the chapters of this book are presented as discrete units, the themes are interrelated. To get a sense of what it is like for blacks to work in architecture, one must take a systems view; systems thinking reflects the relationships that make up the whole. Without an understanding of how social inequality operates, systems theory remains nothing more than an abstract model. As a model, rather than a tool, it remains just another way to keep inequality hidden, another parallel to institutions that are invisible to whites but clearly visible for people of color. What we call individual "parts" are merely threads of the same fabric, "a pattern in an inseparable web of relationships."[2] This book is one view of the complex worlds where black architects live; it is about their relationships and connections—to each other, to the profession, and to the larger culture.

Most of us who are not architects know so little about the profession of architecture it is a useful vehicle for evaluating systemic racism; those of us who are not architects enter a discussion on the topic with few preconceived notions. It is also useful as a research focus because, unlike medicine and law, architecture is not divided into specialties. Although there are affinity groups within the industry associations, there are no additional educational or licensing requirements by area of expertise. This makes it relatively easy to collect data that are comparable across firms.

Although I have written here about architects, the concepts are applicable across our entire culture. I hope to have captured your attention with stories and commentary about well-educated, middle-class blacks, but the issues are not unique to them. Systemic racism has an impact on all of us. Obviously, the disparity of opportunity and access has the most pernicious effect on people of color, but all of us lose the richness of experience and community that comes from enabling and hearing a broader range of voices.

INSTITUTIONAL STRUCTURES

The institutional structures discussed in this volume—the profession, the education, and the practice—can be likened to the background noise of daily life. For some of us, European Americans in particular, the sound is rarely audible. However, for people of color it can often be a deafening roar. It is these systems that make access to successful practice more and less attainable.

The Profession

The structure of the profession puts architects of color at a disadvantage. I very consciously named the chapter on architecture "A White Gentlemen's Profession"[3] because it continues to be dominated by, and most rewarding of, white males.[4] In reality, this system is a network of social connections.

In Renaissance Italy, architects were chosen by the wealthy on the basis of relationships. The legacy of that system of patronage continues.[5] As architecture in the United States moved from being a building trade to being a design profession, the necessity for access to capital, and thus to the wealthy developers and individuals who possessed the capital, increased. As the profession continued to distance itself from the building trade, the ability of blacks to gain access diminished; it became more and more difficult for them to achieve economic parity.

Education

Architecture, with its focus on a Eurocentric aesthetic and its legacy of patronage, could hardly be expected to welcome difference. Like all professional training programs, the architecture curriculum reflects the culture of the practice. According to Larson and others, the education is designed to reproduce the profession.[6] The training program for architects fosters the existing professional systems, thereby also maintaining the cultural disparities.[7] In an arena that is so overwhelmingly white and male, why would we expect the education system to be different?

Criticism of the lack of ethnic diversity in architectural education comes from those who are intimately involved in it. Darell Fields, an associate professor of architecture at the Harvard Graduate School of Design, contributed an essay to a collection the Boston Society of Architects assembled in 2003 on the subject of diversity. Fields said although architecture "remains one of the most segregated disciplines in higher education," nobody cares, because nobody cares about architecture. He continued, "Sadly, diversity, as exemplified by the schools of architecture alluded to here, is becoming nothing more than a mascot for Jim Crow."[8]

What Fields is saying is institutional racism has kept black students out of architecture programs. The system, long an integral part of American culture, continues today in a more sophisticated form.

His point is well taken. Architecture remains invisible in the lives of all but those in the industry. It is particularly invisible in communities of color. Most of the architects interviewed for this book talked about their early desire to be an architect, and they also acknowledged the importance of having had a champion, a family member, an older architect, or an influential teacher who facilitated their entry into the profession. As a result, they understand the importance of role models and mentors. Stevens has pointed out the ways of reproducing the profession's culture—the aesthetic, the access to patrons, and the fame that comes to star architects—are all dependent on a guild system, where young practitioners are taken in hand and allowed to "study at the drafting table of the master."[9] Black architects assume most of the responsibility for providing black students with mentors and serving as role models.

The homogeneity of architecture schools makes it difficult to imagine change. It is for that reason black architects consider it their responsibility to teach in these programs, serve as mentors for younger children, and be visible as role models. If they are not intentionally introduced to architecture, most children of color will never know they could consider architecture as a vocation. We are all the losers when such talent is not developed. The process of introducing new generations to the profession has to start early and be reinforced over time. Some architects work with elementary school children, some in middle school. The continual reinforcement serves to both encourage and inform students about the possibility they, too, can pursue this dream.

"There is just not a critical mass. There are not enough of us to make a difference." I heard that repeatedly in the course of doing these interviews. Without colleagues who share their worldview, it is difficult for students and practitioners of color to build community. In a field where social connections play an important role in business development, the small numbers of nonwhites remain at a distinct disadvantage. Blacks and whites *can* be colleagues and allies; a long heritage of institutional racism keeps us from creating those relationships. As the stories in this book have shown, we remain segregated from each other.

Practice

Understanding the history of architecture and architectural education makes it easier to place architectural practice in context. The whiteness of the profession heightens the problems faced by black, and other nonwhite, practitioners.

Capital and influence have always been required to construct buildings, and work in the community has always been discounted. Unlike in other countries, where architecture is better integrated into the culture, in the United States work outside the limelight of design is regarded as unimportant and insignificant. The thousands of architects whose focus is not specifically designing buildings, those working in academia, government, planning, and so forth, are viewed by the professional mainstream as other than "real" architects. The wealth gap between African Americans and European Americans makes it more difficult for all black business owners to succeed.[10] This is a significant problem for black architects who choose to establish their own practices or firms.

For all architects, the decision to go into architecture requires making a deliberate choice to forgo economic glory. According to Robert Gutman, a professor in the School of Architecture at Princeton University,

> Men and women for whom economic security is the prime consideration do not usually choose a career in architecture. College graduates who focus on the issue of opportunity are more likely to get an MBA or a law or medical degree. The image of these other professions and how much better their members fare financially haunts architects. Not only do architects generally have lower incomes than those in other professions, but the demand for the services of lawyers and physicians is more stable, and they are able to exercise more control over the domains in which they work. The differences are very apparent now as the privileged position of lawyers and physicians has come under scrutiny. Critics, however, are finding it difficult to reduce the autonomy of these professions, while architects are continually losing out to clients and other parties in the building industry in the battle for hegemony.[11]

The reality of the wage structure for architecture makes access to other investment capital even more important. However, the structural racism of capital markets, which has kept blacks out of the most lucrative sectors, means capital is even more difficult for black architects to access.

Even when they achieve a modicum of success, they are still subject to the *perception* that they are neither as competent nor as qualified as their white counterparts. There is no basis in fact for thinking black architects are more, or less, competent than any other architects. (Given that they have to work twice as hard to become architects, it is more realistic to think black architects are *more* competent.) The assumptions many whites make that blacks are "less than" is reinforced in the public sector and seeps into the fabric of the private sector. It is hard to imagine a hiring interview where a potential institutional client would ask a white male architect whether he and his firm had actually completed the projects they were presenting as their own. What gives whites the hubris to ask that kind of question of an experienced architect who is black? It likely does not occur to the client that institutional racism has led him to that query. Bonilla-Silva points out that many well-meaning, decent whites play out the script this culture has written for them.

As the person who told me that story said, "At least he [the potential client] said it out loud. Most don't; they just don't call us back."

POLITICAL CONTEXT

It is not possible to draw a complete picture without including the support and chaos provided by government contracts. Because they have had limited access to private-sector clients, black architects have been reliant on public-sector work. The history and politics of government programs have an impact on whether and how access is improved.

The advent of affirmative action, and the government set-aside programs it spawned, provided some revenue relief to black-owned architectural firms and other black-owned businesses, shut out of most private-sector markets.[12] The irony of these programs, however, is that the supposedly greater access led many businesses to stretch beyond their limits to attain government contracts.[13] Many of these firms dissolved under the load of trying to accomplish this work.[14] There is a tragic irony in programs designed specifically for "minority" businesses resulting in the demise of so many.

Although public projects provide black-owned firms with increased revenue opportunities, there is a stigma associated with doing government work.[15] These firms have to choose between the risk of not doing government work, and limiting both their revenue potential and their visibility, and working government jobs and hearing later they have only gotten these projects because they were handed to them. It is the kind of double bind created when the programs ostensibly established to "help minority firms" were motivated primarily by political goals. The development of government programs to assist "nonmajority" entrepreneurs was seen by many whites as a way to increase access to lucrative government contracts. What whites did not understand was the Nixon administration enacted many of these programs with more of a focus on *appearing* to do something for blacks than on actually building effective programs.

It is much the same story with community work. Black firms are heavily reliant on the revenue from projects in ethnic communities, but the experience of working in communities of color is often discounted by private-sector clients and contractors. Some firm owners reported they had potential corporate clients offer small jobs in the "central area" (usually low-income communities of color), implying these were low-risk projects; if the black-owned firms could not complete them successfully, it would not be the disaster that an improperly completed large job would be.

It is impossible for me to contemplate the indignity of completing a lengthy professional training course, and an impossibly long apprenticeship, only to have your professional credentials questioned at every turn. Even for firms that deliberately choose to do most of their work in the community, there is still the indignity of having to answer funding agencies' concerns about their ability to do the work.

SOCIAL NETWORKS

Social networks are an integral part, and a reflection of, the institutional structures and the political context in which they are formed. The ability to get customers, obtain funding, and have access to professional services and clients is often dependent on behavior, connections, and the political climate. Social networks, and the capital they provide, often increase economic capital. In light of the fact architecture remains a profession based on patronage, the job of developing social networks is vital, difficult, and time consuming. This is a challenging task for all practitioners; it is only more so for blacks.[16]

Working in the community provides a way for black architects to connect with other people of color, a vital connection that is limited working in a profession that is so overwhelmingly white. It is a big price to pay for the chance to maintain identity. The community design movement provided an organized, systematic way to practice architecture *and* work in community, but funding for community design centers became harder and harder to find during the Reagan years and beyond.[17]

The cultural and social capital most black architects bring with them into the profession are generally not the right capital to purchase access to clients and commissions.[18] Obviously, the "right" capital depends on who the prospective clients are, but when black firms are trying to get projects downtown, not only do they have to learn architecture, but they also have to learn how to find a way into the dominant culture, and do it almost entirely without the benefit of mentors. That so many survive, and thrive, is a testament to their tenacity, and to their desire to practice architecture.

RECOMMENDATIONS FOR CHANGE

The following actions are focused on the architecture profession, but they are applicable and readily adaptable to any discipline. Some items are directed specifically at architects, but can be used as the basis for programs and activities in a wide range of milieus. None of them appears difficult to implement, but they all require a commitment to make change and a willingness to spend time. We must be prepared to work together, across ethnicities and across political parties, to dismantle the barriers that are keeping a large segment of the population from achieving parity. In these years of conservative Republican control, that is a tall order.

Based on my years of experience and research in the field with black business owners, I am suggesting small steps that have the potential to make a big difference. These recommendations are not a solution to the problem of institutional racism. However, they do have the potential to bring people together in new ways. Once people start working together across race lines, and begin to listen to each other's stories, the context in which they are operating begins to change. The institutions responsible for creating and maintaining institutional racism have been around as long as the country; changing them is a long process. That knowledge should not keep us from starting the process.

The Children

Start with the children. There are good models of how to involve "disadvantaged" children in architecture; the Steelcase Corporation sponsorship of a program, working with fourth graders who live in a disintegrating housing project, is a great example. Contact your local middle school, and see if you can conduct a design class. If you have ever observed the fascination of toddlers at a construction site, you understand the possibilities for younger children to be introduced to architecture. A nursery school in Seattle created an arrangement with the construction company working on a site next to the school. The children wrote daily questions to the job foreman—Why are you digging such a big hole? What are the posts in the corners for?—and the foreman wrote back answers. The children were thrilled, the foreman was gratified, and a new generation of families got to understand how buildings are constructed.

Firms may consider setting up a field trip to take kids on an architecture adventure; most children have no idea what makes buildings work. Set up joint ventures with nonmajority firms to sponsor outings to familiarize children with architects and with design. Talk to the folks who run your local Big Brothers/Big Sisters program and see if you can get engaged in the program. See if you have Associates in the firm who would be interested in working with youth at the local YMCA. This would be good for children, for the future of the profession, and also for you. Think back to the letter Sharon Sutton received from the woman she mentored decades earlier (see chapter 2). Small steps can bring large rewards.

Existing Models

Look to successful models and understand what made them successful. If we consider the 1968 experiment at Columbia, there are useful lessons to be learned. Granted, it was devised under duress, but its genesis does not negate the results. (The fact it was devised as a response to a strike may be part of the lesson.) The faculty and administration acknowledged the existing disparities; provided mentors of color for the new students; and admitted enough black students that they had the security of a peer group. Almost forty years later, graduates of that class are still talking about how valuable those elements were to their ability to succeed. Can we find ways to increase black participation without shutting down the professional schools?

Give voice to the students of color who are already in architecture programs. Jennifer Newsom's symposium on black architecture was inspired by her outrage when one of her faculty insisted there was no such thing. We need to welcome other voices and encourage new perspectives. A Eurocentric view of the profession is only one view. The demographics of the United States are changing dramatically. It is important to recognize that tomorrow's clients—and practitioners—will be more ethnically diverse. Now is the time for the profession to prepare.

Look Inside the Firm

Make a greater effort to ensure a diversity of opinions and aesthetics within the firm. For those who already have architects of color on staff, take a good look at whether any of them are in positions of power in the firm. Are their voices heard, or are they window dressing? Do they have input into the design and construction processes? Look at other traditions, and be open to new ideas.

For those who have not hired architects of color, consider the reasons. It is easy to think of reasons why there are so few architects of color working in majority firms. The standards responses, "We tried to hire one, but he didn't take our offer," or "We've looked for one, but we can't find any who are qualified," reflect the influences of systemic racism. Why would *one* architect of color want to come to work in a firm? Is there any indication that would be a comfortable situation? We need to be prepared to consider how we create organizations that are welcoming to a wider range of people. Keep in mind, though, if you ask the questions, you have to be prepared to hear the answers. The rewards of struggling through the conversations are well worth the effort. Do not be surprised if your initial efforts are met with skepticism; consider seeking advice from people who have already worked on these questions.

Government Involvement

Create public programs that are designed to be effective. If the SBA 8(a) program had really provided technical assistance, and if the program staff had actually gotten involved in strategic planning that included a realistic marketing plan for phasing firms out of the program, the numbers of firms that failed after "graduation" would never have been 50 percent. If significant public projects were awarded to minority firms, the stigma associated with government work would begin to disappear. Government programs designed to celebrate the competence of black professionals would have the potential to change perceptions in the marketplace. It is unlikely to happen in an atmosphere where affirmative action is considered "reverse discrimination," but it is worth considering the ways existing programs facilitate systemic racism.

I am not suggesting it is easy to learn new ways of listening. It requires a deliberate attempt to see the world through someone else's eyes. As Robert Kegan writes in *The Evolving Self: Problem and Process in Human Development*, "All growth is costly. It involves the leaving behind of an old way of being in the world. . . . [Change] raises the possibility of making relative what I had taken for ultimate."[19] We must be willing to hear that our long-held assumptions about "others" are probably invalid.

When I started working in economic development, I was not aware of the vast cultural chasm that separated me from my clients of color. As I spent more time with the Fund clients, and learned to listen more and talk less, I began to understand how different our worldviews were. Once I began to see the barriers they faced in all aspects of their lives, I started to understand institutional racism. I was able to see what one of my friends refers to as the "ghost in the middle of the room."

The more I learned to reach out across race, the more enlightened I became and the more my life was enriched. By learning how others see the world, my own view has become broader. In addition, at a time when whites in the United States are feeling a loss of community, we have much to learn from the cultures of people of color about how community is developed and maintained.

We still have a long way to go. Growing up in this country, we have all learned the myths of color-blindness. Exploding closely held myths is an arduous task, but one that is necessary if we are truly invested in addressing the reality of racism.

Cultural change is a long-term process. If we begin the journey with realistic expectations, it is surprising and rewarding what the results can be. If we can quit assuming "we are all alike," we can begin to celebrate the fact we are not. Twenty-first-century racism can only be dismantled if we all learn to pay more attention, and more respect, to the differences between us, and begin to take responsibility for the institutions that make those differences insurmountable.

As Jack Travis said in his foreword to *African American Architects in Current Practice,*

> Yet these firms endure. Their work attests to the fact that these men and women of color, having to do better than their white counterparts at each juncture of their lives, are indeed special. They have persevered against prejudice, fear, and ignorance to achieve prominence. I hope that the light of a new day may finally shine on them and future generations of black architects.[20]

NOTES

1. Eduardo Bonilla-Silva, *Racism without Racists: Color-Blind Racism and the Persistence of Racial Inequality in the United States* (Lanham, MD: Rowman & Littlefield, 2003).

2. Fritjof Capra, *The Web of Life: A New Scientific Understanding of Living Systems* (New York: Anchor, 1997): 39.

3. See John Morris Dixon, "A White Gentlemen's Profession?" *Progressive Architecture* 75, no. 11 (November 1994): 55–61; and Melvin Mitchell, *The Crisis of the African-American Architect: Conflicting Cultures of Architecture and (Black) Power* (Lincoln, NE: Writer's Club, 2001).

4. See Kathryn Anthony, *Designing for Diversity: Gender, Race, and Ethnicity in the Architectural Profession* (Urbana: University of Illinois Press, 2001); Max Bond, "The Black Architect's Experience," *Architectural Record* (June 1992); Darell W. Fields, "Diversity Needs a New Mascot," in *20 on 20/20 Vision*, ed. Linda Kiisk, 39–41 (Boston: Boston Society of Architects, 2003); Dennis Alan Mann, "Making Connections: The African-American Architect," *Journal of the Interfaith Forum on Religion, Art & Architecture* (Fall 1993); Mitchell, *Crisis of the African-American Architect*; and Jennifer Reese, "Paul Williams, An Architect," *Via* (September–October 1999), 52–55.

5. See Richard Dozier, "The Black Architectural Experience in America," in *African American Architects in Current Practice*, ed. Jack Travis (New York: Princeton Architectural Press, 1991); Magali Sarfatti Larson, *The Rise of Professionalism* (Berkeley: University of California Press, 1977); Mitchell, *Crisis of the African-American Architect*; and Reese, "Paul Williams, An Architect."

6. See Anthony, *Designing for Diversity*; Dixon, "A White Gentlemen's Profession?";
Larson, *Rise of Professionalism*; and Magali Sarfatti Larson, "Patronage and Power," in *Reflections on Architectural Practice in the Nineties*, ed. William S. Saunders, 130–43 (Princeton, NJ: Princeton Architectural Press, 1996).

7. See Anthony, *Designing for Diversity*; Magali Sarfatti Larson, *Behind the Postmodern Facade: Architectural Change in Late Twentieth-Century America* (Berkeley: University of California Press, 1993); and Susan S. Szenasy, "Designers and Multiculturalism," *Metropolis* 14, no. 3(October 1994): 11, for more on the relationship between the structures of the training and the profession.

8. Fields, "Diversity Needs a New Mascot," 41.

9. Garry Stevens, *The Favored Circle: The Social Foundations of Architectural Distinction* (Cambridge, MA: MIT Press, 1998).

10. See Daniel P. Immergluck, "Progress Confined: Increases in Black Home Buying and the Persistence of Residential Segregation," *Journal of Urban Affairs* 20, no. 4 (1998): 443–57; Melvin L. Oliver and Thomas M. Shapiro, *Black Wealth/White Wealth: A New Perspective on Racial Inequality* (New York: Routledge, 1997); and Gregory D. Squires, *From Redlining to Reinvestment: Community Responses to Urban Disinvestment* (Philadelphia: Temple University Press, 1992).

11. Robert Gutman, "Architects and Power: The Natural Market for Architecture," *Progressive Architecture* 73, no. 13 (1992): 39.

12. See Anthony, *Designing for Diversity*; Max Bond, "Collaborating with Minority Architects," *Architecture* (June 1994): 43–47; Benjamin Forgey, "First Black Designed Building in Downtown DC," *Washington Post*, March 30, 2002, C1, C5; Jane Holtz Kay, "Invisible Architects: Minority Firms Struggle to Achieve Recognition in a White-Dominated Profession," *Architecture* (April 1991); and Mitchell, *Crisis of the African-American Architect*.

13. Manning Marable, *How Capitalism Underdeveloped Black America* (Boston: South End, 1983).

14. Timothy Bates and Darrell Williams, "Preferential Procurement Programs and Minority-Owned Business," *Journal of Urban Affairs* 17, no. 1 (1995): 1–17; and Joyce Jones, "Graduation Day from 8(a)," *Black Enterprise* 28 (February 1998): 161–66.

15. See Jean Barber, "Profile of the Minority Architect," and Roundtable "Today's Minority Architect: A Major Force," Minority Resources Committee of the AIA (MRC), July 1990; Timothy Bates, *Race, Self-Employment, and Upward Mobility* (Washington, DC: Woodrow Wilson Center Press, 1997); and Thomas D. Boston, *Affirmative Action and Black Entrepreneurship* (New York: Routledge, 1999).

16. See Anthony, *Designing for Diversity*; Larson, *Rise of Professionalism*; and Larson, *Behind the Postmodern Facade*.

17. Association for Community Design, "History of ACD"; Anthony, *Designing for Diversity*; and Lily M. Hoffman, *The Politics of Knowledge: Activist Movements in Medicine and Planning* (Albany: SUNY Press, 1989).

18. Yvonne R. Bell, "A Culturally Sensitive Analysis of Black Learning Style," *Journal of Black Psychology* 20, no.1 (1994): 47–61; Stephen L. Carter, "The Black Table, the Empty

Seat, and the Tie," in *Lure and Loathing: Essays on Race, Identity and the Ambivalence of Assimilation*, ed. Gerald Early (New York: Penguin, 1993); Joe Feagin and Melvin Sikes, *Living with Racism: The Black Middle-Class Experience* (Boston: Beacon, 1994); and Donna Langston, "Tired of Playing Monopoly?" in *Race, Class and Gender: An Anthology*, ed. Margaret Andersen and Patricia Collins, 126–35 (Belmont, CA: Wadsworth, 1997).

19. Robert Kegan, *The Evolving Self: Problem and Process in Human Development* (Cambridge, MA: Harvard University Press, 1982), 215, 207.

20. Jack Travis, *African American Architects in Current Practice* (New York: Princeton Architectural Press, 1991), 7.

DISTRIBUTION OF BLACK ARCHITECTURE STUDENTS

**African American Architects and Their Education:
A Demographic Study***

**Working Paper #1
Spring 2005**

Center for the Study of Practice
College of Design Architecture, Art & Planning
University of Cincinnati

Dennis Alan Mann
Professor of Architecture
University of Cincinnati

Bradford Grant
Professor of Architecture
Hampton University

* Courtesy of Dennis Alan Mann and Bradford Grant, Center for the Study of Practice.

Professor Bradford Grant, Chair of the architecture program at Hampton University and Dennis Alan Mann, a professor of architecture at the University of Cincinnati have been tracking licensed African American architects since 1989. Our work has resulted in two hard copy directories (1991 and 1996) and two professional surveys (1995 and 2000). We also maintain a web site at http:// blackarch.uc.edu where we list architects by name and by state of residence.

We continue to be engaged in demographic studies of African American architects. We have concentrated solely on following the careers of licensed architects since licensure is a matter of public record, therefore clearly bounding our demographic group. Our current piece of research work has been to determine at which universities each African American architect received his or her degree(s). This information has been drawn from our data base which currently lists 1487 architects of whom 171 are women.

This project originally arose when we noted in an earlier study that nearly forty five percent of African American students in professional architecture programs (B Arch & M Arch) in the USA were attending Historic Black Colleges and Universities (HBCUs). These programs are located at Florida A&M, Hampton, Howard, Morgan State, Prairie View A&M, Southern, and Tuskegee universities. If this was the case, we hypothesized, would that same percentage transfer through to those who eventually became licensed? And moreover, where did the others receive their degrees? How many continued on to receive graduate degrees? Where did they study?

Since there was no data to draw from, we had to patiently query each architect in our data base to gather this information. We also corresponded with over eighty schools of architecture. We have been successful in identifying universities and degrees for everyone but eight people.

The first general statistic that we discovered was that over thirty seven percent of African American architects hold at least one degree from an HBCU (If someone held one degree from an HBCU and another from a majority university they were listed in the total below under HBCU. There were 81 in this category). This aligns well with our earlier finding on where African American students study architecture (This data was attained from the National Architectural Accreditation Board). Given that there are only seven accredited architecture programs at HBCUs and over 110 other accredited programs in the USA, it became readily apparent that the HBCUs were making a significant contribution in educating future African American architects.

Overall Totals of Where Professional Degrees were Granted

HBCUs*	539	36.2%
MAJORITY SCHOOLS Only	868	58.4%
NO DEGREE (or Assoc. degree)	56	3.8%
INTERNATIONL UNIVERSITY Only	16	1.1%
UNKNOWN	8	0.6%
TOTAL Number Licensed	1487	
Male	1316	88.5%
Female	171	11.5%

* We included North Carolina A&T, Tennessee State, Central State, and Lincoln University in these totals.

THE HISTORIC BLACK COLLEGES AND UNIVERSITIES

The breakdown among the various HBCUs is illustrated in the list below:

AT LEAST ONE DEGREE FROM AN HBCU

		Accredited[1]
Howard University	277	1950/51
Hampton University	79	1970/71
Tuskegee University	67	1970/71
Southern University	37	1970/71
Florida A&M University	23	1979/80
North Carolina A&T	17	*
Prairie View A&M	14	1992
Tennessee State	10	*
Morgan State	10	1991
Central State	1	*
Lincoln University	1	*
Howard & Tenn. State (one degree @ each)[2]	1	
Howard & Tuskegee (one degree @ each)[2]	2	
TOTAL	539	

1. All professional degree programs are accredited on a regular basis by NAAB. The date listed above is when a program first received accreditation.
2. Neither university has an accredited B Arch or M Arch program. Their degree is in architectural engineering.
* Not an accredited architecture program.

THE MAJORITY SCHOOLS

We defined the majority schools as all the accredited programs at American Collegiate Schools of Architecture (ACSA) where a majority of the students were not

African American. (We did not poll the ten Canadian schools who belong to the ACSA, newly accredited programs where there were not likely to be any graduates who have become licensed, or some universities in locations in the USA where there were not likely to be many African American graduates). In all we heard back from eighty three programs at the date of this writing.

This is what we found:

Universities with TEN or more LICENSED African American Graduates

		Accredited
Columbia	54	1945/46
City College of New York	52	1967/68
Pratt	52	1947/48
Illinois/Urbana	50	1945/46
Harvard	47	1945/46
Cal/Berkeley	38	1945/46
Cornell	29	
Michigan	29	1945/46
MIT	28	1945/46
NYIT	21	1977/78
Detroit/Mercy	20	1965/66
Lawrence	20	1974/75
Southern California	19	1945/46
IIT	18	1945/46
Georgia Tech	17	1945/46
Illinois/Chicago	17	1969/70
Syracuse	17	1945/46
Yale	17	1945/46
Kansas State	16	1945/46
Notre Dame	16	1949/50
Washington Univ.	16	1945/46
Kent State	15	1962/63
Texas/Austin	15	1945/46
Cal Poly/San Luis Obispo	14	1966/67
Florida	14	1948/49
Ohio State	14	
Clemson	13	1953/54
Arkansas	12	1958/58
Cincinnati	12	1947/48
Rice	12	1945/46
Virginia Tech	12	1957/58
Catholic	11	1945/46

1. Note that the numbers above only account for a person ONCE at a university even though some may have received more than one degree from that University.
2. If someone received a degree from MORE THAN ONE university, they will show up in the totals for each university.
3. Note that numbers include non-professional degrees, masters degrees, and doctorates.

GRADUATE DEGREES

We were also interested in determining how many African American architects hold graduate degrees. Since we had no national statistics to compare with we only listed the overall totals.

Masters Degree*	463	(31.1% of 1479 known)
PhD, Doctorate, or LLD	18	
Law Degree (LLD)	9	

* Masters degrees are in a wide variety of fields including Architecture, Urban Design, Landscape Architecture, Regional Planning, City Planning, and Business.

INTERPRETATIONS

There are many interpretations and inferences that can be drawn from this data. We can be certain that when nearly forty five percent of African American students attend architecture programs at HBCUs that those figures should eventually transfer through to a similar percent of those who become licensed (37+%). Howard University obviously stands out as the pre-eminent university (as well as the oldest) in providing nearly nineteen percent of African American architects (many of whom have gone on to receive Masters degrees at other universities listed above).

But some fundamental questions remain unanswered. Why do people choose to attend the university that they do? Certainly decisions are made for many, many reasons. Among them would be cost, scholarship support, location relative to family, academic standards, prestige, black experience, and the quality of a program, among others. We do not pretend to understand what reasons a young person chooses to attend one institution over another other than anecdotal stories that we have heard.

We do know that some universities have made a major commitment to diversifying their student body while others are located in areas of the country with a pre-existing diverse population from which to draw students (though from glancing at the numbers above this is no guarantee of success).

We plan to continue and broaden our studies with the long term goal of making public who and where African American architects are so that young people who aspire to the profession can seek out mentors.

SURVEY OF
AFRICAN AMERICAN
ARCHITECTS

African American Architects
Survey 1999/2000*

1. Which category best describes your primary activities?

Private Practice	165	65.7%
Public/Govt. Agency	47	18.7%
University Faculty	12	4.8%
Construction	3	1.0%
Retired	10	4.0%
Other	14	5.6%

2. Which most closely represents the organization of the firm where you work?

Sole Proprietorship	54	21.4%
Partnership	19	7.3%
Ltd Liability Corp.	7	2.8%
Sub-Chapter S Corp.	29	11.5%
Corporation	78	31.0%
Other	1	
N/A	60	23.8%
No Answer	4	1.6%

* Courtesy of Dennis Alan Mann and Bradford Grant, Center for the Study of Practice

3. Please mark your position in your primary place of employment

Principal/Senior Partner	128	50.6%
Junior Partner/Associate	21	8.3%
Project Architect	24	9.5%
Architect	16	6.3%
Faculty Member	8	3.2%
Other	45	17.8%
Proj. Manager	11	
Director	15	
Other	19	
No Answer	11	4.3%

4. My firm or the firm that I work with is

100% African Amer. owned	121	47.3%
Joint Afr. Amer./White owned	25	9.8%
White/Other Minority owned	4	1.6%
White owned	36	14.1%
Female owned	0	
Joint Male/Female owned	4	1.6%
N/A	54	21.1%
No Answer	12	4.7%

5. Which designation best describes your firm or the firm that you work for? (some boxes were checked more than once)

Architecture	154	48.4%
Architecture/Engineering	33	10.4%
Engineering/Architecture	10	3.1%
Interior Design/Space Planning	19	6.0%
Planning	23	7.2%
Construction/Constr. Mgmt	25	7.9%
Other	35	11.0%
No Answer	19	6.0%

6a. How would you characterize the scope of your firm's practice?

Single state or metro area	99	39.3%
Multi-state or regional	75	29.8%
National	21	8.3%
International	30	11.9%
N/A	12	4.8%
No Answer	15	6.0%

6b. **How would you characterize the scope of your firm's practice?**
(OWNERS ONLY)

Single state or metro area	62	41.6%
Multi-state or regional	61	40.9%
National	11	7.4%
International	11	7.4%
N/A	4	2.7%
No Answer		

7. **What year was your firm founded?**
(AFRICAN AMERICAN OWNED ONLY)

1945–1960	7
1961–1975	19
1976–1990	55
1990–	57
N/A	46
No Answer	26

8. **Including you, how many employees did your firm have on the payroll in each of these categories?**

Principals/partners

one	91
two	48
three	16
four	7
five	10
six or more	13
N/A	39
No Answer	28

   Licensed architects other than Principals or Partners

zero	61
one	49
two	27
three	16
four	4
five	11
six or more	43
N/A	12
No Answer	29

Total Staff Size (full-time)

one	26
two	11
three	10
four	10
five	17
six	11
seven	13
eight	10
nine	7
ten to fifteen	25
16–20	8
20–30	19
31–50	11
50+	36
N/A	11
No Answer	28

9. Including you, how many principals/partners are African American?

none	0
one	107
two	40
three	2
four	1
five	1
N/A	41
No Answer	27

10. Not including yourself how many licensed African American architects (not including principals/partners) are employed in your firm?

none	113
one	70
two	13
three	10
more than four	5
N/A	15
No Answer	25

11. **How many other professionals (engineers, interior designers, etc.) are African American?**

none	151
one	33
two	15
three	6
four	4
five or more	6
N/A	10
No Answer	27

12. **What year were you born?**

1920–30	16
1931–40	34
1941–50	65
1951–60	91
1961–68	36

Average Age = 51 years old

13. **Estimate the percentage of your 1998 billings that are private contracts and public contracts.**

%	Private	Public
0–25%	39	43
26–50%	30	26
51–75%	35	34
76–100%	65	33
N/A	32	
No Answer	42	

14. **Approximately what percentage of your active clients in 1998 were African American?**

0–25%	100	54%
26–50%	26	14%
51–75%	29	15.8%
76–100%	30	16.2%
N/A	27	
No Answer	38	

15. **Approximately what percentage of your 1998 net billings were the result of a joint venture with a majority firm?**

0–25%	138	(all but 21 wrote in 0%)
26–50%	10	
51–75%	6	
76–100%	2	
N/A	46	
No Answer	46	

16. **Approximately what amount of time do you or your firm members participate in community volunteer work, neighborhood assistance work, or community "pro bono" work?** (Please estimate the number of hours *per week* over a year)

zero	18
one	18
two	38
three	17
four	26
five	16
six	7
seven	4
eight	8
nine	0
ten	22
11–20	11
20+	6
No Answer	50
N/A	13

17. **Which of the following includes your average total compensation received in 1998 (including bonuses, profit sharing, and/or other incentive compensations)?**

less than $25,000	9
$25,001–$37,500	11
$37,500–$50,000	26
$50,001–$62,500	36
$62,501–$75,000	41

$75,001–$100,000	42
$100,001–$150,000	29
$150,001–$200,000	14
$200,001–$250,000	4
$250,000 or more	5
No Answer	42

C

AFFIRMATIVE ACTION SUITS

Opposition to affirmative action, particularly elucidated in the *Adarand* case,[1] is illustrative of both the ways the dominant culture struggles to remain dominant and, especially, the lack of understanding of institutional racism. An *Economist* article entitled "Orwell and Beyond" is a telling example of this view. The opening line is "The Supreme Court should kill a programme whose time has passed."[2] The article contends that the historical argument for racial preference no longer adds up to much. The gist of the article is "racism is history, so get over it." It is illustrative of the misperception the existence of a black middle class indicates an end to racism. Although the popular press is full of arguments against affirmative action, there is ample evidence of the need for some way to ameliorate continuing disparities.

Four court cases have had the biggest impact on commercial affirmative action programs: *Fullilove*;[3] *Metro Broadcasting*;[4] *Croson*;[5] and *Adarand*.[6] *Fullilove* attempted to reverse congressional action that established at least 10 percent of federal funds granted for local public works projects must be used by the state or local governments to procure services from businesses owned by minority group members. In its decision, the Supreme Court viewed affirmative action as a necessary effort to "address a contentious political issue and social problem."[7]

The legislative history shows that there was a rational basis for Congress to conclude that the subcontracting practices of prime contractors could perpetuate the prevailing impaired access by minority businesses to public contracting opportunities, and that this inequity has an effect on interstate commerce.[8]

"Until Metro [Broadcasting] the Court as a whole conceived of race-based affirmative action as remedial, temporary measures to achieve an individualistic society in which race would be irrelevant to governmental action."[9] Mishkin goes on to quote Justice Blackmun in Bakke:[10] "In order to get beyond racism, we must first take account of race. There is no other way."[11]

Croson was a suit brought against a local (Richmond, Virginia) affirmative action ordinance that set aside 30 percent of contracting work for minority businesses. The justices agreed on the doctrinal standard of "strict scrutiny" for state and local agencies. Croson requires evidence of specific, relevant discrimination to justify affirmative action programs. One way to prove such discrimination is through the use of disparity studies.[12]

Andrew Brimmer, in an article in Black Enterprise, makes the point disparity in hiring minority contractors is based on racial discrimination. In his view, Croson showed the need to continue and enlarge race-conscious programs in the construction industry. "Racial discrimination is widespread and deeply rooted in the construction industry."[13] "Common threads, such as apprenticeship systems and trade unions, help connect the construction industry. Moreover, there is the old-boy network composed entirely of white males."[14] Both in my research and my decade of working with businesses of color, I have been made aware of the truth of this statement. I also am very clear most European Americans don't perceive the ways the system works to their advantage, and thus to the disadvantage of people of color. While it is true a lot of business gets done through personal connections, I have observed the construction industry to be especially that way. Most of the uproar about affirmative action is about economics. Before these lawsuits, any construction project that involved federal funds had a portion of work "set aside" for minority and other disadvantaged businesses. With the constraints on affirmative action, owners are now free to revert to a system more like that used in private development, where the bulk of the bidding is by invitation.

The issue in the Metro case was the preference policies of the Federal Communications Commission (FCC). This case was seen as one more attack on the right of Congress to mandate set-asides. The decision allowed that "benign race-conscious measures" are permissible even if they're not "remedial."[15] It was an admission of sorts that race-based discrimination didn't seem to be going away, and the public interest could be served by mandating affirmative action programs.

In the ten years between *Metro* and *Adarand*, public sentiment and policy shifted. *Adarand*, brought by a Colorado contractor against then U.S. Department of Transportation Secretary Pena, led to the strict scrutiny standard for federal affirmative action programs. While it is still possible to create constitutional affirmative action programs, it is a very tedious and expensive process, made only more so by the vigilance of the anti-affirmative action adherents.[16] Without the political mandate to fund economic justice programs, the availability of programs to increase access to government contracts will likely continue to dwindle. Although affirmative action has not been the perfect solution to hundreds of years of economic disparity, it was a significant start. The idea that affirmative action should be eliminated reflects an attempt by the dominant culture (those in positions of power) to remain dominant; a lack of knowledge on the part of most European Americans about institutional racism; and a desperate attempt by the right wing to convince whites one more time that people of color are responsible for their economic problems.

NOTES

1. *Adarand Constructors v. Pena*, 515 US 200 (1995)
2. "Orwell and Beyond: Affirmative Action in America," *Economist*, December 7, 2002, 16.
3. *Fullilove v. Klutznick*, 448 US 448 (1990).
4. *Metro Broadcasting, Inc. v. FCC*, 497 US 547 (1990).
5. *Richmond v. J.A. Croson Co.*, 488 US 469 (1989).
6. See Thomas D. Boston, *Affirmative Action and Black Entrepreneurship* (New York: Routledge, 1999); Richard A. Epstein, "A Rational Basis for Affirmative Action: A Shaky But Classical Liberal Defense," *Michigan Law Review* 100, no. 18 (2002): 2036–62; and Paul J. Mishkin, "Foreword: The Making of a Turning Point—*Metro* and *Adarand*," *California Law Review* 84, no. 4 (1996): 875–86.
7. Paul J. Mishkin. "Foreword: Making of a Turning Point," 877.
8. *Fullilove v. Klutznick*, 475–76.
9. Mishkin. "Foreword: Making of a Turning Point": 880.
10. *University of California Regents v. Bakke* 438 US 265 (1978).
11. Mishkin. "Foreword: The Making of A Turning Point," 880.
12. The requirement for disparity studies created a new market for diversity consultants. There are several studies both supporting and refuting the credibility of these studies. All agree, however, this requirement made it much less likely jurisdictions could prove the constitutional need for affirmative action. See Boston, *Affirmative Action and Black Entrepreneurship*; Andrew E. Brimmer, "A Croson to Bear," *Black Enterprise* 22, no. 10

(1992); Richard A. Epstein, "A Rational Basis for Affirmative Action"; and Mishkin, "Foreword: The Making of A Turning Point."

13. Brimmer, "Croson to Bear," 43.

14. Brimmer, "Croson to Bear,": 44.

15. *Metro Broadcasting, Inc. v. FCC* (89-453), 497 U.S. 547 (1990).

16. See Boston, *Affirmative Action and Black Entrepreneurship*; Epstein, "Rational Basis for Affirmative Action"; and Mishkin, "Foreword: The Making of A Turning Point," for discussions about the difficulties of creating programs that will hold up in the courts.

REFERENCES

Agar, Michael H. *The Professional Stranger: An Informal Introduction to Ethnography.* New York: Academic, 1980.

Althusser, Louis. "Ideology and Ideological State Apparatuses: Notes Towards an Investigation." Pp. 127–86 in *Lenin and Philosophy and Other Essays.* New York: Monthly Review Press, 1971.

American Bar Association. *Commission on Racial and Ethnic Diversity in the Profession.* www.abanet.org/minorities/links/2000census and www.abanet.org/legaled/statistics. Accessed September 16, 2005.

American Institute of Architects. "AIA Firm Survey 2000/2001." Washington, DC: 2000.

American Institute of Architects. "AIA Firm Survey, 2000/2002." Washington, DC: 2000.

American Institute of Architects, National Associates Committee. "Diversity in the Architecture Profession." May 6, 2004. www.aia.org/SiteObjects/files/NACDiversity/WhitePaper.pdf. Accessed September 15, 2005.

Andersen, Margaret, and Patricia H. Collins, eds. *Race, Class and Gender: An Anthology.* Belmont, CA: Wadsworth, 1998.

Anthony, Kathryn H. *Designing for Diversity: Gender, Race, and Ethnicity in the Architectural Profession.* Urbana: University of Illinois Press, 2001.

"Architect Jack Travis Explains a Black Aesthetic in Architecture and Design." One Life, Inc. www.onelifeinc.org/black_homes.html. Accessed March 16, 2005.

Aschaffenburg, Karen, and Ineke Maas. "Cultural and Educational Careers: The Dynamics of Social Reproduction." *American Sociological Review* 62 (August 1997): 573–87.

Association for Community Design. "History of ACD." Washington, DC, 1989. www.communitydesign.org/rex/supportdocs/History.pdf. Accessed September 2004.

Association of American Medical Colleges. "Minorities in Medical Education: Facts & Figures, 2005." Washington, 2005.

Bandura, Albert. *Social Learning Theory*. Englewood Cliffs, NJ: Prentice-Hall, 1977.

Barabasi, Albert-Laszlo. *Linked: How Everything Is Connected to Everything Else and What It Means for Business, Science and Everyday Life*. New York: Penguin, 2003.

Barber, Jean. 1990. "Profile of the Minority Architect" and Roundtable "Today's Minority Architect: A Major Force." Minority Resources Committee of the AIA. July.

Bates, Timothy. *Race, Self-Employment and Upward Mobility: An Illusive American Dream*. Washington, DC: Woodrow Wilson Center Press, 1997.

Bates, Timothy, and William D. Bradford. *Financing Black Economic Development*. New York: Academic, 1979.

Bates, Timothy, and Darrell Williams. "Preferential Procurement Programs and Minority-Owned Business." *Journal of Urban Affairs* 17, no. 1 (1995): 1–17.

Behr, Peter. "Contract Woes for Small Firms: 'Bundling' Found to Undermine Minority-Owned Companies." *Washington Post*, July 20, 2000, A23.

Bell, Yvonne R. "A Culturally Sensitive Analysis of Black Learning Style." *Journal of Black Psychology* 20, no. 1 (1994): 47–61.

Bender, Eve. "Complex Factors Keep Many Blacks from MH System." *Psychiatric News* 39, no. 21 (2004): 14.

Bernstein, Fred A. "For African-Americans, a Chance to Draft History." *New York Times*, June 24, 2004, F1, F8.

Blackwell, Angela G. "Promoting Equitable Development." *Indiana Law Review* 34, no. 4 (2001): 1273–90.

Bond, Max. "The Black Architect's Experience." *Architectural Record* (June 1992): 60–61.

——. "Collaborating with Minority Architects." *Architecture* (June 1994): 43–47.

Bonilla-Silva, Eduardo. *Racism without Racists: Color-Blind Racism and the Persistence of Racial Inequality in the United States*. Lanham, MD: Rowman & Littlefield, 2003.

Boston, Thomas D. *Affirmative Action and Black Entrepreneurship*. New York: Routledge, 1999.

Bourdieu, Pierre, and Loic Wacquant. *An Invitation to Reflexive Sociology*. Chicago: University of Chicago Press, 1992.

Bradford, William D. "Black Family Wealth in the United States." Pp. 103–143 in *The State of Black America, 2000*. Washington, DC: National Urban League, 2000.

——. "The Wealth Dynamics of Entrepreneurship for Black and White Families in the US." Author's manuscript. Seattle, 2001.

Branch, Mark A. "Chicken Little Critics." *Progressive Architecture* 75, no. 6 (June 1994): 25.

Brimmer, Andrew E. "A Croson to Bear." *Black Enterprise* 22, no. 10 (1992): 43–44.

Buchanan, Mark. *Nexus: Small Worlds and the Groundbreaking Science of Networks*. New York: Norton, 2002.

Burt, Ronald S. *Structural Holes*. Cambridge, MA: Harvard University Press, 1992.

Capra, Fritjof. *The Web of Life: A New Scientific Understanding of Living Systems*. New York: Anchor, 1997.

Carroll, Grace. "Mundane Extreme Environmental Stress and African American Families: A Case for Recognizing Different Realities." *Journal of Comparative Family Studies* 29, no. 2 (1998): 271–84.

Carter, Robert T. "Is White a Race? Expressions of White Identity." Pp. 198–207 in *Off White: Readings on Race, Power, and Society*, edited by Michelle Fine, Lois Weis, Linda C. Powell, and L. Mun Wong. New York: Routledge, 1997.

Carter, Stephen L. "The Black Table, the Empty Seat, and the Tie." Pp. 55–79 in *Lure and Loathing: Essays on Race, Identity and the Ambivalence of Assimilation*, edited by Gerald Early. New York: Penguin, 1993.

Caskey, John P. "Bank Representation in Low-Income and Minority Urban Communities." *Urban Affairs Quarterly* 29, no. 4 (1994): 617–38.

Conley, Dalton. *Being Black, Living in the Red: Race, Wealth, and Social Policy in America.* Berkeley: University of California Press, 1999.

Cose, Ellis. *Rage of a Privileged Class.* New York: Harper Perennial, 1995.

Craig-Taylor, Phyllis. "To Be Free: Liberty, Citizenship, Property, Race." *Harvard Blackletter Law Journal* 14 (Spring 1998): 45–90.

Crosbie, Michael J. "AIA: Worth the Price of Admission?" *Progressive Architecture* 75, no. 4 (April 1994): 60–65, 100–102.

Cunningham, Phyllis. "The Adult Educator and Social Responsibility." Pp. 134–41 in *Ethical Issues in Adult Education*, edited by Ralph G. Brockett. New York: Teachers College Press, 1988.

Dawson, Patricia. *Forged by the Knife: The Experience of Surgical Residency from the Perspective of a Woman of Color.* Seattle: Open Hand, 1999.

DeLisser, Eleena. "SBA Program Falls Short on Helping Firms Win Jobs." *Wall Street Journal*, August 1, 2000, A2.

Denton, Nancy A. "The Role of Residential Segregation in Promoting and Managing Inequality in Wealth and Property." *Indiana Law Review* 34, no. 4 (2001): 1199–1211.

Dixon, John Morris. "A White Gentlemen's Profession?" *Progressive Architecture* 75, no. 11 (November 1994): 55–61.

Dozier, Richard K. "The Black Architectural Experience in America." *AIA Journal* 65, no. 7 (1976): 162–68.

——. "The Black Architectural Experience in America." Pp. 8–9 in *African American Architects in Current Practice*, edited by Jack Travis. New York: Princeton Architectural Press, 1991.

Du Bois, W. E. B. *The Souls of Black Folk.* New York: Penguin, 1903/1995.

Duke, Lynne. "Blueprint of a Life." *Washington Post*, July 1, 2004, C1, C4.

Epstein, Richard A. "A Rational Basis for Affirmative Action: A Shaky But Classical Liberal Defense." *Michigan Law Review* 100, no. 18 (2002): 2036–62.

Farkas, George, Robert P. Grobe, Daniel Sheehan, and Yuan Shuan. "Cultural Resources and School Success: Gender, Ethnicity and Poverty Groups within an Urban School District." *American Sociological Review* 55 (February 1990): 127–42.

Feagin, Joe. *Racist America: Roots, Current Realities, and Future Reparations.* New York: Routledge, 2001.

Feagin, Joe, Kevin E. Early, and Karyn D. McKinney. "The Many Costs of Discrimination: The Case of Middle-Class African-Americans." *Indiana Law Review* 34, no. 4 (2001): 1311–60.

Feagin, Joe, and Melvin Sikes. *Living with Racism: The Black Middle-Class Experience.* Boston: Beacon, 1994.

Fields, Darell W. "Diversity Needs a New Mascot." Pp. 39–41 in *20 on 20/20 Vision,* edited by Linda Kiisk. Boston: Boston Society of Architects, 2003.

Fine, Michelle. "Witnessing Whiteness." Pp. 57–65 in *Off White: Readings on Race, Power, and Society,* edited by Michelle Fine, Lois Weis, Linda C. Powell, and L. Mun Wong. New York: Routledge, 1997.

Fine, Michelle, Lois Weis, Linda C. Powell, and L. Mun Wong, eds. *Off White: Readings on Race, Power, and Society.* New York, Routledge 1997.

Forgey, Benjamin. "First Black Designed Building in Downtown DC." *Washington Post,* March 30, 2002, C1, C5.

Franklin, Vincent P. "Introduction: Cultural Capital and African-American Education." *Journal of African-American History* 87 (Spring 2002): 175–81.

Galves, Fred. "The Discriminatory Impact of Traditional Lending Criteria: An Economic and Moral Critique." *Seton Hall Law Review* 29, no. 4 (1999): 1467–87.

Gates, Henry Louis, and Cornel West. *The Future of the Race.* New York: Knopf, 1996.

General Accounting Office. "Questionable Effectiveness of the 8(a) Procurement Program." Report to the Congress, Washington, DC: 1975.

——. "The SBA 8(a) Procurement Program—A Promise Unfulfilled." Report to the Congress, Washington, DC, 1981.

——. "Problems Continue with SBA's Minority Business Development Program." Report to the Chairman, Committee on Small Business, House of Representatives, Washington, DC, 1993.

Gladwell, Malcolm. *The Tipping Point: How Little Things Can Make a Big Difference.* Boston: Back Bay; Little, Brown, 2002.

Gordon, Colin, ed. *Power/Knowledge: Selected Interviews and Other Writing by Michel Foucault.* New York, Pantheon, 1980.

Grant, Bradford C., and Dennis A. Mann, eds. *Directory of African American Architects.* Cincinnati, OH: Center for the Study of Practice, 1995.

Gutman, Robert. "Architects and Power: The Natural Market for Architecture." *Progressive Architecture* 73, no. 13 (1992): 39.

Haggerty, Maryann. "Behind the Design of a New Headquarters: High-Profile Freddie Mac Contract a Bittersweet Victory for Devrouax & Purnell." *Washington Post,* June 19, 1995, F5.

Harding, Vincent, Robin D. G. Kelley, and Earl Lewis. "We Changed the World: 1945–1970." Pp. 445–543 in *To Make Our World Anew: A History of African Americans,* edited by Robin D. G. Kelley and Earl Lewis. Oxford: Oxford University Press, 2000.

Hartman, Chester, ed. *Double Exposure: Poverty and Race in America.* Armonk, NY: Sharpe, 1997.

Hayden, Dolores. *The Power of Place: Urban Landscapes as Public History*. Cambridge, MA: MIT Press, 1995.

Herbert, James I. *Black Male Entrepreneurs and Adult Development*. New York: Praeger, 1989.

Hernandez-Trujillo, Bertha E., and Shelbi D. Day. "Property, Wealth, and Human Rights: A Formula for Reform." *Indiana Law Review* 34, no. 4 (2001): 1213–41.

Hoffman, Lily M. *The Politics of Knowledge: Activist Movements in Medicine and Planning*. Albany: State University of New York Press, 1989.

Holtz Kay, Jane. "Invisible Architects: Minority Firms Struggle to Achieve Recognition in a White-Dominated Profession." *Architecture* (April 1991): 106–113.

hooks, bell. *Killing Rage: Ending Racism*. New York: Holt, 1995.

——. *Where We Stand: Class Matters*. New York: Routledge, 2000.

Horton, Miles, and Paulo Freire. *We Make the Road by Walking*. Philadelphia: Temple University Press, 1990.

Hudson, Karen E. *Paul R. Williams, Architect: A Legacy of Style*. New York: Rizzoli, 1993.

Hughes, David. *Afrocentric Architecture: A Design Primer*. Columbus, OH: Greyden, 1994.

Immergluck, Daniel P. "Progress Confined: Increases in Black Home Buying and the Persistence of Residential Segregation." *Journal of Urban Affairs* 20, no. 4 (1998): 443–57.

Immergluck, Daniel P., and Erin Mullen. "New Small Business Data Show Loans Going to Higher-Income Neighborhoods in Chicago Area." Woodstock Institute Reinvestment Alert no. 11, November 1997, www.woodstockinst.org/document/allert11.pdf. Accessed April 7, 2002.

Immergluck, Daniel, and Geoff Smith. "Bigger, Faster . . . But Better? How Changes in the Financial Services Industry Affect Small Business Lending in Urban Areas." Woodstock Institute. 2001. brookings.edu/cs/urban/publications/immerglucklending.pdf. Accessed January 21, 2001.

Jarvis, Peter. "Meaningful and Meaningless Experience: Toward an Analysis of Learning from Life." *Adult Education Quarterly* 73, no. 3 (1987): 164–72.

Johnson, Brian P., and David D. Horowitz. "Table of Brotherhood: Variety in the Field of Architecture." *Arcade* (Spring 1994): 14–15, 30.

Jones, Joyce. "Graduation Day from 8(a)." *Black Enterprise* 28 (February 1998): 161–66.

Kalmijn, Matthijs, and Gerbert Kraaykamp. "Race, Cultural Capital and Schooling: An Analysis of Trends in the United States." *Sociology of Education* 69 (January 1996): 22–34.

Kaplan, Victoria. *Against All Odds: An Ethnographic Case Study of One African American Architect*. Doctoral dissertation. Santa Barbara, CA: Fielding Graduate Institute, 2004.

Kaplan, Victoria, and Robert Kunreuther. *The A to Z of Managing People*. New York: Berkley, 1996.

Kegan, Robert. *The Evolving Self: Problem and Process in Human Development*. Cambridge, MA: Harvard University Press, 1982.

Kelley, Robin D. G. "Into the Fire: 1970 to the Present." Pp. 543–613 in *To Make Our World Anew: A History of African Americans*, edited by Robin D. G. Kelley and Earl Lewis. Oxford: Oxford University Press, 2000.

Kelley, Robin D. G., and Earl Lewis, eds. *To Make Our World Anew: A History of African Americans*. Oxford: Oxford University Press, 2000.

Kim, Hyoun K., and Patrick C. McKenry. "Social Networks and Support: A Comparison of African Americans, Asian Americans, Caucasians, and Hispanics." *Journal of Comparative Family Studies* 29, no. 2 (1998): 313–34.

King, Peter H. "Putting Away New Orleans." *Seattle Times*, October 9, 2005, A2.

Kivel, Paul. *Uprooting Racism: How White People Can Work for Racial Justice*. Philadelphia: New Society, 1996.

Kleinman, Sherryl, and Martha Kopp. *Emotions and Fieldwork*. Newbury Park, CA: Sage, 1993.

Kong, Deborah. "The 2000 Census: Looking Beyond Color Lines." *Seattle Post-Intelligencer*, June 29, 2001, A1.

Kotlowski, Dean. "Black Power–Nixon Style: The Nixon Administration and Minority Business Enterprise." *Business History Review* 72, no. 3 (1998): 409–445.

Langston, Donna. "Tired of Playing Monopoly?" Pp. 126–35 in *Race, Class and Gender: An Anthology*, edited by Margaret Andersen and Patricia H. Collins. Belmont, CA: Wadsworth, 1998.

Larson, Magali Sarfatti. *The Rise of Professionalism*. Berkeley: University of California Press, 1977.

——. *Behind the Postmodern Facade: Architectural Change in Late Twentieth-Century America*. Berkeley: University of California Press, 1993.

——. "Patronage and Power." Pp. 130–43 in *Reflections on Architectural Practices in the Nineties*, edited by William S. Saunders. Princeton, NJ: Princeton Architectural Press, 1996.

Levitt, Mitchel R. "Flying with Eagles: An Interview with Curtis J. Moody, FAIA." *SMPS Marketer* (October 2002): 4–15.

Littlefield, Daniel C. "Revolutionary Citizens: 1776–1804." Pp. 103–168 in *To Make Our World Anew: A History of African Americans*, edited by Robin D. G. Kelley and Earl Lewis. Oxford: Oxford University Press, 2000.

Lofland, John, and Lynn Lofland. *Analyzing Social Settings: A Guide to Qualitative Observation and Analysis*. Belmont, CA: Wadsworth, 1995.

Mann, Dennis Alan. "Making Connections: The African-American Architect." *Journal of the Interfaith Forum on Religion, Art & Architecture* (Fall 1993): 22–23, 31.

Mann, Dennis Alan, and Bradford Grant. "African American Architects Survey 1999/2000." University of Cincinnati Center for the Study of Practice. blackarch.uc.edu/publications/survey1999.html.

Marable, Manning. *How Capitalism Underdeveloped Black America*. Boston: South End, 1983.

——. "Beyond Racial Identity Politics: Towards a Liberation Theory for Multicultural Democracy." Pp. 360–65 in *Race, Class and Gender: An Anthology*, edited by Margaret Andersen and Patricia H. Collins. Belmont, CA: Wadsworth, 1995.

McIntosh, Peggy. "White Privilege and Male Privilege: A Personal Account of Coming to See Correspondences Through Work in Women's Studies." Pp. 94–105 in *Race, Class and Gender: An Anthology*, edited by Margaret Andersen and Patricia H. Collins. Belmont, CA: Wadsworth, 1988.

Merriam, Sharon B., and Rosemary S. Caffarella. *Learning in Adulthood*. San Francisco: Jossey-Bass, 1999.

Mezirow, Jack. "Transformation Theory of Adult Learning." Pp. 39–70 in *In Defense of the Lifeworld: Critical Perspectives on Adult Learning*, edited by Michael R. Welton. Albany: State University of New York Press, 1995.

Mezirow, Jack, et al., eds. *Fostering Critical Reflections in Adulthood: A Guide to Transformative and Emancipatory Learning*. San Francisco, Jossey-Bass, 1990.

"Minorities in Medical Education: Facts & Figures 2005." Association of American Medical Colleges. 2005. services.aamc.org/Publications. Accessed September 15, 2005.

Mishkin, Paul J. "Foreword: The Making of a Turning Point—*Metro* and *Adarand*." *California Law Review* 84, no. 4 (1996): 875–86.

Mitchell, Melvin. *The Crisis of the African-American Architect: Conflicting Cultures of Architecture and (Black) Power*. Lincoln, NE: Writer's Club, 2001.

Mitgang, Lee D. "Saving the Soul of an Architectural Education: Four Critical Challenges Face Today's Architecture Schools." *Architectural Record* (May 1997): 124.

——. "Back to School: Architects Sound Off on 10 Critical Issues Facing Architectural Education." *Architectural Record* 187 (September 1999): 112.

Myers, Samuel L. "'The Rich Get Richer and . . .': the Problem of Race and Inequality in the 1990s." *Law & Inequality: A Journal of Theory and Practice* 7, no. 2 (1993): 369–89.

Newsom, Jennifer. "Does African-American Architecture Exist?" Metropolismag.com. September 12, 2004. www.metropolismag.com/cda/story.php?artid=63.

"Norma Sklarek." PageWise. www.ni.essortment.com/normasklarek_rqbo.htm. Accessed June 2, 2004.

Oliver, Melvin L., and Thomas M. Shapiro. *Black Wealth/White Wealth: A New Perspective on Racial Inequality*. New York: Routledge, 1997.

Omi, Michael, and Howard Winant. *Racial Formation in the U.S.* New York: Routledge & Kegan Paul, 1986.

"Orwell and Beyond: Affirmative Action in America." *Economist*, December 7, 2002, 16.

Overstreet, Harry L. "The Bastion of Hope." P. 12 in *African American Architects in Current Practice*, edited by Jack Travis. New York: Princeton Architectural Press, 1991.

Peters, B. Guy. *American Public Policy: Promise and Performance*. New York: Seven Bridges, 1999.

Piven, Frances Fox, and Richard A. Cloward. *Poor People's Movements: Why They Succeed, How They Fail*. New York: Vintage, 1979.

Rapoport, Amos. "Cross-Cultural Aspects of Environmental Design." Pp. 7–46 in *Human Behavior and Environment: Advances in Theory and Research, Vol. 4*, edited by Irwin Altman, Amos Rapoport, and Joachim F. Wohlwill. New York: Plenum, 1980.

Reese, Jennifer. "Paul Williams, An Architect." *Via* (September/October 1999): 52–55.

Reilly, Mary. "African Americans, Especially Women, Build Up Their Numbers in Architecture." University of Cincinnati, September 26, 2005, www.uc.edu/news/NR.asp?id=1222.

Roscigno, Vincent J., and James W. Ainsworth-Darnell. "Race, Cultural Capital, and Educational Resources: Persistent Inequalities and Achievement Returns." *Sociology of Education* 72 (July 1999): 158–78.

Rosenbaum, David B. "Expanding the American Dream: For Its $2.4 Billion Airport Expansion, San Francisco 'Spread Out the Work as Much as Possible' for Designers, CMs." *ENR New York* 240, no. 25 (1998): 32.

Rushefsky, Mark E. *Public Policy in the U.S.: Toward the 21st Century.* Belmont, CA: Wadsworth, 1996.

Ryan, William. *Blaming the Victim.* New York: Random House, 1976.

Schwartz, Alex. "Bank Lending to Minority and Low-Income Households and Neighborhoods: Do Community Reinvestment Agreements Make A Difference?" *Journal of Urban Affairs* 20, no. 3 (1998): 269–301.

Shapiro, Thomas M. *The Hidden Cost of Being African American: How Wealth Perpetuates Inequality.* New York: Oxford University Press, 2004.

Simpson, George, and Milton Yinger. *Racial and Cultural Minorities: An Analysis of Prejudice and Discrimination.* New York: Harper & Row, 1985.

Sklarek, Norma Merrick. "Norma Merrick Sklarek." *California Architecture* (January/February 1985): 22–23.

Squires, Gregory D. *From Redlining to Reinvestment: Community Responses to Urban Disinvestment.* Philadelphia: Temple University Press, 1992.

——. *Capital and Communities in Black and White.* Albany: State University of New York Press, 1994.

Stack, Carol. B. *All Our Kin.* New York: Harper Colophone, 1974.

Stevens, Garry. *The Favored Circle: The Social Foundations of Architectural Distinction.* Cambridge, MA: MIT Press, 1998.

Stevenson, Howard C., and Gary Renard. "Trusting Ole' Wise Owls: Therapeutic Use of Cultural Strengths in African-American Families." *Professional Psychology: Research and Practice* 24, no. 4 (1993): 433–42.

Stout, Linda. *Bridging the Class Divide and Other Lessons for Grassroots Organizing.* Boston: Beacon, 1996.

Sutton, Sharon E. "Finding Our Voice in a Dominant Key." Pp. 12–15 in *African American Architects in Current Practice*, edited by Jack Travis. New York: Princeton Architectural Press, 1991.

——. "Practice: Architects and Power." *Progressive Architecture* 73, no. 5 (1992): 65–68.

——. "Expand Architects' Leadership." *Architecture* 85, no. 12 (1996): 51.

Szenasy, Susan S. "Designers and Multiculturalism." *Metropolis* 14, no. 3 (1994): 110–15.

Talvi, Silja J. A. "No Dreams Deferred: Donald King Builds Community through Diverse Architecture." *ColorsNW* 3 (September 2003): 15–16.

Tennant, Mark, and Philip Pogson. *Learning and Change in the Adult Years: A Developmental Perspective.* San Francisco: Jossey-Bass, 1995.

Travis, Jack, ed. *African American Architects in Current Practice*. New York: Princeton Architectural Press, 1991.

——. "Hidden in Plain View." *National Associates Committee Quarterly* (Spring 2003): 1–4.

Watts, Duncan J. *Six Degrees: The Science of a Connected Age*. New York: Norton, 2003.

Weems, Robert E., and Lewis A. Randolph. "The National Response to Richard M. Nixon's Black Capitalist Initiative." *Journal of Black Studies* 32, no. 1 (2001): 66–83.

West, Cornel. "Race Matters." Pp. 120–25 in *Race, Class and Gender: An Anthology*, edited by Margaret Andersen and Patricia H. Collins. Belmont, CA: Wadsworth, 1998.

——. *Race Matters*. New York: Vintage, 2001.

Wilson, Dreck Spurlock, ed. *African American Architects: A Biographical Dictionary, 1865–1945*. New York: Routledge, 2004.

Yanow, Dvora. *How Does a Policy Mean: Interpreting Policy and Organizational Actions*. Washington, DC: Georgetown University Press, 1996.

Young, Whitney M., Jr. "Man and His Social Conscience: The Keynote Address by the Executive Director of the Urban League." *AIA Journal* (September 1968): 44–49.

INDEX

ABOUT THE AUTHOR

Victoria Kaplan has worked in finance for the last twenty years. She served as a corporate financial analyst and managed a community development venture capital fund. She brings her MBA in finance and her PhD in human and organizational development together to work for economic and social justice. She is the founder of *writing for change*, an organization that uses storytelling as a vehicle to educate audiences about systemic racism.